F
Ami
PBK.   An Amish cradle.

PCG   GRG   MCG   SDG   MGG   PTG

76-6473   F
                                       AMI
                                       PBK.

An Amish cradle

Other Novels by the Authors

BETH WISEMAN

The Daughters of the Promise novels
Plain Perfect
Plain Pursuit
Plain Promise
Plain Paradise
Plain Proposal
Plain Peace

The Land of Canaan novels
Seek Me with All Your Heart
The Wonder of Your Love
His Love Endures Forever

Need You Now
The House that Love Built
The Promise

KATHLEEN FULLER

The Hearts of Middlefield novels
A Man of His Word
An Honest Love
A Hand to Hold

The Middlefield Family novels
Treasuring Emma
Faithful to Laura
Letters to Katie

VANNETTA CHAPMAN

The Shipshewana Amish
Mystery novels
Falling to Pieces
Perfect Square
Material Witness

The Amish Village Mystery novels
Murder Simply Brewed
Murder Tightly Knit
Murder Freshly Baked (Available
May 2015)

AMY CLIPSTON

The Hearts of the Lancaster
Grand Hotel Series
A Hopeful Heart
A Mother's Secret
A Dream of Home
A Simple Prayer (Available April 2015)

The Kauffman Amish Bakery Series
A Gift of Grace
A Place of Peace
A Promise of Hope
A Life of Joy
A Season of Love

A Plain and Simple Christmas
Naomi's Gift
Roadside Assistance (young adult)
Reckless Heart (young adult)
Destination Unknown (young adult)

A Spoonful of Love, included
in An Amish Kitchen
A Son for Always, included in An
Amish Cradle (Available
February 2015)

Nonfiction
A Gift of Love

**OTHER AMISH NOVELLA
COLLECTIONS**
An Amish Christmas
An Amish Gathering
An Amish Love
An Amish Wedding
An Amish Kitchen
An Amish Miracle
An Amish Garden
An Amish Second Christmas

An Amish Cradle

BETH WISEMAN,
AMY CLIPSTON,
KATHLEEN FULLER,
AND VANNETTA CHAPMAN

THOMAS NELSON
Since 1798

NASHVILLE   MEXICO CITY   RIO DE JANEIRO

Published in Nashville, Tennessee, by Thomas Nelson. Thomas Nelson is a registered trademark of HarperCollins Christian Publishing, Inc.

Thomas Nelson titles may be purchased in bulk for educational, business, fund-raising, or sales promotional use. For information, please e-mail SpecialMarkets@ThomasNelson.com.

HOLY BIBLE: NEW INTERNATIONAL VERSION®. © 1973, 1978, 1984 by International Bible Society. Used by permission of Zondervan Publishing House. All rights reserved.

Publisher's note: This novel is a work of fiction. Names, characters, places, and incidents are either products of the author's imagination or used fictitiously. All characters are fictional, and any similarity to people, living or dead, is purely coincidental.

Library of Congress Cataloging-in-Publication Data

An Amish cradle / Beth Wiseman, Amy Clipston, Kathleen Fuller, and Vannetta Chapman.
    pages cm
  ISBN 978-0-529-11867-7 (pbk.)
1. Amish--Fiction. 2. Christian fiction, American I. Wiseman, Beth, 1962- II. Clipston, Amy. III. Fuller, Kathleen. IV. Chapman, Vannetta.
  PS648.A45A36 2015
  813'.01083823--dc23

              2014032853

Printed in the United States of America

15 16 17 18 19 RRD 6 5 4 3 2 1

CONTENTS

In His Father's Arms

BETH WISEMAN

To Raelyn Cutbirth

GLOSSARY

ach—oh

danki—thank you

Englisch—non-Amish person

gut—good

kapp—prayer covering or cap

kinner—children or grandchildren

maedels—girls

mamm—mom

mammi—grandmother

mei—my

mudder—mother

nee—no

sohn—son

ya—yes

PROLOGUE

Ruth Anne squeezed her eyes closed and held her breath as she sat beside her husband in the hospital waiting room. They left Bethany's room because her best friend's wailing was more than Ruth Anne could bear. Levi leaned closer to her, the roughness of his brown beard grazing her cheek as he whispered, "You know your delivery won't be like this. Bethany has never had *gut* tolerance for pain."

She opened her eyes, glanced around the waiting room, then also spoke softly. "Having babies hurts. Even *Mamm* said that God makes sure we shed the memory. Otherwise, we'd all just have one child." She squeezed her lips together and held her breath again, remembering Bethany's cries.

Ruth Anne looked around the room again. Both of Bethany's parents were here, along with her in-laws and cousins. About twenty folks waiting for little Esther Rose to arrive.

Levi leaned close to her again. "Ruthie, you're gonna do real fine. Mary Elizabeth is going to see to that." He gave a taut nod at the mention of the midwife who would be delivering their baby. Unlike her best friend, Ruth Anne had chosen not to deliver in a hospital, and she'd also opted not to have an ultrasound. Or pain medication. But as she listened to Bethany struggle, she was starting to second-guess her choices. But her husband was right. They'd all grown up together, and Bethany made a fuss over the smallest of ailments.

Ruth Anne stood and walked down the hall to listen at her friend's door. She strained to hear something since Bethany had grown quiet. She silently prayed that the worst of the pain was over and that little Esther Rose had made a safe and healthy arrival into the world.

It was about twenty minutes later when John walked into the waiting area, a tiny bundle swaddled in his arms. His ear-to-ear smile was proof that all was well. Everyone rushed toward him, and Levi helped lift Ruth Anne from her chair. As scared of the delivery as she was, she had to admit she was ready to hold her own baby in her arms.

She waited until the grandparents and other family members had a chance to see Esther Rose before she and Levi moved toward the proud father.

"She's beautiful," Ruth Anne said as she eyed the tiny infant with a hint of Bethany's red hair. "Welcome, Esther Rose."

Ruth Anne and Bethany had both found out they were pregnant the same week, and they'd spent the last nine months knitting baby clothes, setting up nurseries, and preparing for these blessed events. She thanked God for Esther's safe arrival.

"The doctor said she's just perfect." John beamed as he gazed down at his daughter. He didn't lift his eyes when he added, "And Bethany did just great."

Ruth Anne swallowed hard. If that was great, she wondered what not-so-great would have sounded like. She put a hand across her tummy, wondering if God would bless her with a boy or a girl.

Levi said it didn't matter to him if they had a daughter or a son, but Ruth Anne knew he wanted a son. All three of his brothers had daughters. Five total. Levi was hoping to give his parents their first grandson.

Ruth Anne smiled as John said he needed to get back to Bethany, and then he gave both sets of grandparents a final peek at Esther Rose before he left the waiting room. Ruth Anne and Levi said their good-byes and left through another door that led to the parking lot where a line of buggies were tethered. Levi reached for her hand and squeezed.

"I can't wait to see who shows up in our life—Joshua or Eva Mae."

Waddling alongside him as fast as she could, she said, "Me either."

And if truth be told—Ruth Anne was secretly hoping for a boy too. Somehow she sensed that Joshua would be making his entrance soon.

CHAPTER ONE

Ruth Anne held off pushing when Mary Elizabeth said to, even though she was sure the baby was going to come out anyway. Levi stood at the end of their bed, white as the sheet that covered Ruth Anne. He apparently had forgotten everything he was supposed to do during the birthing process. Ruth Anne had asked for her mother to come in four hours ago, and she'd only just arrived. And she'd asked for pain medication. Repeatedly. As she focused on a stuffed elephant on her bedroom dresser, she tried to recall the day she and Levi had gone to the fair, but the pain wouldn't allow her to shift her thinking. She'd packed a small red suitcase, which now sat in the corner, in case of an emergency and they needed to rush to the hospital, but Mary Elizabeth had assured her that everything was going well.

"Not quite yet," Mary Elizabeth said as she positioned herself on the stool at the end of Ruth Anne's bed. She pulled the sheets to the side and checked Ruth Anne again. "Levi, I see the head. Look."

Ruth Anne hadn't cried out and wailed the way Bethany had, but this was indeed the worst pain she'd ever felt in her life. Even worse than when she broke her leg in three places when she was seven. But when she saw her husband move in closer and a smile light up his face, she knew that Joshua was almost here.

"Wow," her husband whispered before he looked up at Ruth Anne. "I can see the head. I can see the head."

"Oh, blessed be the Lord," Ruth Anne's mother said as she reached for her daughter's hand.

"It's time, Ruth Anne. You can push." Mary Elizabeth edged Levi to the side as Ruth Anne held tightly to her mother's hand.

Ruth Anne pushed with all her might, knowing she sounded like Bethany and not caring. She followed Mary Elizabeth's instructions and kept pushing and pushing and pushing—and crying. The pain, the anticipation, the miracle of birth . . . Her emotions were all over the place. But when she heard a tiny cry and felt the pressure ease from her body, she drew in a deep breath and wept. Her mother walked to the end of the bed, her eyes tearing up.

"It's a boy," *Mamm* said as she brought both hands to her chest.

Thank You, God. She closed her eyes and thanked Him again. After a couple more deep breaths, she looked up just in time to see her mother and Mary Elizabeth exchange looks, both leaning closer to the baby.

"What? What's wrong? What is it?" She tried to lift herself, but couldn't. "Levi!" she screamed. "What's *wrong*?"

Levi was sure he'd never seen a more precious sight in his life. He quickly counted his son's fingers and toes. Ten. And he was breathing. And beautiful. He looked at Mary Elizabeth, waiting for confirmation that everything was okay since his wife was acting concerned all of a sudden.

"*Ya*, dear. *Ya*. Everything is fine." Mary Elizabeth smiled as she and Ruth Anne's mother cleaned the baby. Once they were done, both women touched Joshua's feet, and as Levi leaned closer, he saw why they were studying his son in such a way.

"His big toes are a long way from the other ones." It was almost like an extra toe could fit there. "Will he be able to walk okay?"

Mary Elizabeth nodded. "Everything is fine." She swaddled Joshua and handed him to Levi. He couldn't take his eyes off his son. He'd always heard that the love a person has for a child isn't like any other kind of love, but experiencing the emotion had caught him off guard. He hated to cry, but a tear slipped down his cheek just the same.

"Let me see. Let me see." Ruth Anne had both arms stretched toward him.

Levi didn't want to turn his son loose, but Ruth Anne was anxious. He handed her their baby boy, then put a hand on his wife's arm. He wished his mother were here. Levi's parents and siblings lived in Hershey, too far to travel by buggy, so he didn't get to see his family as often as he would like. Had it not been for a mutual friend's wedding in Paradise, Levi might not have ever met Ruth Anne. His mother had planned to hire a driver so she could be here, but a feverish cold had kept her away today.

"You did *gut*, Ruthie. You did so *gut*. Isn't he the most beautiful person you've ever seen?"

Ruth Anne met eyes with her son, each studying the other. There was no doubt that it was love at first sight for her too. "His eyes are so blue. Will they stay that color?" She glanced toward the end of the bed, but both the midwife and Ruth Anne's mother were talking in low voices in the corner of the room. After a few seconds, Mary Elizabeth walked back to the bed.

"He is a beautiful baby." She shrugged, smiling. "And who knows if his eyes will stay so blue. Some do and some don't."

Both Levi and Ruth Anne had brown eyes, so Levi figured the likelihood of Joshua's eyes staying blue were slim. And that was fine by him. Joshua was perfect in every way. Except maybe his toes, but that was certainly something they could live with.

"Mary Elizabeth said we need to cart little Joshua to the pediatrician. Maybe tomorrow if you feel up to it." Carolyn smiled, but Ruth Anne's mother had never been good at hiding her emotions, and Levi could tell the smile was forced.

"What's wrong?" Ruth Anne's eyes grew round, and Levi could feel his pulse quickening.

"Everything is fine," Mary Elizabeth said again. "Remember, we talked about this, that the baby would need to be thoroughly checked out by a doctor."

"But you said we could wait a few days as long as everything looked okay." Ruth Anne peeled back the swaddling and began inspecting their son, eventually latching onto one of his tiny feet. "Are you worried about his feet?" She glanced at Levi before she looked at Mary Elizabeth. "Because no one will see his little toes most of the time anyway." She smiled.

Levi helped her bundle Joshua back up. Their son had closed his eyes, but Levi could see him breathing.

"So beautiful." Levi's mother-in-law folded her hands in front of her as she stared at Ruth Anne and Joshua. But Levi saw her blink back tears before she asked, "Shall I go get the others?"

Mary Elizabeth finished cleaning up Ruth Anne and draped

fresh covers on her. "Are you ready to show the world your precious son?"

Ruth Anne and Levi both nodded. Levi was anxious for their family to see their boy. There were probably twenty people in the living room waiting to visit.

Levi gazed upon his son with so much love in his heart that it almost hurt. When he finally pulled his eyes from the baby, he saw that Ruth Anne's mother and Mary Elizabeth were back in the corner again. Despite the fact that everyone kept saying everything was fine, in the pit of his stomach, Levi knew it wasn't.

CHAPTER TWO

Two days after Joshua's birth, Ruth Anne was sore, tired, and disappointed that Joshua hadn't latched onto her breast, so she'd been pumping her milk and feeding him with a bottle. Mary Elizabeth had set the appointment with the pediatrician in Lancaster for today. What made the niggling worry bearable was the love that was growing by the minute for little Joshua.

Watching Levi interact with Joshua was deepening her love for her husband in a way she didn't know was possible. And he wasn't only attentive with Joshua, but also with her. She didn't remember her father ever being so involved in their lives. Just five years ago they'd gotten a surprise when Katie came along. Ruth Anne tended to her mother while her father headed back to the fields within an hour of Katie's delivery.

"Do you think everything is okay?" Ruth Anne twirled the string on her *kapp* as Levi held their sleeping infant. "Dr. Prescott said they were doing some blood tests. Is that normal?"

"I'm sure Bethany's baby had all that stuff done too. It's routine." Levi continued to gently rock Joshua, not taking his eyes off of him, while they waited in Dr. Prescott's office. Ruth Anne looked at the clock on the wall. They'd been waiting for almost thirty minutes. She jumped a little when the door opened.

Dr. Prescott was young. The woman must have had to go through lots of schooling to be a doctor, but Ruth Anne didn't think she looked old enough for that.

"Hey, you guys," she said as she walked around her desk and sat down. *She even talks like a young person.* Ruth Anne scanned the doctor's desk. On the desk sat a wedding picture of Dr. Prescott and her husband, lots of file folders, and a stack of books on the doctor's left. "Sorry it took so long." She opened a folder. Smiling, she said, "What a beautiful boy Joshua is. Isn't he just amazing?"

"*Ya.* He is." Ruth Anne glanced at her baby in his father's arms, then back at the doctor. "Is he of *gut* health?" The doctor had examined Joshua earlier for what seemed like a long time. Then they'd been asked to wait in her office until she finished with another patient.

Dr. Prescott opened her mouth to speak, but pressed her lips together when the door opened and an older man walked in. He was slightly hunched over, with gray hair and gold-rimmed glasses, and wearing a white coat.

Dr. Prescott nodded toward the man. "Ruth Anne and Levi, this is Dr. Calhoun. I've invited him to join us."

When the doctor offered his hand, Ruth Anne shook it. The older man gave Levi time to shift Joshua into the nook of his left arm, and they shook hands as well.

"Listen, guys." Dr. Prescott sat taller and folded her hands on her desk. "I've brought Dr. Calhoun in so that he can talk to you about a condition we believe your son has."

Ruth Anne swallowed back a lump in her throat, but quickly thought about the power of prayer. She'd prayed away problems, ailments, worries, and the like her entire life. She held her breath. *Please, God. Don't let it be bad. Please, God. Please, God. Please. Don't let anything be wrong with our baby.* Ruth Anne looked at her husband, sure he wasn't breathing either, but a glance at Joshua let her know that even if they weren't, their son was breathing just fine.

"Have either of you heard of Down's syndrome?" Dr. Calhoun took a step farther into the room, but he remained standing despite the fact that there was another chair against the wall. Ruth Anne shook her head, then looked at Levi. Her husband blinked back tears.

"Don't tell me our Joshua has Down's syndrome," he said as he shook his head. "He doesn't. I know he doesn't. I've seen *kinner* with Down's syndrome. Their faces look different. Our Joshua looks just fine." He lifted the baby a little bit. "Look at him. He looks like a normal baby."

Ruth Anne felt light-headed. She'd never heard of this Down's disease, but it was scaring her the way Joshua was reacting. "Can you tell us what this is? This disease?"

"It's not really a disease. It's a syndrome, and I know this is a lot to handle for anyone, to get word of this about your child. Especially since you are both young and first-time parents." Dr. Calhoun pulled the chair closer to Ruth Anne. Maybe he sensed that she might keel over. He sat down, put his hands on his knees, and focused on Ruth Anne since Levi was scowling and wouldn't even look at him.

"How sick is he?" Ruth Anne wished her mother were here holding her hand. *Mamm* had offered to come, but Ruth Anne was trying to be a grown-up, so she'd declined. She'd only been married to Levi for a year, and while he'd been very nurturing throughout her pregnancy, right now he was trembling and just staring at Joshua. But they were both nineteen. Mature adults.

Levi glared at the doctor. "He doesn't have it. My third cousin had Down's syndrome and this isn't it." He looked at his son again.

"Doesn't have what? I don't understand what this is. Will he be all right?" Ruth Anne's voice was cracking, and the woozy feeling in her head was getting worse. "Is there medicine for it?"

Dr. Prescott cleared her throat. "Ruth Anne, like Dr. Calhoun said, it isn't really a disease. When a person has a full or partial extra copy of a certain chromosome, chromosome 21, it can genetically alter development, and we call this Down's syndrome." She paused, but Ruth Anne still didn't have a clue what she was talking about or what was wrong with her baby. "Your midwife noticed the gap between Joshua's big toes and second toes. This is a clue that a child could have this syndrome."

"So, do we fix his feet? I don't think it looks bad, but if it will help him to walk or—"

"It's not just his feet, Ruthie!" Levi's face was red, his bottom lip trembling. "It's . . . it's . . ." He finally lowered his head after his eyes teared up. "Explain it to her."

Ruth Anne started to cry. "I'm scared. What does this mean?"

"Honey, I know you're upset," Dr. Prescott said. "I brought in Dr. Calhoun because his office is in this building, and I wanted to be sure before I told you. This condition has all kinds of physical distinctions, and some won't become apparent until little Joshua gets a bit older. But he does already have some of the common traits." She nodded toward their baby. "Do you see how his eyes have an upward and outward slant?"

Ruth Anne swiped at her eyes, then leaned closer to her son.

"My aunt has eyes kind of like that." She shrugged. "We can live with that."

Dr. Prescott turned to a computer that was on the desk in front of her and began to type. After a few moments, she turned the screen so that Ruth Anne and Levi could see it along with her. "Here are some varying degrees of Down's syndrome. See how the mouth is small and the lips are thin in this picture?" She pointed to another one. "The head is a bit smaller than average sometimes, and the ears are lower set. The arms and legs are—"

Ruth Anne sobbed, waiting for Levi to offer comfort, but he just sat staring at Joshua. Then he started to cry also. She touched his arm. "But we will love him no matter what." She looked at Dr. Prescott and spoke in a shaky voice. "We already love him more than life. He is perfect."

Dr. Prescott reached over and put her hand on Ruth Anne's. "Of course you love him. And I have always believed that God chooses special people to raise special children. It isn't what any parent expects, but every child is a blessing."

Ruth Anne couldn't catch her breath. "What . . . what . . . do we . . ." She raised her shoulders and dropped them slowly.

Dr. Calhoun handed her a box of Kleenex. "We need to run a series of tests. Babies with Down's syndrome are at high risk for other medical conditions, and we need to rule those out." He handed Ruth Anne a card. "Dr. Prescott said her initial exam of Joshua didn't indicate anything that is urgent, and he is breathing well on his own. But I'd like to see him next week. You can call the number on the card. Ask for Kayla. She'll be expecting your call and will make sure to fit you in."

"I love him. I don't care if he looks a little different." Ruth Anne scanned the faces on the computer screen, and most of them were cute in their own way. "Look how adorable some of those children are. And we are simple people. Plain people. Our looks don't rule our lives like—" She stopped herself before saying, "Like the *Englisch*."

"Awe, sweetie. Of course you will love him no matter what. He is precious." Dr. Prescott closed her computer and pushed it aside. "And I know you said you felt badly because you couldn't get Joshua to latch on. That's very common with Down's babies. So don't feel guilty about it, okay?"

Ruth Anne wished she could bring Joshua back to Dr. Prescott instead of the older man. Her mind was awhirl with thoughts, questions, and fears. She wasn't sure what to ask, so she just nodded.

Levi had stopped crying, but he wouldn't look at anyone. After a few moments, he stood up and looked back and forth between the two doctors. They all waited for him to say something. Looking out the window, Ruth Anne could see dark clouds rolling in and that it had begun to rain. She was glad her parents had hired a driver since Lancaster was a bit too far to go by buggy. Besides, she couldn't have managed all the jostling of a buggy ride just yet, and August in Lancaster County was still too warm to be carting around a newborn.

On shaky legs, Ruth Anne stood up. As best she could, she thanked the doctors, then extended her arms so that Levi could hand her Joshua. She waited as her husband leaned down and kissed Joshua gently on the forehead. Then he handed their son to her and walked out of the room.

"He just needs time to process this information," Dr. Calhoun said as thunder boomed in the background.

Dr. Prescott opened the drawer of her desk, then handed Ruth Anne another card. "This is a local support group. After Dr.

Calhoun finishes testing and things settle down, you might want to call that number. Everyone in the group is raising at least one child with Down's syndrome."

Ruth Anne swallowed hard as she pulled Joshua closer to her. After a few moments, she eased him into the baby carrier, fearful of dropping him. Her legs were shaking, her lip trembling. "I have to go find Levi," she said as she leaned down to grab the carrier.

"I'm going that way. Let me carry that for you. I doubt you need to be lifting anything so soon." Dr. Calhoun lifted the carrier, and together they left the office and headed toward the exit. Ruth Anne still thought she might pass out. But she didn't have that luxury. She had a baby to care for. In the distance, she saw Levi standing underneath the awning, staring out into the darkness of the storm, and she tried to picture a future that neither of them saw coming.

CHAPTER THREE

The next morning Levi got ready for work earlier than normal, even though he'd already gotten permission to be off for a few days. He'd heard Ruth Anne getting up and down every few hours, heating bottles, changing diapers, and comforting their son when he cried. It was a tiny cry, and to Levi, he seemed to be struggling to make the sound. A better man would have let his wife rest and handled things during the night, but instead, he'd lay sleepless, pretending to be in a sound slumber. He knew that his mother-in-law would be over this morning, as would some of the other women, each bringing meals and wanting to see the new baby.

He put on his straw hat and was almost out the door when Ruth Anne called his name. He turned around.

"*Ya?* Are you okay?"

She nodded but didn't say anything. She shuffled toward him, barefoot in her white nightgown, her dark hair tousled and circles

21

under her eyes. "I just wanted to make sure *you* are okay. I thought you were going to take a few days off from work."

He hung his head, sighed, then looked back at her. She was always thinking about everyone else. "*Ya.* I-I'm fine," he stammered. "I'm going to check in at work, that's all. Just make sure everything is okay. Jake's been real *gut* to me, so if he needs me, I figure I can work a few hours each day. I know you'll be having lots of company."

She took a couple of steps toward him. "But we talked about this. We planned it all out, that you would stay home with me and the baby. You said—"

"I know, Ruthie, but I have responsibilities." He scratched his cheek as he recalled all the conversations they'd had. "I gotta go."

He gave a quick wave, then turned and closed the door behind him. By the time he crossed Lincoln Highway in his buggy, it had started to rain again. Not as hard as the previous night, but it was coming into the buggy from the north and pelting against the side, enough that he was soaking wet by the time he got to the bishop's house. He'd considered talking to his father, but they'd never been close, and such a heartfelt conversation would seem strange. Levi and his brothers might as well have been raised solely by their mother. She'd done everything. And Levi had promised himself a long time ago that he would be involved in his children's upbringing.

He'd also considered talking to his mother, but he assumed she would be by to visit Ruth Anne and the baby later, and Levi felt the need for some fatherly advice. Bishop Lantz had been the bishop of their community since before Levi was born. He was a wise man, someone Levi respected and trusted. And Levi sensed that the man would have a better understanding than most, due to his own handicap. He was sure that word was out by now about Joshua.

Ruth Anne had tearfully called her mother from a cell phone they kept for emergencies.

Susanna Lantz walked onto the front porch, the screen door slamming behind her. The older woman had a towel in one hand. She waited until Levi had tethered his horse and was trotting toward the house before she called out to him.

"We were going to pay you a visit within the week. We're so anxious to meet little Joshua." She smiled as Levi hurried up the steps to the covered porch. Susanna passed him the towel, then put her hands on her plentiful hips, smiling broadly. "Congratulations, dear."

Levi wiped his face, his arms, and then his hands. "*Danki.* The rain was coming sideways into the buggy, and the drop-down window cover on my side ripped while I was pulling it down." He dabbed at his pants and shirt as best he could. "I don't want to drip on your floors."

Susanna chuckled. "It wouldn't be the first time, young Levi. Now you come in here for some iced tea and a slice of cinnamon raisin bread I just pulled from the oven." She motioned for Levi to follow her. "Are you here to see John?" she asked over her shoulder.

"*Ya.* If he has time to talk with me." Levi crossed the threshold and followed the bishop's wife into the living room. "Do you . . . do you know . . ." He didn't want to say it. "That our Joshua is, uh . . ."

Susanna pointed to a rocking chair in the corner, then winked at Levi as she nodded. "*Challenged* is the word I think you're looking for. How special you and Ruth Anne are for God to have chosen you both for this unexpected role." She smiled. "Very blessed indeed." She pointed toward the corner again. "Now, you sit. I will find John, then get you both some warm bread while you chat."

Susanna scurried in her bare feet out of the living room, and Levi sat down in the rocking chair. He put his hat in his lap. Dr.

Prescott also had said God chose special people. Levi didn't think that was the right word to describe how he was feeling. He'd spent the entire night calculating all the bad things he'd ever done in his life and wondering if they warranted this kind of punishment.

Bishop Lantz walked into the room wearing the black glasses he always wore, although he wasn't carrying the cane he usually had with him. Levi suspected he knew his way around his own house well enough not to need it. He walked toward the rocking chair and extended his hand. Levi started to stand up, but the bishop quickly said, "Keep your seat, *sohn*." Then he sat in a nearby tan recliner and stroked his gray beard. "I've had to smell that cinnamon raisin bread for the past hour. I sure hope Suzie is bringing us a slice."

Levi tried to smile. "It does smell real *gut*. She said she was bringing us some." Although he didn't have much of an appetite.

"It needs to cool a bit before I slice into it," Susanna hollered from the kitchen. A moment later she poked her head in. "So I'm going to fold some clothes that I luckily got down from the line before this rain started. You boys talk, and I'll be back with your snack later."

Susanna's eyes were always twinkling, and she didn't seem to have a worry in the world. But it couldn't have been easy for her, taking care of a husband who was blind.

"Tell me about your new son." Bishop Lantz lifted his chin and kept his black sunglasses directed at Levi. He grinned. "I always wanted one of those—a son. But after our fifth girl, we figured a son wasn't in our future." He paused, still smiling. "I bet your family is happy to have a boy." He pointed a finger at Levi, and Levi braced himself for what might be coming. Bishop Lantz leaned closer to Levi and spoke in a whisper. "I think the Lord is intentionally gifting the world with more girls. Eventually they are going to just take over."

"I heard that," Susanna said as she walked past them with a basket of laundry. "Sorry to interrupt. But keep in mind that you are the bishop in this community, so don't fill the boy's mind with silliness." She winked at Levi again, then closed a bedroom door behind her. Levi loved the bishop and his wife.

"Our Joshua has Down's syndrome." Levi needed someone to understand how he was feeling, and he'd been spending too much time crying quietly in the bathroom since leaving Dr. Prescott's office. He didn't want to show weakness in front of Ruth Anne. It was his job to take care of his family. He wanted Bishop Lantz to tell him that everything would be okay, that he wasn't being punished, and that his worries would subside. Fear was suffocating him.

"It's going to be a hard road, Levi, and some will say that you and Ruth Anne have been chosen to raise a special child."

Levi nodded but realized Bishop Lantz couldn't see him, so he said, "*Ya.* We've been told that."

The bishop was quiet for a few moments. Then he ran a hand down his long beard again. "*All* children are special, Levi. And I sense that you have come to me for several reasons." He smiled. "One, because I'm the bishop. And two, because I am blind."

Levi could feel himself blushing and was glad Bishop Lantz couldn't see it. He sighed, but the bishop went on before Levi had a chance to say anything.

"And sometimes I'm at a disadvantage, but I never one time heard my mother say that I was sick, and she didn't treat me any different from the other *kinner.* I had to clean my room and do chores just like everyone else in the household. My father was the same way. I worked with him in the fields as soon as I was of age. He didn't cut me any slack either."

"I'm fearful, Bishop Lantz, and I know that's a sin."

The bishop sighed as he leaned against the back of the couch. "My advice to you, Levi, is to set the standard by which you want your son treated by others in the community. If you want to treat him like he is different, then others will too. And it's understandable to have fear and worry. You are blessed to be raising him here, in a place where judgment is limited, where pride and vanity have no place. God sees your fears, and He will lead you and Ruth Anne in the right direction. Does this help?"

"*Ya,*" he said softly, even though the bishop hadn't addressed Levi's biggest fear, the one that had kept him from going to check in on his son during the night—the self-imposed detachment Levi was creating.

Susanna apologized for interrupting again as she crossed through the living room toward the kitchen, but she was quickly back with two slices of bread and two glasses of iced tea. Then she was on her way out of the room.

"*Danki.*" Levi put his plate in his lap, took several large gulps of the tea, then set the glass on a small table next to him. Sweat beaded on his forehead as he lifted the bread, but he didn't bring it to his mouth. He'd made this trip for one reason, and he wanted to leave with an answer. "Bishop Lantz, *mei* cousin . . ." His voice cracked, and he was glad the bishop couldn't see his tears. "*Mei* cousin died when he was nine. He was the cutest little fellow, but he had this Down's syndrome, like Joshua. And I loved Joshua the minute I laid my eyes on him, but my fear is causing me to . . . to not want to love him as much as I do." He swallowed back a sob. "What kind of man does this?" His voice rose an octave. "What kind of man doesn't want to love his own son? But I love him so much it hurts, and I don't know how to explain it—even to Ruthie. I know in my mind that the right thing to do is to love him for however long we have him, to be the best father I can, and . . ." He paused, took a breath. "And I just can't understand how I will ever go on if we only have him for a short time, Bishop." A tear slid down his cheek, and Levi didn't think he'd ever felt worse about himself than he did in that moment. "I love the Lord. I know that Joshua will be with Him, but . . . but what about me? And Ruthie? If my love for Joshua is this strong now, how would I ever get by if something happened to him?" Levi didn't even try to hide the fact the he was crying now. His emotions were pouring out, as if a bottle had been uncorked. "How will I survive after loving him for years?" He shook his head. "It just ain't natural for a *kinner* to go before their parents. I need you to tell me what to do and how not to be fearful."

Bishop Lantz put his uneaten bread on the small table by his own chair. He set his glass down too. "I can't help you, Levi."

Levi felt his stomach lurch as his pulse picked up. *You're the bishop. It's your job to help me.*

"And let me tell you why. Every man, woman, and child faces fear differently. You already know that fear and worry block the voice of God. You know it's a sin. I will pray for you, of course, but ultimately you have to figure this out on your own. But . . ." The bishop sighed. "It wonders me about what the *Englisch* doctors have told you. I am familiar with Down's syndrome. And the percentage of those who live well into adulthood is very high. Some have emotional challenges, and I'm not saying that your cousin's death is rare." He shrugged. "I honestly don't know. But you must educate yourself, learn about your son's diagnosis. That in itself might eliminate a lot of the fear you are feeling."

Levi didn't say anything as he tried to process the bishop's words.

"My boy, there are no guarantees. You might still lose him. We don't know the Lord's plan. People die unexpectedly every day. We can't know the future, or we would all live in fear all the time. The fact is, fear is not going to change one thing. It's simply an outlet for Satan to find his way into our hearts and detach us from our Savior."

Levi took a deep breath and let it out slowly, determined not to let the enemy into his heart, but still unsure how God could do this to him and Ruth Anne.

He finished the slice of bread quickly and thanked the bishop for his wise words. Then he stopped at the lumberyard. And told his boss he wouldn't be needing any time off. He set quickly to work.

CHAPTER FOUR

Ruth Anne sat down on the couch in a freshly ironed maroon dress, not a strand of hair out of place beneath her *kapp*. She gently rocked Joshua. Despite her exhaustion and worry, she wanted everything to appear as normal as possible. She would have visitors all day long, and she was dreading it. She'd thought Levi would be with her to receive everyone, that he would lead the conversations, but her husband couldn't even look at their newborn son, and for Ruth Anne, that fact was almost worse than Joshua's diagnosis. She pulled her son even closer, fighting tears. How could Levi not be as in love with Joshua as she was? He hadn't held Joshua even once since they'd returned from Dr. Prescott's office. Maybe he just needed some time.

She stood up when she heard a buggy coming up the drive, and she wondered who her first visitor would be. Looking out the window, she saw a line of buggies. Had they all gotten together ahead of time and rehearsed what they would say and how they'd act? She swallowed back the lump in her throat as she continued to rock Joshua. Even if her baby's face had a flatter appearance than most and his legs and arms were a little shorter than normal, Ruth Anne didn't care. She'd never known such love. She kissed him on the forehead and moved toward the front door. Her mother and little sister were the first ones to come up the porch steps.

"I'm an auntie," Katie said proudly as she pulled the screen door open and marched toward Ruth Anne. "So I'm the boss of him." She stood on her tiptoes to have a better look. "*Ach*, he's pretty."

"*Maedels* are pretty. Boys are handsome," Ruth Anne's mother said as she slid up to her daughters. Her face lit up when she saw Joshua, and she quickly lifted him from Ruth Anne's arms. "Look at you, my darling bundle of joy."

This was one of the many moments Ruth Anne had dreamed of—when family and friends came calling for a visit with their son. But in the daydream, Levi had always been by her side, the proud father he'd been throughout her pregnancy. She glanced over her mother's shoulder, wondering if Levi would be returning soon.

Ruth Anne welcomed her guests, offered them iced tea and cookies, and did her best not to crumble in front of everyone. People always fussed over a new baby, but everyone seemed to be going overboard. As though it were a miracle that Joshua was even born.

The one person she'd expected hadn't shown up, and she was trying not to show her disappointment. Levi's mother, sister-in-laws, and grandmother were busy ogling over Joshua, and Ruth Anne excused herself to go get more cookies.

"I know this is hard for you."

Ruth Anne looked over her shoulder at the sound of her mother's voice. Then she turned back and finished putting the cookies on the tray. "No one is saying anything about the Down's syndrome.

It just feels weird, like everyone is pretending that he isn't different from other babies." She turned around, blinked back tears, and gazed into her mother's eyes. "But he is."

Mamm walked closer. "*Mei maedel*, could you possibly love Joshua any more or any less if he were just like other *kinner*?"

She shook her head. "I can't even explain the kind of love I feel for him, and he's only a few days old."

Mamm smiled. "It's a very different kind of love." She reached up and pushed back a strand of Ruth Anne's hair that had fallen from beneath her *kapp*. "You are going to be fine. You are going to be a wonderful *mudder*."

Ruth Anne leaned to her left to look in the living room. In addition to Levi's family, several cousins on Ruth Anne's side were there and three older women who lived alone. "It's . . . ," she whispered, bit her lip for a few moments, and then looked back at her mother. "It's Levi, *Mamm*. He hasn't held Joshua since we got home from the doctor's office." She blinked back tears. "When he was born, you saw Levi. He loved Joshua instantly." She lifted her shoulders and raised her palms. "How could he change like this just because his child isn't . . . isn't . . . normal?" She fought the urge to run into her mother's arms, bury her face into her chest, and sob.

"*Ach, mei maedel*. Levi is a *gut* man. He will find his way. He might just need some time." She sighed, a slight smile on her lips as she touched Ruth Anne's arm. "You are both so young, but if God didn't feel like the two of you could handle this, He wouldn't have gifted you with a special-needs child. You will do fine." She glanced toward the living room. "And everyone is already in love with Joshua. You will have plenty of help." She chuckled. "I think Katie probably wants to come live here now." She nodded toward Ruth Anne's sister sitting on the couch holding Joshua. "He is all she's talked about."

Ruth Anne pulled a tissue from the pocket of her apron, dabbed at her eyes, then smiled at her mother. "He really is the most beautiful little person on the planet."

"*Ya*. He truly is."

Levi spent the day taking inventory, the part of his job he disliked the most. His boss had told him it wasn't necessary until next month, but Levi wanted to bury himself in a project he hated. He deserved that for not staying home with his wife and new baby.

When he got home, Ruth Anne was sitting on the porch rocking their son, and by the time Levi hit the porch steps, the aroma of roast and potatoes wafted through the screen window of the old farmhouse. His stomach rumbled. He'd skipped lunch today, and despite the circumstances, he was hungry.

"Did you have a *gut* day?" He took off his straw hat and ran his arm across his forehead. "Lots of company today?"

She nodded. "*Ya.*"

As she listed all the people who'd come by, Levi let his eyes drift to the bundle in her arms. Ruth Anne stood up quickly and walked toward him. She held out Joshua, tucked in a blue blanket, his blue eyes wide and searching. "I have to go check on the rolls. Can you please hold him?"

Levi shifted his feet as Ruth Anne brought Joshua closer to him. Then she glared at him. "Can you please hold your son while I finish supper?"

Levi took his tiny son into his arms, and once he'd locked eyes with him, the pang of fear took hold. He sat down in the rocking chair and didn't look up when the screen door slammed shut behind his wife. Instead, he just gazed at his boy. He recalled what Bishop Lantz had said, about how many Down's syndrome children live a full life. Maybe Levi's cousin truly had been an exception. He squeezed his eyes closed for a few moments as he recalled Saul's funeral.

When he opened his eyes, Joshua's eyes were closed. He held his breath as he waited for his son's chest to rise and fall. Would it always be this way? Would he never have peace because he would be worrying about this new person in his life? It was all consuming. But when Joshua opened his bright-blue eyes again, all Levi could do was stared at him in total awe.

There wasn't much conversation during supper. Ruth Anne told Levi some of the news she'd heard from the women who had visited, but beyond that, she was having a hard time even being in the same room with him.

Later in the evening, she eased Joshua into the cradle Levi had built, remembering how he'd made sure the slats were a safe distance apart, and how he'd finished it with a varnish he'd researched would be safe for an infant. She gave the cradle a gentle rock, then turned to her husband, who was already in bed. She lowered the flame in the lantern and crawled in beside him. "Are you awake?"

Facing away from her, Levi groaned a little but didn't turn her way. She'd watched them together out the kitchen window earlier while she was finishing supper, how Levi had gazed at Joshua.

Ruth Anne and Levi hadn't interacted the rest of the evening. A large part of her wanted to poke Levi in the back and make him talk to her, but she was exhausted, and Joshua would be ready for a bottle again in a couple hours. She just didn't have the energy to fight with him.

She eased atop the covers, extinguished the lantern, and curled into a ball on her side facing Joshua, thankful there was a slight breeze blowing into the room through the open window. Crying wasn't an option because once she started, she wouldn't be able to stop, and she needed to get some rest to keep up this pace. She thought about the card Dr. Prescott had given her, but quickly tossed the thought aside. Ruth Anne loved Joshua more than anything, and she would answer God's call to be his mother. She didn't need a support group.

Ruth Anne's problem was with her husband. And she wasn't sure who to talk to about that.

Chapter Five

"You are two weeks old today," Ruth Anne whispered to Joshua as she leaned down and touched her nose to his. She glanced at the clock on the wall behind Dr. Calhoun's desk. She'd spent most of the day taking Joshua from one lab to another for tests she didn't understand. She'd expected Levi to be with her today, although she wasn't sure why since the man she'd married two years ago felt like a stranger to her, leaving earlier and earlier for work each day and coming home later and later. He would give her the obligatory kiss on her cheek, kiss Joshua, then bathe, eat, and go to bed. She wished her mother were with her today, but she'd been too embarrassed to tell her *mamm* that Levi was a weasel of a man who'd chosen not to accept his own son into his heart and that, so far, time hadn't propelled Levi the way her mother had said it might.

Dr. Calhoun walked into his office and wound around to the chair behind his desk. His office wasn't as tidy as Dr. Prescott's, and it smelled of antiseptic, whereas Dr. Prescott's office had smelled like lilac. Ruth Anne forced a smile, but when Dr. Calhoun's eyebrows drew together and he sighed, she was wishing more than ever that her mother were here with her.

"Where is your husband?" Dr. Calhoun asked as he opened a file folder and slipped on a pair of wire-rimmed glasses.

"He is . . . uh, doing inventory at work." She paused, glanced down at Joshua in his carrier, then added, "He's very busy." *Too busy to care about his own son.*

Dr. Calhoun leaned back in his chair and took off the reading glasses. He stared at her for a few moments. "Ruth Anne, is everything okay at home? I know that being thrust into a situation you weren't expecting can be confusing."

She nodded, trying to smile again. "*Ya*, everything is *gut. Danki* . . . I mean, thank you."

The doctor folded his arms across his chest. His gray hair was much too long for a man his age, and his eyes were dark and scary, tucked beneath bushy gray eyebrows. His voice was deep and raspy. Ruth Anne wished Dr. Prescott were here. Or her mother. Levi. Someone.

"Ruth Anne, do you know what kind of doctor I am? Do you know why Dr. Prescott asked me to oversee some special testing for Joshua?"

She sat taller, hoping it would make her appear smarter, despite her eighth-grade education. She knew doctors had schooling for a dozen years or so. "You're a pediatrician for babies with Down's syndrome."

"I'm a pediatric cardiologist. My focus is on the heart." He unfolded his arms and leaned forward. "Do you remember one of the first tests they did this morning at the hospital lab? It was called an echocardiogram."

Ruth Anne nodded. "*Ya*, the nurse said it took a picture of Joshua's heart."

"That's right." Dr. Calhoun smiled, but Ruth Anne recognized the way he was talking to her, the same way she often heard her mother talking to Katie. "And what we found is that Joshua has a heart defect and—"

"*Nee.*" Ruth Anne gasped and brought a hand to her mouth.

"It's all right, Ruth Anne. It's minor and can be controlled with medication right now. We just have to keep an eye on it."

She allowed herself a breath, but before she could say anything, Dr. Calhoun went on.

"Ruth Anne, Joshua is going to need to undergo a lot of testing. He is going to need to see a pediatric ophthalmologist." He paused, scratching his forehead. "Do you know what that is?" She shook her head and waited for him to explain. "It's a doctor who will check Joshua's eyes for cataracts, something common to Down's syndrome. And there will be other specialists who'll need to examine Joshua. Dr. Prescott will oversee all of these other appointments. Today's was to have Joshua's heart checked and to run some other blood work. I'll need to see him every month for a while."

Ruth Anne looked at her baby boy and wondered how someone so beautiful could have anything wrong with him. "He is finishing almost all of his bottles at each feeding. He goes to the bathroom like normal, and he sleeps really well." She spat the comments at the man, as if these things would undo what he'd told her. He nodded.

"And those are all good things. Joshua seems to be doing very well. But, Ruth Anne, it can be exhausting emotionally to adjust to the changes in your life, and physically, too, running around from one appointment to the next. Can your husband take time off work to help you? Or maybe your mother or another family member?"

"Of course." She shifted her weight in the chair, not planning to ask anyone for help. She may be nineteen, but she was capable of taking care of all Joshua's needs.

After she'd thanked Dr. Calhoun, she found her way to the exit and stopped at the receptionist's window right before the door. "Is this where I pay?" She pulled out her wallet, hoping that two hundred and forty dollars would cover all of the tests. The community account had funds available, but she'd never had to draw from that account, and she hoped she wouldn't have to now.

"Dr. Calhoun wants to see Joshua in one month." The receptionist didn't look up from writing something. "Do you want the same day and time?"

"*Ya.* That's fine."

Finally, the woman looked up at her with huge brown eyes that had lots of makeup around them. She handed Ruth Anne a piece of paper. "Okay, you were charged seven hundred dollars. And here's your receipt."

Ruth Anne felt the breath rush from her lungs, and she wasn't sure she'd be able to breathe in enough air to keep from passing out. She brought a hand to her chest. "What?" She blinked a few times and asked again, "What? I . . . I don't have that much." She held up the wad of twenties she'd pulled from her small black purse.

The girl on the other side of the partition straightened her back and shook her head. "No, sweetie, I'm sorry. You don't owe that. It's a receipt. I figured you understood."

Ruth Anne didn't understand anything, and why was this woman that couldn't be any older than her calling her sweetie? It seemed inappropriate. She just wanted to be at home, away from everyone, so she could cry her eyes out. She felt like she was going to explode. "Understand what?"

"All of your bills are being paid by an anonymous person. So you'll never have to worry about payments."

"Anonymous?"

"Yes. Isn't that great?" The woman smiled, showing her bright white teeth.

Ruth Anne was waiting for the woman to tell her what *anonymous* meant, but she did understand that someone else was paying her bills. Aside from that, nothing was great.

"Who would do such a thing?"

The woman shrugged. "I don't know. That's why it's *anonymous*."

Ruth Anne felt her face flushing, so she rushed to get her things together and hurried out of the office. *Joshua has a heart problem. He will have lots of appointments. Someone is paying our bills.*

She slung the diaper bag onto her shoulder as she carted Joshua in his carrier down the hall toward the exit. She rounded the corner but slowed down when someone came into the hallway from Dr. Prescott's office. A few moments later she looked up and locked eyes with Bethany. Her friend's jaw dropped.

"Ruth Anne!" She glanced at her husband who was toting Esther Rose in a carrier, the same type Joshua was in. "We've been meaning to pay you a visit." She hurried to Ruth Anne, then leaned down and brought a hand to her chest. "Isn't he a handsome fellow." She stood up and smiled. "Are you here to see Dr. Prescott?"

"*Nee.* I saw her awhile back. I was here to see a doctor around the corner. A heart doctor."

Bethany glanced at Joshua but quickly pulled her eyes away. "I hope everything will be all right." Even though public affection was frowned upon by their people, Bethany had always been affectionate. So it was even more of a kick in the shins when her friend gave a quick wave instead of a hug. "It was *gut* to see you. Let's get together soon."

Ruth Anne's feet were rooted to the floor as she watched the couple disappear into the elevator. *Let's get together soon? Really, Bethany? You are my best friend.* She set the carrier down next to her, reached for the tissue in her pocket, and blew her nose. Loud and unladylike, but she didn't care. As a tear spilled down her cheek, she swished it away with her hand and sniffled. Why was Bethany acting like this? All the hours knitting blankets, booties, and caps. They'd spent days at their sewing machines making baby outfits. And they'd laughed, talked about what their children would be when they grew up, and shared every detail of their pregnancies with each other.

"Ruth Anne, is that you?"

She stuffed the tissue in her pocket and turned to face Dr. Prescott. "What's wrong?" The doctor put a hand on Ruth Anne's arm.

"Everything. Everything is wrong. I don't understand what is happening!" She threw her hands in the air and started to cry again. "I don't understand everything I need to about Joshua. Levi isn't the same man I married. And now"—she pointed toward the elevator—"my best friend won't have anything to do with me. Dr. Prescott, what is happening?" She covered her face with her hands until she felt the doctor put an arm around her.

"Hey, sweetie. Everything is going to be okay."

Ruth Anne uncovered her face, realizing that it didn't feel inappropriate for Dr. Prescott to call her sweetie.

"I don't have another patient for about an hour. Let's go into my office and see if I can help you put the pieces together."

Dr. Prescott led Ruth Anne and Joshua into the reception area, then down the hallway and into her office, where a wave of lilac welcomed her.

Dr. Prescott waited while Ruth Anne changed Joshua's diaper

on a pad in her lap. Once she had him curled into the nook of her arm, Ruth Anne said, "I am embarrassed and so sorry. So much has been happening lately, so much to understand, and . . ."

"I know. Where is your husband?"

Ruth Anne figured she would be hearing that a lot from now on. "Working. It's inventory time, so he's very busy."

Dr. Prescott nodded. "Now, tell me everything that's going on. Was today your appointment with Dr. Calhoun?"

"*Ya.* Joshua has something wrong with his heart, but won't need surgery. Just medicine. And he has to go to an eye doctor, and I don't know what all else. And then there's Levi and Bethany and . . ."

Before she knew it, Ruth Anne had spilled her private feelings to a complete stranger. "I'm sorry," she said again.

Dr. Prescott was sitting beside Ruth Anne instead of on the other side of her desk. She put a hand on Ruth Anne's arm again. "A newborn is a lot of work, Ruth Anne, even one who doesn't have the medical problems that Joshua has. You have a lot more on your plate than most new mothers. And you're a first-time mom. You are going to need some help. Your husband just might need some time to come around. Some men get a little weird right after their baby is born, even under the best of circumstances. They see the woman they love loving someone else more than them. Give Levi time."

"No one is giving *me* any time. What if I was acting like Levi?" Fear, sadness, and worry were burrowing into her heart and changing quickly to anger.

"Do you still have the card I gave you with the information about the support group? I really think you need to check that out, Ruth Anne, and find out how other parents are coping. They share ideas and help each other."

Sitting around with a bunch of *Englisch* parents discussing how sick their children were did not sound appealing to Ruth Anne.

But yelling at Levi and telling him to grow up *was* on the agenda. She had one more question for Dr. Prescott.

"Do you know why a person would secretly pay Joshua's medical bills? I mean, I paid my bill to you. But at Dr. Calhoun's office, they said all the bills were covered." She cocked her head to one side. "Who would do that?"

Dr. Prescott shrugged. "I don't know. Is that something the bishop or someone in your community would do?"

"I don't think so . . ." She couldn't think of anyone, even her parents. They didn't have that kind of money, and they would have no reason to hide their help anyway.

She thanked Dr. Prescott again and went to find her driver. She had a thing or two to say to her husband when he got home.

CHAPTER SIX

Levi walked in the door and immediately recognized the look on Ruth Anne's face. His wife had beautiful brown eyes, but when she was mad, all her fury centered beneath her frowning eyebrows. Levi pushed back his shoulders and reminded himself that he was the head of the household. He raised his chin, lifted his straw hat from his head, and hung it on the rack by the door. But the closer he got to her, the more his manhood withered until his shoulders slumped, and he cautiously eased into the chair next to hers.

"What's wrong, Ruthie? Is Joshua okay?" He swallowed hard as he watched her take a deep breath.

"*Nee*, Levi. He is not okay." She threw her words at him like stones, and Levi felt a burst of adrenaline shoot through his body. "He has something wrong with his heart. Right now medicine can fix it, but he has to go back to the doctor every month." She paused long enough to shoot daggers from her eyes. "And he will need a lot more appointments. I am tired. I am worried. I am sad. But I love that child more than my own life. He is in his cradle, the one you lovingly made for him." She stood up and smoothed the wrinkles from her blue dress, then raised her chin and scowled even more. "There is chicken salad in the refrigerator. There are six bottles of formula with the exact right amount in each. Your son will need a bottle in two hours, so I suggest you bathe and eat now. If you don't burp him, he will spit up."

Levi opened his mouth to tell her that he didn't know anything about such things, but she pointed a finger at him.

"Shame on you." Then her cold eyes filled with tears. "You're acting just like your father, a man you said you didn't want to be. And you are ignoring your son because he isn't perfect—"

"That's not true." He started to get up, but her finger was in his face now.

"I'm going to bed! Upstairs!"

She stormed off toward the stairs, and he was tempted to follow her into the spare bedroom, but instead, he just sat there, knowing that's how it must seem—that he was a man who didn't love his own son. If she only knew how wrong she was, maybe she could understand the fear and worry that caused his heart to pound so hard he felt like he was having a heart attack. He worried so much it was hard to function sometimes; it was easier just to detach from them both. But he knew Ruth Anne was at her wit's end to talk to him like that. He sat there until he was completely convinced he was an awful person and was going to make a pretty lousy father as well. Then he skipped supper and took a bath. The moment he stepped out of the claw-foot bathtub, he heard faint crying.

There it was again—the adrenaline—pulsing through his body like a freight train racing through his veins. He darted naked from the bathroom, down the hall, and into their bedroom, leaving droplets of water across the wood floors. He stopped about two feet from the cradle and stared at his son. Hungry? Wet? Sad? Probably hot. Levi reached over and unwrapped him from the blanket cocoon, but when he did, the baby's arms and legs went wild, and his cry turned into a scream. *Why isn't Ruth Anne coming to help me?*

Fear. Fear. Fear. But without even thinking, he rebundled Joshua in the blanket and scooped him into his arms. The baby's screaming ratcheted up another notch as droplets of water splashed onto his tiny face from Levi's wet hair. He laid the baby back down, grabbed the towel and dried his body and hair as best he could, then wrapped a towel around his waist, picked up Joshua again, and began pacing the room.

Ruth Anne sat at the top of the landing, her knees curled to her chest, wanting more than anything to go comfort her son, but she held her position, knowing she could be downstairs in ten seconds if she needed to be. She'd rarely talked to Levi like that before. Maybe twice over the course of their entire relationship, from dating to marriage. It just wasn't their way for a woman to behave in such a manner. She and Levi had been raised in traditional Old Order households without some of the luxuries their friends had and with rules stricter than most. But one thing had clearly been instilled in both of them. The man is the head of the household and is to be respected always.

But Ruth Anne needed some help. She needed Levi. She inched down the stairs on her behind, careful of the creak on the third step down. She kept going until she was far enough down the stairs that she could see into her bedroom. She latched onto the handrails and peered through to the opened bedroom door, quiet as a mouse and thankful that her son wasn't crying anymore.

She leaned away and grimaced. *Levi, why are you wearing just a towel around your waist?* Her husband paced the room, gently bouncing Joshua in his arms. Finally. Even though it had been forced, at least they were interacting. After a couple of minutes, Levi kissed Joshua on the forehead and then held him up until they were cheek to cheek. Then he put him back in the cradle and took three steps backward until he was sitting on the edge of their bed. He covered his face with his hands and wept.

She watched her husband, not bothering to swipe at the tear that slipped down her own cheek. She'd never seen him cry prior to Joshua's birth and then again at Dr. Prescott's office. A huge part of her wanted to run to him, to comfort him. But an underlying worry was embedded in her heart. Was he crying because he was so incredibly sad that his child wouldn't be like other children? Why couldn't he love Joshua for the person he was? Or maybe he did, and he just felt as lost as she did.

She scooted quietly back up the stairs until she was out of sight. She crawled into the twin bed in her sewing room. She'd never slept in the bed. Only her mother had when she'd stayed over a couple of times when Ruth Anne had been sick during the early months of her pregnancy. As she curled into a ball and cried, she wished her mother were here now. Joshua needed her. Apparently her husband did too.

But who is going to take care of me?

She awoke in the middle of the night, checked the time, and hurried down to the refrigerator. Relief washed over her when she saw that two of the bottles in the refrigerator were gone. She tiptoed back up to the sewing room, but before she got there, in silhouette against the light of an almost full moon, she saw Levi standing over the cradle, dressed in his night clothes. She walked into the bedroom and stood beside him.

They were both quiet as they stared at their tiny boy, listening to the sweet sound of him breathing. Ruth Anne reached for Levi's hand, then squeezed it.

"I know you have to get up in the morning. I'll take it from here and catch the next feeding." Even though she was exhausted, this exercise hadn't been about that. She'd just wanted Levi to spend some time with his son, and in that respect, she'd accomplished what she'd hoped for.

"Okay," he said softly as he slipped his hand out of hers, then headed toward the door.

"Levi."

He turned around. *"Ya?"*

"Aren't you going to sleep in here?" Maybe he was mad about the way she'd talked to him.

"Nee. I'm going upstairs."

She took a couple of steps to follow him, but stopped.

What is happening to us?

○⃝⃠

Levi got into the small bed, wanting nothing more than to be curled up with his wife, her arm draped across him, holding him close. Even more so, he wanted to rest his head against her chest while she stroked his hair as he let his guard down, hearing her say that everything would be okay. But that wasn't his role. His role was to provide for his family, to be strong and not cry like a little baby, even though that's all he wanted to do lately.

He put his hands behind his head and stared at the ceiling. He'd been taught his entire life that everything was God's will, that the Lord always had a plan. But each time he let his thoughts run away from him, they circled back to the same place. *God, don't You dare take my son from me.*

The thought went against everything he believed—or thought he believed—and had been taught. But each time he tried to rely on his faith, to pray like he had before Joshua was born, anger reared up instead.

So, for the first time that he could remember, he closed his eyes for sleep without acknowledging God at all.

CHAPTER SEVEN

Ruth Anne walked into the fellowship hall at a nearby *Englisch* church where the support group met every Thursday at four. Apparently Dr. Prescott had gotten together with Ruth Anne's mother, and between the two of them, they'd convinced Ruth Anne to give it a try. The idea of talking to strangers—especially *Englisch* strangers—about her problems felt strange. She hadn't gotten much sleep last night even though after two months, Joshua wasn't taking a bottle as often. She'd been dreading this meeting, and it was the first time she'd left Joshua with her mother.

She'd begged Levi to attend the meeting with her, but he said he had to work late. He worked late most days. They'd settled into a routine, and even though Levi was spending more time with Joshua, it seemed forced, and he remained detached. Not only from Joshua, but from Ruth Anne as well.

At a table on the far side of the room sat four ladies and a man. On shaky legs, Ruth Anne walked toward them.

"You must be Ruth Anne, the young woman I spoke with on the phone." A pretty woman dressed in a red dress with matching heels and long blond hair stood up, walked to Ruth Anne, and extended her hand. "I'm Julie Hicks."

She motioned to one of the empty chairs.

"Sometimes there are as many as ten of us, but we are the regulars." Julie pointed to her left. "This is Angie." Julie introduced the other two women and the man, and Ruth Anne made an effort to remember their names. Angie was much older than the rest of them, maybe fifty. Julie and the other two women—Tonya and Elaine—looked to be in their thirties. With Elaine was her husband, Elmer, which seemed like a funny name for an *Englisch* man.

"We're very casual here. We mostly share ideas, discuss doctors we like, offer advice and encouragement, and generally support one another through the good and the bad of having a child with Down's syndrome." Julie smiled. "So, Ruth Anne, tell us about you, your family, and your new baby."

Ruth Anne could feel herself blushing. She wasn't used to being the center of attention, but as she glanced around the table, everyone was smiling, waiting. "My . . . my baby is Joshua. And . . . and you know I'm here because he has Down's syndrome. I'm here to learn more about it." There was a lot more to it, but she figured it was a starting point.

"Great," Julie said. "And how old is Joshua? Tell us all about him."

Ruth Anne took a deep breath. "He will be three months old next Thursday, November fifteenth. He . . . has Down's syndrome." She paused. *They know that.* She felt herself starting to sweat. "And he has a heart defect, so I take him to the heart doctor once a month. It isn't the kind that he will have to have surgery for, they don't think. And he doesn't see real *gut*, so he will eventually need glasses. He has lots of doctor appointments. My mom mostly goes with me." Ruth Anne had finally accepted her mother's offer to go with her, and it helped to have two sets of ears at the appointments. Half the time it took both Ruth Anne and her mother to understand what the doctor was saying.

"Are you married?" the older woman, Angie, asked.

Ruth Anne nodded.

Angie leaned back against her chair and folded her arms across her chest. She was a heavyset woman with short, silver hair. To Ruth Anne, she looked much too old to be having children. "Does his job prevent him from going to the doctor visits with you? And what about you? Do you work?"

Ruth Anne thought about all the hours Levi worked at the lumberyard now, voluntarily. "*Ya.* He works many hours. I only work at our house, keeping our home tidy, working in the garden, sewing, and now caring for Joshua."

"You're lucky to have a husband," Tonya said. "Mine bailed not long after Matthew was born."

"How awful." Ruth Anne bit her lip right away, knowing she shouldn't have blurted out her first thought. In some ways, Levi had left her too. That was her main reason for being here, but she wasn't about to bring it up on her first visit. Maybe never.

Tonya let out a little snort. She was pretty, too, but different from the others, who all looked like they may be professional types. Tonya had bleached white hair with dark roots and a tattoo on one of her arms—of a cross. "Believe me, I'm better off without him."

Angie chuckled. "I'd have to agree with you." She looked at Ruth Anne. "This is our safe place, Ruth Anne. We laugh, we cry, we share. And it all stays right here in this room. Having a Down's child is challenging, but they are amazing, and we've shared some wonderful times in this room over the years. Sometimes people come once or twice, or they might pop in when they are facing an unexpected challenge. We're always available. We get new people who just need help and advice during the infant and toddler years. So whether you come only today or for the next ten years, or even three or four times a year, we're fine with anything."

"How old is your baby?" Ruth Anne asked since it sounded like maybe Angie had been coming for a while.

She chuckled. "Kenny is hardly a baby. He's twenty-five. But mentally he is about fifteen. He lives on his own, though. It was scary at first, for both of us, but I check on him every day. He has a job at a burger place nearby, and he pays his own rent." She smiled. "But I guess they are always our babies, no matter how old they get."

Ruth Anne nodded. She wondered if Joshua would be behind in his mind too. Dr. Prescott said that was a possibility, and she'd given Ruth Anne some books to read. She'd glanced through them, but she didn't understand a lot of the big words, so it was frustrating.

Julie cleared her throat. "Let me give you a little briefing about each of us." She took a sip from a water bottle she had in front of her. "I am an attorney, so I can help you with any legal issues you might run into, and I'm pretty good at dealing with the insurance companies as well, so if you need to appeal any claims, I'm your gal."

"The Amish don't have insurance," Tonya said. "They draw from a community fund, right?" She looked at Ruth Anne, who nodded, recalling the mystery person who was paying her bills. She wasn't ready to share that with this group of strangers either.

"Right, right. I knew that," Julie said. "But anyway, Ruth Anne, if there is anything you don't understand, you can come to me. For example, if your son ends up needing surgery and you don't understand what you're signing, things like that."

Ruth Anne felt herself blushing. Most people who lived in Lancaster County knew plenty of Amish folks, and they all knew that Amish children only went to school through the eighth grade. She couldn't help but wonder if these people thought she was stupid. Especially Julie, who'd had lots of schooling.

"My daughter is six. Her name is Destiny. And like your Joshua, she has vision problems, but she loves her pink-framed glasses we just bought her." Julie paused, smiling. "She goes to public school, but we have a tutor who comes to the house twice a week." She leaned down and reached into her purse, pulling out a picture. She handed it to Ruth Anne.

"She's pretty," Ruth Anne said, hoping she didn't sound surprised. The little blond girl in the picture looked like some of the pictures Dr. Prescott had shown Ruth Anne. "And I like her pink glasses." She handed the photo back.

"Thank you. Rob and I adore her." She pointed to Elaine. "Elaine, you go next. I think it would be best if Ruth Anne heard from everyone, instead of me giving a summary."

"Elmer and I have been coming here for almost a year," Elaine said in a soft voice. She was a tiny little redhead who reminded her of Bethany. "Our daughter, Jamie, just turned two. She has congenital heart disease and has had two surgeries so far—she's done great with both of them." She turned to her husband, then back to Ruth Anne. "She is the love of our lives."

Ruth Anne wanted to burst into tears when Elmer leaned over and kissed Elaine on the cheek. *I miss you, Levi.*

"Half of the children born with Down's syndrome have heart problems," Julie said, then she nodded to Tonya. "Your turn."

Tonya was slumped against her chair with her hands in her lap. "Well, like I said, I'm doing this on my own. It wasn't in my husband's life plan to raise a special-needs child, and Matthew and I are doing just fine without him. Matt is three. He has a healthy heart, no vision problems, and so far the only issue we've had to deal with is that he has celiac disease, so it's gluten free at our house."

Ruth Anne had no idea what that meant, so she just smiled and nodded.

Julie took over again. "So, what's on everyone's plate this week?"

Ruth Anne listened to them mention various doctor appointments and tell stories about new things the children had done, but what she noticed most was the laughter. These people joked, laughed, shared, and amidst it all, there was a hopefulness that she could feel rubbing off on her.

After an hour, it was Tonya who offered to close the meeting. "Ruth Anne, we like to close with a prayer every week. Okay with you?"

"Of course." Ruth Anne knew better than to judge a person by their appearance, but she was surprised that Tonya was the one offering to lead the prayer.

"Dear Lord," Tonya began, "it is only through Your grace that we face each and every challenge head-on with courage, faith, and hope. Please continue to guide us as we nurture and love these children You've put in our charge. May we always make the best decisions we can for their well-being, and please guide each and every doctor who lays hands on our children. Special blessings for Ruth Anne and her family, and we're glad You guided her into our circle. In Jesus' name we pray. Amen."

Ruth Anne gulped hard, wanting to cry. But happy tears this time. This was a meeting she would look forward to attending. It hadn't been as strange as she'd feared, but more than ever, she wished Levi could have been here. She followed the others to the door, and after everyone said good-bye, Ruth Anne realized she didn't have a ride home. The church was too far from home to travel by buggy, so she'd hired a driver to drop her here, someone she didn't know well who wouldn't ask a lot of questions. But she'd forgotten to set up a return ride home. She reached into her purse and realized that wasn't the only thing she'd forgotten. Her cell phone, which was only to be used for these kinds of situations. She waved as Julie, Elaine and her husband, and Angie pulled out of the parking lot, knowing she should flag someone down to take her home, but she felt embarrassed. Then she covered her ears when a loud noise startled her. It was Tonya firing up a huge motorcycle and giving it gas over and over again. She eventually pulled up to where Ruth Anne was standing.

"Need a ride?" Tonya yelled over the roaring engine.

On that? Are you crazy? "No, thank you." She spoke as loudly as she could.

"Do you have a ride coming?" Tonya turned off the engine.

"Uh, no. Do you, um . . . do you have a cell phone I can borrow?"

"Sure." She reached into the pocket of her black leather coat, then handed Ruth Anne a phone. "But I have an extra jacket and helmet. Where do you live?"

Ruth Anne eyed the motorcycle with two large seats and the word *Harley* etched across the bright-pink finish. She'd never been on anything like that in her life.

"I live not too far from Gordonville Bookstore," she finally said as she wondered what it would feel like to be on a motorcycle.

"Well, I'm happy to drop you off. It'd be faster than you waiting for someone to come get you."

Ruth Anne stared at Tonya's phone and realized she didn't know anyone's phone number by heart. She handed back the phone. "Is it safe?"

Tonya grinned. "Probably safer than those buggies you people take out on the main highways."

Ruth Anne couldn't argue with that. She bit her lip, eyeing the pink motorcycle. Tonya got off of the seat and went around to the front of the bike and pulled out another black leather coat and a black helmet from a storage compartment. Tonya's helmet was pink. "Here," she said. "Hop on before you change your mind. Only thing is, my house is on the way to the bookstore. I need to stop there before I drop you off. It's time for Matt to get his medicine, and it's new so I want to be there. I forgot to tell Missy—the babysitter—about it." She smiled. Ruth Anne wanted to tell her what pretty teeth she had, but that seemed inappropriate. "And you can meet Matt." She pushed the coat and helmet at Ruth Anne. "Button up. Might be a bit chilly."

Tonya swung a leg over the motorcycle and started the engine, then put on her helmet. Ruth Anne felt ridiculous as she grabbed the small bar in front of the rear seat, which was higher than the one Tonya was sitting on, and swung a leg over. Once she'd tucked her dress underneath her legs as best she could, she put on the coat, buttoned it up, then put on the helmet. The temperature was in the fifties, so her legs were going to be cold, but she was anxious to do something she'd never done before.

"Ready?" Tonya yelled above the roar.

Ruth Anne nodded as she took a deep breath and grabbed on to the bar in front of her.

CHAPTER EIGHT

Levi paced the living room, wondering when Ruth Anne would be home. He'd already given Joshua a bottle, bathed him, and put him down for a nap. He loved his alone time with his son. It was okay to cry, be silly, or just cuddle him without having to worry what Ruth Anne thought. He was still angry at God, still worried if Joshua would be snatched away from them at a young age, but it was impossible not to love him, no matter the risks to Levi's heart. But somewhere over the past three months, he'd lost Ruth Anne. It was like she no longer needed him. She was quiet, did her household chores, and tended to Joshua. But it seemed like they'd lost whatever had drawn them together in the first place. Levi suspected that was mostly his fault, but he wasn't sure what to do about it.

He sat down on the couch, hungry. And waited. Then Joshua started to cry, so Levi went to his son, changed his diaper, brought him into the living room, and held him. "I love you," he whispered. "And I'm sorry it took me so long to tell you that. I just don't want to lose you. Not ever." He pulled the baby closer, careful not to let the tip of his beard brush against Joshua's soft face. Joshua smiled, and Levi smiled back at him. "It's a *gut* thing I took off work so early, or no one would have been home when your *mammi* came to drop you off." Levi walked to the window and peered outside, still wondering when his wife would be home.

∞

Ruth Anne waited until Tonya got off the motorcycle before Ruth Anne eased herself down. She removed the helmet, and with chattering teeth, she said, "So fun!"

Tonya put her helmet on her seat, so Ruth Anne did the same. "I thought you might like it." Tonya laughed. "I wonder how many people did a double take when they saw an Amish chick on the back of a Harley."

Ruth Anne laughed, too, then she noticed where she was. She thought she knew every house in Lancaster County, but Tonya's was tucked off the main road. A huge brick house with three cars in the driveway, plush landscaping, and a horse arena. "Is this your house?" Ruth Anne asked, not even trying to hide the surprise in her voice.

Tonya grinned. "Yep. My husband might have left me and Matt, but it cost him." She waved a hand for Ruth Anne to follow her.

Ruth Anne followed Tonya through a grand entryway and into a living room where a young girl was sitting on the couch reading to a little boy.

"Hey, you." Tonya hurried to her son and scooped him up. Then she smiled at the girl who looked to be not much younger than Ruth Anne. "Everything go okay?" she asked.

"Yep. He was a perfect angel as always." The girl closed the book, set it on the coffee table, and stood up. She extended her hand to Ruth Anne. "I'm Missy."

"Oops," Tonya said. "I was so busy loving on my little man I forgot to make introductions." She buried her face against her son's belly and wiggled her head back and forth as Matt laughed. Finally, she put him down and squatted in front of him. "This is my new friend, Ruth Anne."

"Hello, Matt." Ruth Anne smiled at the small boy with hair as white as his mother's, albeit natural. As she squatted down in front of Matt, Tonya explained Matt's new medication to Missy.

Matt edged closer to Ruth Anne, then threw his arms around her.

"I forgot to warn you," Tonya said. "He's a hugger."

Matt had startled Ruth Anne at first, but she squeezed him gently, and after a while, Matt eased away. "You are pretty."

"Aw. *Danki*—I mean, thank you, Matt." He was a darling little boy with big blue eyes, characteristically slanted, against a pale complexion. Ruth Anne stood up when Tonya walked toward them and lifted Matt into her arms, smothering him with kisses.

"My sweet boy. I have to take Ruth Anne home, but in a few minutes Missy is going to give you your medicine, and I will see you shortly." She gave him a final kiss. Ruth Anne told Missy and Matt it was nice meeting them both, then she followed Tonya to the door. Tonya stopped and turned to her. "It's cold now. We can take one of the cars. It was so nice outside earlier, especially for November. I felt like taking the bike for a spin."

"*Nee*, I'm fine on the bike if you are." Ruth Anne's adrenaline spiked just thinking about another ride.

Tonya grinned and shrugged. "Okeydokey."

Ruth Anne thanked Tonya a few minutes later when they'd pulled into Ruth Anne's driveway. Tonya gave a quick wave to

Levi, who was standing on the porch, but told Ruth Anne she'd meet him another time. She wanted to get home before dark. Ruth Anne was excited to tell Levi about the group, but when she saw the scowl on his face, sharing was suddenly the last thing on her mind.

"Is Joshua okay?" She hurried up the porch steps and stopped in front of him.

"*Ya.* Your *mamm* brought him home two hours ago. *Gut* thing I left work early and was here."

"Sorry. I meant to be home before now, but Tonya—the girl who brought me home—needed to stop and give her babysitter some instructions about a medication for her son." She paused, teeth chattering. "Can we talk inside? I'm freezing."

"I bet," Levi mumbled as he followed her into the living room. "I would have made a fire, but I was busy feeding and bathing Joshua. Then I had to find something to eat."

Ruth Anne wondered if he heard how pitiful and helpless he sounded, but instead of falling into a fight, she went to check on her son.

"Why would you accept a ride on a motorcycle?" Levi asked when she walked back into the living room.

She shrugged. "Because I didn't have a ride home, and I thought it would be fun."

"Fun?" Levi edged closer. "They are dangerous."

"So are our buggies. We have to trust God and His plan for us." Levi was itching for a fight, she could tell, and if he wasn't careful, he was going to get one. She'd had a nice afternoon and really didn't want it ruined, but if he was ready to talk, she was willing to listen. And she had plenty to say. "I'm going to heat up the soup."

"*Ach*, well, don't do it on my account. I ate a sandwich." He followed her into the kitchen.

She took a deep breath and blew it out slowly. "Maybe you will want some soup, too, and I'm hungry." She poured the leftover chicken noodle soup in the pot and turned on the burner before she turned to face her husband. "I was nervous about going to the support group meeting today, but I'm so glad I went. You should think about going."

Levi shook his head. "*Nee*. I don't need a group of strangers telling me how to act or feel."

"It's not like that. Everyone there has a child with Down's syndrome, and they share information about doctors, development, all kinds of things. I really liked everyone. I felt comfortable there. It's nice to know we aren't the only ones going through something like this."

"It's just not for me, Ruthie." Levi sat down in one of the kitchen chairs. It felt nice to hear him call her that since he hadn't in a while. She pulled out the chair across from him.

"Levi, we have to talk. Joshua is a precious gift from God, and I know you love him, and—"

"Why would you even say that? Of course I love him. I love him with all my heart. Why would you say that?" He scooted the chair back and stood up, his eyes fierce, his cheeks above his beard turning red.

She stood up also. "Stop yelling. It's just that we haven't talked about our feelings the past few months. I know you're scared, hurting, worried, and fearful. I am too. We need to be able to talk, Levi." She waited, but he didn't say anything.

After he left the room, she sat down at the kitchen table and tried not to cry. Again. She suddenly missed Bethany more than ever. They'd spoken at worship service, and every time they would mention getting together, but neither made the effort for it to actually happen.

She finally gave in to her sadness—despite her brief reprieve at the support group—and allowed herself a good cry before it was time to feed Joshua.

CHAPTER NINE

Levi tethered his horse outside the bishop's house, not surprised he'd been summoned for a visit. He'd missed the last three worship services, and Ruth Anne had told him people were asking about him, specifically the bishop.

"Come in out of the cold, young fellow," the bishop's wife said as she swung the door wide. The smell of pumpkin and spice wafted through the living room, and Bishop Lantz was sitting in his recliner near the fireplace as orange sparks shimmied upward.

Susanna Lantz excused herself, and after Levi had shaken the bishop's hand, he sat down in the rocker and braced himself for a talking to. He'd already made up his mind that he wasn't going to lie. He'd been a heel to his wife, stopped communicating much with the Lord, and stayed worried and fearful day in and day out. He wasn't going to add lying to the bishop to his list of sins.

"How's that new baby? Come Thanksgiving, he'll be how old?

Almost four months?" Bishop Lantz crossed one leg over the over as he pushed his dark glasses up on his nose.

"*Ya.* In two weeks he'll be four months old. It's hard to believe."

The bishop shifted his weight in the chair and uncrossed his legs. "Much to be thankful for this Thanksgiving."

Levi nodded, but then quickly said, "*Ya, ya.*" He decided not to mention all of Joshua's doctor appointments. It seemed like every time Ruth Anne and her mother returned from the medical clinic, something else was wrong with Joshua. The doctor now feared their son might not hear very well.

His nervous stomach growled, and he glanced at the clock on the wall. Ruth Anne was at her support group. This was the third week she'd attended. It seemed to make her happy, so Levi didn't begrudge the fact that it meant leftovers or a sandwich for supper. And Ruth Ann's mother enjoyed her time with Joshua each week. Ruth Anne's friend Tonya picked her up and took her home—in her car, thankfully, instead of that motorcycle. November had brought much cooler temperatures.

He took a deep breath, hoping Bishop Lantz would get on with it so he could get home to his supper and his family.

"I'll get to the point." Bishop Lantz cleared his throat and Levi's stomach did a little flip. Sometimes, he was sure the bishop had received another gift to replace his inability to see. *Mind reading.*

"It wonders me why you haven't been at worship service the past six weeks. And before you say anything, I want you to speak freely, Levi. Don't tell me what I want to hear. That's not what this visit is about. Then you can be on your way home for supper."

Levi sighed. "I don't feel very *gut* about myself right now, and I'm just trying to work out some things in my head."

"Worship service doesn't take on the task to make you feel bad or *gut*, although most people feel *gut* when they leave. It's about worshipping the Lord with your brethren. Plain and simple. But aside from that, what has you troubled, *sohn?*"

Levi didn't say anything. Why was it that all of his emotions bubbled to the surface so easily these days? Part of him wanted to cry out to the bishop for help, but he was a grown man with a family to take care of, and he doubted the bishop would understand or approve of the way Levi was feeling. "I'm fine, Bishop Lantz," he said. *So much for not lying.* "I'll be at the next worship service."

"*Gut* to know since it's at your *haus.*" The bishop grinned. Levi swallowed. He hadn't realized that it was their turn to host church service. This would be their first time. He wondered if Ruth Anne remembered. They only had ten days to get their farmhouse and yard in tip-top shape.

"*Ya*, that's right," he finally said.

Levi and the bishop were both quiet for a while. Then Bishop Lantz sighed and said, "Go home to your family, Levi. It is clear you are not ready to talk about what is bothering you, but know that I am here for you." He paused, and Levi felt like the bishop was burning a hole to his soul from behind those black glasses. "And the Lord is here for you too. But you must reach out to Him. Don't shut Him out."

⧲

Ruth Anne buckled up as Tonya started the car. "I wonder where the others were," Ruth Anne said as Tonya backed out of the church parking lot.

"Who knows?" Tonya shrugged as she put the car in reverse. "Maybe everyone is just busy getting ready for Thanksgiving next week. Angie goes through periods where she doesn't attend, but Julie rarely misses."

Ruth Anne tucked a loose strand of hair beneath her *kapp*. "It was nice chatting with Elaine and Elmer. They're such a nice couple and seem so in love and devoted to each other and their daughter." She thought about how she and Levi were at the beginning of their journey, how they got off to a rocky start. "They've been through a lot with Jamie's surgeries, but I love how upbeat and positive they are." She wanted to talk to someone about her marriage, but she just wasn't comfortable doing it during the group meeting. "What happened with you and your husband? Do you mind me asking?"

Tonya turned down the radio, a Christian station she always had on low. "No, I don't mind." She glanced at Ruth Anne, then set her eyes back on the road. "I guess a lot of things caused the marriage to fail. For me, my cup is always half full. Allen's cup was always half empty. I can find hope in any situation, but he was like someone drowning in despair—all the time. And if I tried to throw him a life vest, he'd just get mad. I wasn't going to let him pull me under with him. I couldn't. I had Matt to think about." She paused, sighed. "He was older than me, and he really didn't want any kids. I knew that, but I pushed him. I wanted a child so badly, and then when Matt was born, Allen had a really hard time dealing with the fact that he wasn't perfect, the way Allen expected everything in his life to be."

Ruth Anne nodded as she thought about her and Levi.

"Anyway, he left me the house and loads of money. And he keeps Matt on his insurance, even though he rarely sees him."

"I'm sorry." Ruth Anne folded her hands in her lap, shook her head.

"Don't be. I'm fantastic. Matt is fantastic. We love the Lord with all our hearts." She smiled as she turned into Ruth Anne's driveway. "Cup is half full, remember?"

Ruth Anne nodded. She wondered what she would be walking into. Levi seemed cranky on most Thursdays when she got home from the meeting, but she knew that he'd met with the bishop earlier as well. "Thank you again for the ride."

"You are very welcome."

Ruth Anne pulled her black coat snug around her as she walked past Levi's buggy and up the porch steps. He met her at the door holding Joshua, and he was barefoot in black slacks and no shirt.

"He threw up everywhere!" Levi's eyes were round as saucers. "Over and over again. I didn't know what to do." His eyes teared up. "What do I do? I called nine-one-one from the cell phone."

"What?" She eased over the threshold and took Joshua from him. He smiled and cooed, and she pressed his face to hers to see if he had fever. He didn't. "Levi, please tell me you did not call nine-one-one because our son threw up! Babies throw up. Sometimes they eat too much or . . . did you burp him after his bottle?" She scurried around the kitchen looking for the cell phone so she could cancel the emergency call.

"I don't know." Levi threw his hands in the air. "I've never seen such a little person throw up so much."

Ruth Anne looked at Joshua, who was still smiling, then back at her husband. "Levi. Calm down. Joshua is fine." She quickly called and canceled the emergency, explaining to the operator that everyone was okay. *Everyone but my husband.* She set Joshua in his carrier atop the kitchen table and sat down across from Levi, who was holding his head in his hands. When he finally looked up at her, he was crying.

"Levi," she said gently. But he scooted the chair away from the table and avoided her eyes.

"I gotta bathe." He strode across the living room, closing their bedroom door behind him.

Ruth Anne slowly stood up as she tried to figure out how he'd turned a simple tummy ache into a crisis.

Levi sat down on the side of the bathtub and put his head in his hands again, his stomach churning, his chest tight. *Why, Lord, do You give us the ability to love this much, so much that it hurts like this? I stay scared and afraid all the time, and I can't talk to anyone about it. Please help me.*

He realized that this was the first time he'd reached out to God since Joshua was born. Maybe God wasn't going to help him because Levi hadn't kept the Lord in the forefront of his life. Instead, he'd threatened Him, demanded that Joshua not be taken from him and Ruth Anne at a young age. But right now he was desperate to feel better, to attain some sort of control, to slow his heartbeat. He took several deep breaths, knowing that he needed help. He longed to talk to Ruth Anne, but instead, he sat on the side of the bathtub. And prayed.

Ruth Anne ran a brush the length of her hair as she watched Joshua gently breathing in his cradle, the dim light from the lantern casting a slight glow across his angelic face. The nursery she'd set up was ready, but when she'd tried to move him to the crib in that room a couple of weeks ago, Levi had thrown a fit and said they couldn't hear him if he cried. Ruth Anne had woken up several times during the night to find Levi standing over the cradle watching Joshua sleep. When she'd asked him about it, he'd said he was on his way to the bathroom.

"Levi," she whispered softly. "Are you awake?"

As usual, he was facing away from her. "We need to talk if you're awake. We have Thanksgiving at your parents coming up, and we have worship service here after that." Those were not the things she wanted to talk about, but she thought she'd have more luck getting her husband to respond to those topics. But when he didn't, she lowered the flame on the lantern until it was extinguished and buried herself beneath the covers. She missed her husband and the way things used to be. She missed Bethany, still confused why her friend had just walked away from her. But as she closed her eyes and prayed, she tried to remember what Tonya had said, that her cup was always half full and that she found hope in everything. So instead of asking God to fill up the other half of her own cup, Ruth Anne thanked Him for what she had.

CHAPTER TEN

Thanksgiving Day came and went, and while it had been a nice time with family, Ruth Anne missed her friends in the support group, and unfortunately, next week she was going to have to miss the session again. Bethany had gotten word to her, asking to meet for coffee at four. Ruth Anne was fighting bitterness toward her friend, but she missed her so much that she'd agree to go at the only time that worked for Bethany.

After an awkward hug, they each slid into a booth at a local café that Bethany's *Englisch* great-aunt owned. They positioned Joshua and Esther Rose on the seats next to them in their identical carriers. She hoped that Bethany would explain why she'd walked away from the friendship. Ruth Anne had scoured her mind, but nothing made sense.

"*Ach*, my. Look at little Joshua dressed so cute in his black slacks and sweater." Bethany pulled her eyes from Joshua and looked at Ruth Anne. "He truly is a handsome little fellow."

Ruth Anne nodded toward Bethany's baby, stretching taller to see her on the other side of the table. "Esther Rose looks very pretty too."

Bethany twisted the string of her *kapp* and was tapping her foot against the base of the table hard enough that the table shook to the beat of her foot. Bethany avoided looking Ruth Anne in the eye.

"What's wrong, Bethany?"

The foot tapping got faster as her friend blinked back tears while twisting the string of her *kapp* so tightly around her finger, Ruth Anne feared she was cutting off the circulation.

"I'm sorry. I'm so, so sorry." Bethany reached across the table and put her hand on Ruth Anne's for a few moments before she took it back and dabbed at a tear coming down her cheek. "I'm sorry for the way I've acted. And I miss you so much."

Ruth Anne took a deep breath. "My feelings are hurt. We planned and planned, and then once the babies came, that was it. No more friendship." She glanced at Joshua as her lip trembled. "Is it because Joshua is different?" She was sure Bethany would absolutely deny that, but Ruth Anne knew she'd be able to read Bethany's expression, to see if she was telling the truth.

Bethany nodded.

Ruth Anne was too shocked to say anything. Not that she condoned lying, but if Ruth Anne had been sitting where Bethany was, she would have lied.

"I just couldn't look at Joshua," Bethany said with her head down. Ruth Anne waved the waitress away, telling her they needed more time before ordering.

Ruth Anne stared across the table, then shook her head and reached for her purse. She slung her purse over her shoulder and lifted the handle of the carrier. "I'm leaving."

"Wait. Don't go. Please. I need to explain." Bethany dabbed at her eyes again. "Please, Ruth Anne. Just let me explain, and then if you still want to go, I'll understand."

Ruth Anne had hoped that there would be a reasonable explanation for Bethany's absence in her life, that they'd somehow find their way back into the friendship they'd shared for years. Ruth Anne needed to talk to someone about her relationship with Levi. She swallowed back the bile in her throat. "You just told me you couldn't look at my child." She glanced at Joshua. "He is the light of my life, and I love him. How can you say that?"

"I . . . I need you to understand," Bethany whispered. "And I'm afraid you won't."

"*Ya*, well. I'm doubting I will either."

Bethany blew her nose, and Ruth Anne ordered water for both of them and told the waitress that was all for now.

"I need to ask you something," Bethany said, her voice cracking. "If you'd have known that Joshua would be born . . . born . . . you know . . . with—"

"It's called Down's syndrome," Ruth Anne said as she straightened her back.

"*Ya*, I know." Bethany sniffled, then searched Ruth Anne's eyes. "If you'd have known that Joshua would be born with it, would you have . . . you know . . . done something else?"

"What?" Ruth Anne was sure she was reading the wrong meaning into what Bethany was asking. "Are you asking me if I'd known that Joshua would be born with Down's syndrome if . . . if . . . I would have terminated the pregnancy?"

"*Ya*. That's what I'm asking." Bethany clamped her lips together, still blinking back tears.

Ruth Anne brought a hand to her chest, glanced at her precious Joshua, and said softly, "Never in a million years."

Bethany took a sip of her water. "*Ach, ya.* That's easy to say because you didn't know he had it while in the womb since you didn't have any ultrasounds or testing."

"Is that why you had all those tests? Because if anything would have been wrong, you would have aborted your baby?" She glanced at Esther Rose, then back at Bethany. "Is that what you're saying?"

"You can't judge me, Ruth Anne. Only God can do that." Bethany sniffled. "Remember my miscarriage?"

"*Ya.* Of course." Ruth Anne recalled how devastated Bethany was when she miscarried her first pregnancy not long after she and John had married. Her great-aunt's *Englisch* son was a doctor, and that's who Bethany had gone to when she miscarried and who had also delivered Esther Rose.

"I didn't miscarry."

"What?"

Bethany closed her eyes for a few moments, then locked eyes with Ruth Anne. "Prenatal testing showed that my first pregnancy . . . that the baby had something wrong, something genetic."

Ruth Anne felt her pulse quickening as she brought a hand to her heart. "*Nee,* Bethany . . ."

"Don't judge me, Ruth Anne. John and I made a decision based on the information we had, and my uncle was fine with our choice and agreed not to tell anyone."

"But was God fine with your choice?" Ruth Anne asked softly, her chest tightening.

"I'm sorry. I never wanted to tell you, but I need you to understand why it is hard for me to be around Joshua. He is a reminder about what we did. But I treasure our friendship too much to let this stay in the way. I want things back to the way they used to be."

Ruth Anne wasn't sure if things could ever get back to the way they were. And as she searched Bethany's eyes, she longed to see even a shred of regret. Bethany was sorry—about the friendship ending. But Ruth Anne couldn't see any remorse about terminating her pregnancy, other than Joshua being a reminder that she'd ended a life.

Ruth Anne stood up, picked up the carrier, and looked at Bethany. "*Danki* for your honesty. I thought maybe I'd done something, but now that I know the truth . . . I have to say, Bethany, that I will be praying for you, but it would hurt me just as much to be around you, knowing what I know."

Bethany called out to her several times, and when Ruth Anne didn't turn around, Bethany yelled, "My inheritance from my uncle is paying Joshua's medical bills."

Ruth Anne stopped dead in her tracks, but her feet were rooted to the floor. Bethany had two *Englisch* uncles. The doctor she'd spoken of, and an uncle who had passed of cancer a few years ago. Ruth Anne bit back all the hateful things floating through her mind. She wanted to go back and tell Bethany that she could keep her guilt money. And first thing tomorrow morning she would make things right and take care of her own bills. She wanted to tell her friend how awful it was that she couldn't look at Joshua and how terrible to think she could lessen her guilt by paying his bills. There were so many things she wanted to say. But Bethany's decision was not Ruth Anne's cross to bear, only Bethany's. And Bethany had been right when she said that only God could judge. So Ruth Anne forced one foot in front of the other and moved toward the exit. And she didn't look back.

CHAPTER ELEVEN

Levi was pleased with the way everything went for their first time hosting worship service. He and Ruth Anne had paid special attention to details over the past week, scrubbing places in their house that Levi didn't think had ever seen a sponge. And Levi had cleaned up the barn and yard as well as put a fresh coat of white paint on the picket fence that surrounded the house. The food was good. The weather was great. And even the bishop had been in a good mood, cracking jokes after the service. People fussed over Joshua, and for the first time in a while, Levi felt pretty good. Except for one thing. Something was wrong with Ruth Anne. It wasn't anything he could put his finger on, but something was bothering her, and Levi suspected he was probably to blame for it.

Once everyone had left, he walked into the living room to where Ruth Anne was feeding Joshua a bottle. "What's wrong?"

"Nothing." She lifted the baby to her shoulder and patted his back. Levi was relieved to hear a healthy burp after the vomiting episode he'd endured.

"You just seemed quiet." He took his hat and hung it on the rack by the door, then added another log to the fire. He knew that "nothing" didn't mean nothing, and he wondered if his wife would let him in on whatever was bothering her. He decided not to push it. Lately—despite their detachment from each other—Levi had been trying to be more loving, communicative, and involved with Joshua. And he'd prayed a lot . . . mostly for forgiveness. Forgiveness for turning away from the Lord, for the fear and worry he'd kept bottled up, and for not trusting in God's plan for him. And Levi could feel the power of prayer working in his life. He was still afraid and fearful of what medical issues they might face with their son, and even more so about Joshua's future. But he felt stronger in his core, more firmly rooted, and not like he might burst into tears all the time. He glanced at Ruth Anne and saw tears welling in her eyes. He walked to where she was sitting on the couch with Joshua and sat down beside her.

"Ruthie." He put a hand on her leg. "What is it?"

She shrugged and wouldn't look at him. "Nothing."

There it was—that word again. The most misused word in the dictionary. He slipped out of his Sunday dress shoes, then pulled his suspenders down and untucked his shirt.

"I think everything went *gut* today. Especially for our first time." He kicked his socked feet up on the coffee table. "Don't you?"

"*Ya*. I guess."

He reached over and stroked her cheek. "You look really pretty."

She turned and glared at him.

"What? I just said you look pretty." He wasn't sure what was wrong, but apparently he couldn't say anything right.

She left the room with Joshua, but came back alone a few minutes later, stood in the middle of the living room with her hands on her hips, and said, "I want you to come with me to the support group on Thursday."

He pulled his feet from the coffee table, put them on the floor, and straightened from his spot on the couch. "*Nee*, I told you how I feel about that." Besides, he had been doing really well lately. He was working his way through his fears and worries, performing his duties as head of the household, and even trying to make another baby with his wife. "I don't need that group."

Her eyes blazed as she stared down at him. "It's not about you. It's about me! I want you to come for me. I have fears and worries, but I have to keep them bottled up until I'm about to explode. I have a baby to take care of, but I'm scared. I need my husband to talk to me, to understand, to be on the journey with me, not just riding silently beside me on a similar path."

Levi stared at her. Everything she'd just said mirrored what Levi had been feeling until lately, but he had no idea Ruth Anne felt that way too. But he still wasn't going to go air his innermost feelings with a group of *Englisch* strangers.

"If you had known that Joshua would have Down's syndrome, would you still have wanted him?" She thrust the question at him like a big boulder to his gut.

"Ruthie . . . are you kidding me? Of course I would have. I love that child more than my own life. I can't imagine not having him." He paused, his mouth downturned. "What brought this on?"

"Nothing," she said as she turned and headed toward the bedroom.

That word again.

He stood up to follow her, but sat back down again when he

heard her crying, torn between going to her or giving her the space he had longed for when he was feeling frustrated. After a little while, he tiptoed quietly to the bedroom door and knocked gently. "Ruthie."

"I'm fine, Levi."

He pressed his ear and both palms to the door and could hear her lightly whimpering. "I love you," he said softly.

"I love you too."

Ruth Anne was glad to see that all the regulars were in attendance the following Thursday. She needed the comfort of people who understood how she was feeling, and over the weeks she'd spoken freely about most everything to these people—everything except her relationship with Levi. He was spending more time with Joshua, and Ruth Anne could tell he was trying hard to be a good husband and father. But she was exhausted from all the doctor visits and from a scare earlier in the week when Joshua had a high fever that turned out to be an ear infection. And she was still devastated about Bethany. She needed something from Levi she wasn't getting, and she wasn't sure how to tell him that. And this group was support for parents with Down's syndrome children, not marriage counseling, so maybe her persistence that he come with her was wasted effort anyway.

As usual, Tonya had picked her up, and for the first half hour, they'd gotten hung up on some medical terms that Julie was trying to explain within a document that Elmer and Elaine were being pressured to sign, consenting to another surgery that they didn't fully understand. Ruth Anne found herself mentally checking out, which she usually didn't do here. Then, without any warning at all, she burst into tears. Everyone got quiet and stared at her. Tonya got up from where she was sitting a few chairs over and squatted down in front of her.

"Honey, what's wrong?" Tonya put a hand on Ruth Anne's knee. "What is it?"

She shook her head, feeling the flush creep up her neck and into her cheeks, so embarrassed about her outburst. "I'm sorry," she said as she sobbed.

Julie walked over to her and kneeled in front of her too. "Ruth Anne, sweetheart. Remember, this is a safe place to share anything that's going on in your life. Don't apologize to us."

One by one they all gathered around her and offered words of comfort. "It's just . . . I'm tired. I'm scared. I'm young. I don't know if I'm doing things right. I'm anxious all the time. The doctor said he thinks Joshua has hearing problems, and I had suspected that, but it was hard to learn that something else is wrong. I worry about losing him." She looked at Elmer and Elaine. "I know you are facing another surgery with your little Jamie, and you're both so brave . . . and . . ."

Elaine reached for her hand and squeezed. "Darling, sweet girl. Don't you know that we all have these kinds of meltdowns? Parenting is hard under the best of circumstances. We all fall apart sometimes. It's okay to be scared."

"I need my husband. I need him to understand. I keep all my feelings bottled up until I just can't take it anymore. I've been so worried about him for the past few months that I've been walking on eggshells, but I'm tired of doing that. I know he's trying, and he is a *gut* man. But I need him to understand what I'm feeling . . . that I'm scared!"

"I'm scared too, Ruthie."

She spun around in her chair, then leapt to her feet. "Levi! What are you doing here?"

He walked toward her with tears in his eyes. "I've been trying to be strong for you, to be a better man, a better husband, a better father. But I'm scared too. I'm scared of the fact that I love Joshua so much that I can't bear to think of anything happening to him, and that makes me fearful all the time. I love you. I want us to be there for each other, not walking separate paths."

She eased around the others and ran into his arms. "*Danki* for coming," she said through her tears. "I love you too."

She finally gathered herself and led Levi back to the others. Julie and all the women welcomed Levi with hugs. A teary-eyed Elmer extended his hand, but eventually pulled Levi into an embrace as well.

"Welcome, friend," Elmer said as he patted Levi on the back.

Levi sat and listened during the session, but Ruth Anne felt a sense of calm that she hadn't felt in a long time. Somehow she knew that things were going to be different. No hiding feelings or bottling things up.

"Well, we have some news," Elaine said at the end of the session. She glanced at Elmer and smiled. "We are going to have another baby."

Both Elmer and Elaine were clearly happy about this, despite all that they had coming up with Jamie's surgery. A sense of celebration lingered in the air until Elaine brought up a tender subject.

"In light of Jamie's condition, our doctor asked us if we would like to know if this baby I'm carrying has Down's syndrome." She glanced at her husband, then back at the group. "We have decided to find out."

Ruth Anne felt sick, nervous of what was coming next.

"We want to know, but it won't change anything. We know there are choices in life, and we choose to accept God's plan for us no matter what that is."

Ruth Anne breathed a sigh of relief as she thought about Bethany. And her friend had been right. Ruth Anne couldn't judge her. But Ruth Ann was human, and she was having trouble getting over what Bethany and John had done. Ruth Anne wasn't ready to resume the friendship. Maybe she never would be. But she planned to spend time praying for Bethany. Even though her friend had tried to defend her actions, Ruth Anne knew Bethany well enough to know that she was hurting.

She turned to Levi and smiled, knowing that her little family would face a lot of challenges and everything wasn't going to be okay overnight. But through faith, hope, and love, she and Levi would travel the path together. No matter what the future held for them.

READING GROUP GUIDE

1. Ruth Anne and Levi are young, 19 years old. Do you think that they have the emotional maturity to handle the needs of a child with Down's syndrome? Would an older couple have been better prepared for this undertaking?

2. Ruth Anne and her best friend, Bethany, chose different ways of birthing their children, as well as medical options prior to delivery. With all of the testing that is available to us these days, most mothers-to-be choose to have an ultrasound. What would you do if you were told that you were carrying a child with Down's syndrome?

3. As women, most of us are caregivers. But there is a place in the story where Ruth Anne thinks *Who is going to take care of me?* Has there ever been a time in your life when you felt overwhelmed and needed mothering? How did you get through it?

4. Levi struggles with his roles as a father and husband. He

wants to be good at both, but he is thrown completely off-guard by how much he loves Joshua. Instead of embracing these feelings, he tries to reject them, fueled by the fear that he might lose his child at a young age, and afraid his heart couldn't take loss. Bringing us to the age-old question: Is it better to have loved and lost, or to have never loved at all?

5. Following Bethany's confession about her abortion, Ruth Anne has a hard time with this news and chooses to walk away from Bethany. Do you think that Ruth Anne will eventually want to resume the friendship? Did you feel that Ruth Anne was judging Bethany? What if a close friend chose to terminate a pregnancy based on information from medical testing? Would you support their decision?

6. This story largely focuses on Levi; his joy, fears, worries, and struggles as a new father of a special-needs child. While having these feelings, he works hard to maintain a manly outward appearance. He wants to be a good provider and strong head of the household. Do you think that the majority of men put unnecessary pressures on themselves because they are expected to behave in a certain way?

7. Levi reaches out to Bishop Lantz, and the bishop seems to see beyond Levi's words and into his heart. What do you think was the best advice that Bishop Lantz gave to Levi? What advice would you give to Levi?

ACKNOWLEDGMENTS

It is an honor to dedicate this novella to the bravest little four-year-old I know—Raelyn Cutbirth. Your beautiful smile and loving soul left an imprint on my heart and the hearts of many. I love you, sweet angel.

Much thanks to my fabulous partners at HarperCollins Christian Fiction and to my awesome agent, Natasha Kern. It always takes a team effort, and I'm glad we're on this journey together.

Amy Clipston, Kathy Fuller, and Vannetta Chapman—love working with you gals. You all rock!

To my husband Patrick, my assistant Janet, friends and family, I could never do this without your love and support. I'm blessed to have you all in my life.

And God gets the glory for all that I am and all that I do. I pray He will continue to bless me with stories to tell.

Author Bio

Photograph by Saxton Creations

Award-winning, bestselling author Beth Wiseman is best known for her Amish novels, but her most recent novels, *Need You Now* and *The House That Love Built*, are contemporaries set in small Texas towns. Both have received glowing reviews. Beth's highly anticipated novel, *The Promise*, is inspired by a true story.

A Son for Always

AMY CLIPSTON

To my husband, Joe, with love

GLOSSARY

ach—oh

aenti—aunt

appeditlich—delicious

Ausbund—Amish hymnal

bedauerlich—sad

boppli—baby

brot—bread

bruder—brother

bruderskinner—nieces/nephews

bu—boy

buwe—boys

daadi—granddad

daed—dad

danki—thank you

dat—dad

Dietsch—Pennsylvania Dutch, the Amish language (a German dialect)

dochder—daughter

dochdern—daughters

Dummle!—hurry!

Englisher—a non-Amish person

fraa—wife

freind—friend

freinden—friends

froh—happy

gegisch—silly

gern gschehne—you're welcome

grossdaadi—grandfather

grossdochder—granddaughter

grossdochdern—granddaughters

grossmammi—grandmother

Gude mariye—Good morning

gut—good

Gut nacht—Good night

haus—house

Ich liebe dich—I love you

KAPP—prayer covering or cap

kichli—cookie

kichlin—cookies

kind—child

kinner—children

kumm—come

liewe—love, a term of endearment

maed—young women, girls

maedel—young woman

mamm—mom

mammi—grandma

mei—my

mutter—mother

naerfich—nervous

narrisch—crazy

onkel—uncle

Ordnung—The oral tradition
    of practices required and
    forbidden in the Amish faith.

schee—pretty

schmaert—smart

schtupp—family room

schweschder—sister

Was iss letz?—What's wrong?

Willkumm—welcome

Wie geht's—How do you do? or
    Good day!

wunderbaar—wonderful

ya—yes

CHAPTER ONE

Carolyn Glick hefted her tote bag onto her weary shoulder as she climbed the porch steps and headed toward the back door of her farmhouse. The bag felt as if it weighed a hundred pounds while the warm afternoon sun kissed the back of her neck. She opened the door, stepped into the mudroom, and walked through the kitchen to the family room, where she dropped the bag onto the floor.

She sank onto the sofa and moved her fingers across her protruding belly. Her legs were achy, and her swollen feet throbbed as if she'd walked her back pasture two hundred times. With her elbow propped up on the arm of the sofa, she rested her chin on her palm. Her head felt heavier than usual, and she was certain every muscle in her body was sore after spending the morning working at the Lancaster Grand Hotel. She still had two more months before her baby was born, but it felt as if she'd been pregnant for years. The exhaustion gripped her, nearly stealing her breath.

Would she always feel this tired? Would this level of exhaustion continue after her baby was born?

Before long, the back door creaked open and then closed, and footsteps sounded like they were coming from the mudroom.

"Carolyn?" Joshua appeared in the family room doorway. *"Wie geht's?"* Her husband's handsome face clouded with concern. He must have noticed the pained look on her own face. "Are you all right?"

Carolyn nodded. *"Ya.* It was a long day at the hotel. Linda called in sick, and I had to help finish her rooms along with mine." She tried to smile, but it felt more like a grimace.

"You look worn out." He sat close to her on the sofa and pulled her legs up and toward him, placing her feet on his lap. Gently, he massaged her feet, his fingers carefully working through the pain and soreness that she'd felt building all day long.

"I'm fine. It was just a long day." It was a sin to lie, but she didn't want to worry Joshua. Lately he seemed to become concerned every time she complained that she felt a twinge of soreness. "How are the boys doing?" she asked. Her son, Ben, and Joshua's assistant, Danny, both worked on the horse farm with Joshua.

"They're fine. I was out in the pasture, and I didn't see you get home. But when I stopped in at the stables, Ben said he heard your van pull up." He continued to move his fingers over her feet, softly relieving the stress. "How does this feel?"

She nodded. *"Danki.* That definitely helps."

"How are your shoulders?" he asked.

She reached up and felt her right shoulder. "They are hard as rocks."

"Would you let me try to help you?" He gently moved her legs to the floor and patted the sofa beside him. "Spin around, and I'll see if I can give you some relief."

She gingerly moved her achy body, turning her back to him. She closed her eyes and relished the feel of his strong fingers soothing her tight shoulders. The tension in her muscles slowly dissipated, and she blew out a deep sigh. Joshua always seemed to know what she needed, and sometimes he knew before even she realized it. Her shoulders drooped slightly as she looked back toward him.

"*Danki.* My shoulders don't feel like boulders anymore." She leaned back against the sofa.

"*Gern gschehne.*" He took her hand in his and his blue eyes sparkled. "I'm glad I could help you a little bit."

"How has your day been?" she asked.

"*Gut.*" He fingered his dark brown beard. "Two customers came by this morning and another customer called and asked to come out tomorrow to see a couple of horses. It's getting busy now that spring is here. Sales are definitely picking up." His expression clouded with concern. "You still look tense. Is the *boppli* okay? Are you feeling sick?"

"I'm certain the *boppli* is fine," she insisted. "I'm feeling better. Being home always helps. You don't need to worry. I'll start supper after I sit for a little bit." The truth was that she needed a nap, but she couldn't admit it out loud. After he went back out to the stables, she'd sneak into the bedroom and lie down. Just thirty minutes would do her and the baby a world of good. After she awoke, she would figure out what to cook for Joshua and Benjamin for supper.

"Okay." He pointed toward the pile of books on the coffee table. "Since you need to sit, I wonder if you would look at the books for the farm. Some bills arrived today, and I haven't had a chance to look at them because we've been so busy with customers."

Carolyn's lower lip began to quiver as she stared at the pile of books. How could she possibly find the brainpower to balance the books when she felt as if she might fall asleep just sitting at the table? All she wanted was a nap. Just one short, little nap.

"I can't." Her voice cracked as tears splattered her hot cheeks. "I'm too tired to possibly do any more work today. My legs hurt, my feet feel like they're swollen two sizes bigger than usual, and my body is completely worn out. I'll have to do the books tomorrow. I'm sorry." She stared down at the table to avoid his gaze.

"*Ach, mei liewe.*" He moved her into his arms, and his voice was warm and soothing in her ear. "Maybe you should quit the hotel. The *boppli* will be here in only two months. Now is the time for you to slow down."

Carolyn shook her head while clearing her throat. "I can't quit." Her voice was still weak, but she willed herself to stop crying. She had to pull herself together. She was too strong to act like this.

"Why not?" He dipped his chin and his eyes searched hers.

"I just can't." She scooted forward on the sofa and pointed toward the stack of books. "I'll do them right now." She reached for the top book.

"They can wait until tomorrow." Joshua touched her arm. "You need a *gut* night's sleep."

"I'll be fine." She opened the book and swiped her hand over her wet cheeks. "I can do it now."

"Carolyn," he began. "You're pushing yourself too hard. It's not *gut* for you or the *boppli*. Why won't you slow down? You just told me how exhausted you are."

"I just can't." She studied the record book and hoped he'd go back outside. She didn't want to have this conversation now. She wasn't strong enough to admit the truth.

She could feel him studying her while she began opening the stack of bills on the table.

"I'm going back out to the field," he said as he stood. "Call me if you need me."

"*Danki.*" She forced a smile as she looked up at him. "I'll get these done and then start supper."

"Fine." He kissed her forehead and headed through the kitchen toward the mudroom and back door.

Carolyn waited until she heard the door close and then heaved herself up from the sofa, gathered the pile of books and bills in her arms, and walked into the kitchen. After placing everything on the table, she moved to the sink where she filled a glass with water and sipped it. She looked out the window to where Benjamin, her sixteen-year-old son, walked from the stables to the pasture alongside Daniel King, Joshua's assistant. Benjamin grinned as he spoke to Daniel.

Benjamin was the spitting image of Carolyn with his sandy blond hair and brown eyes, and he'd been born when Carolyn was only sixteen. She had given in to the pressures of her then boyfriend and found herself pregnant and alone. Her boyfriend had abruptly left the community before she found out she was going to be a teen mother.

Carolyn had been convinced she'd always live with her parents and never find love, until she met Joshua Glick. They quickly fell in love and married last fall.

She turned back toward the kitchen table and blew out a puff of air. She had to find the strength to do the books for Joshua. The task was daunting when she was this tired, but she was strong and had faced adversity in her life before. She could do this for him.

As Carolyn sank into a chair, she felt the baby kick, and she smiled. She'd get through this exhausting time with God's help. And she couldn't wait to meet her new baby.

Mustering all the will she could find in her body and spirit, Carolyn set out to balance the books. She was determined to keep her promise to her husband and also to her son.

CHAPTER TWO

Carolyn hummed to herself while hanging out the laundry the following morning. She'd finished the books after supper last night and was thankful to have that task completed. This morning she'd made breakfast for Joshua and Benjamin before starting on the laundry.

Although she was moving slowly, she was making progress. She pinned up a pair of Joshua's trousers as she watched Benjamin help Joshua work with a horse in the pasture. She was thankful for the joy that Joshua had brought into her son's life. Thanks to Joshua, Benjamin found a love for horses and training.

She only wished she could feel secure in Benjamin's future. Would he have the same support most Amish children with two biological parents had? Most prosperous Amish parents helped their sons buy land and build a home. They would also help furnish their daughters' homes. Would she be able to help Benjamin build a home when he was ready to go out into the world?

She pushed the thoughts away and finished hanging out the wash before returning to the kitchen to make lunch. She was pouring four glasses of water when Joshua, Benjamin, and Daniel walked into the kitchen.

"*Danki* for lunch," Daniel said to Carolyn as he washed his hands at the sink.

"*Gern gschehne.*"

Joshua surveyed the table. "It smells *appeditlich, mei liewe.*"

"I thought you might like potato salad along with your sandwiches." Carolyn filled the last glass and set the pitcher on the table. "Everything is ready."

Joshua and Benjamin washed their hands before they all sat down at the table. Carolyn sat across from Joshua and, like the men, bowed her head in silent prayer before they all began reaching for the platters. Carolyn took a roll and then a slice of cheese and two slices of turkey from a platter before passing it to Benjamin. Utensils scraped the dishes, and the kitchen filled with noise.

"Your potato salad is amazing, Carolyn," Daniel said between bites. "I'd love to give your recipe to *mei mamm.*"

"*Danki*, Danny. I'll write it down for you." Carolyn glanced at Joshua, who was smiling at her. "How is your day going?"

"*Gut.*" Joshua wiped his mouth with a napkin. "Some customers are coming out this afternoon to look at two horses. We're all ready for them to arrive." He turned to Ben and Danny. "The horses are brushed and ready to be seen, right?"

"Oh, *ya.*" Benjamin nodded as he added mayonnaise and mustard to his sandwich. "We're all set."

"We had more messages this morning from people interested in seeing horses," Joshua added. "Business is booming."

"It's a blessing." Carolyn lifted her glass of water. "God is *gut.*"

"*Ya*, He is," Joshua agreed with a nod.

When the meal was over, Benjamin and Daniel thanked her again for lunch and headed back outside. Carolyn carried a stack of dishes to the counter and began to fill the sink with hot, frothy water.

"It's nice having you home today." Joshua came up behind her and set the empty platters on the counter before leaning his lanky body against it. He reached over and touched her arm.

"I'm always off from work on Tuesdays." She glanced up at him and then set the dishes in the hot water. "I've been working the same schedule for a long time."

"I know that, but I'm just saying I like having you here at the farm." He gently squeezed her arm. "I enjoy having lunch with you. I'd love to have you home every day so we can work together and enjoy all our meals together."

Carolyn averted her eyes by focusing on the dish she was washing. She knew what was coming next. Joshua was going to ask her to quit her job at the hotel, but she had to hold fast to her commitment to Benjamin's future.

"You seem happier when you are at home during the day," he continued. "You're much more relaxed today than you were yesterday when you got back from the hotel. And you always smile when you're working in the garden. I think you long to be here, too, but for some reason you just won't admit it."

She placed a clean dish on the drain board. The baby suddenly kicked, and she gasped while gripping her abdomen with a wet hand.

"Carolyn?" Joshua asked. "Are you all right?"

"*Ya*." She smiled up at him. "The *boppli* kicked. I'm certain the *boppli* recognizes your voice."

Joshua's eyes were warm and tender as he smiled in return. He reached out, touched her belly, and bent down closer to his child. "Hi, little one. Do you know your *dat's* voice?"

The baby kicked again, and Carolyn couldn't stop smiling at Joshua. "I'd take that as a yes."

Carolyn's heart warmed as Joshua's face lit up again. He held his hand to her abdomen and seemed fascinated as the baby continued to kick. She relished the moment between her husband and her unborn child.

"I can't wait to meet our *boppli*," Joshua finally said as he let his hand drop from her belly. "I hope he has your milk-chocolate eyes."

"Well, I hope *she* has *your* blue eyes instead." Carolyn wagged a finger at him. "But we don't know if we'll have a he or a she. We won't know until our baby enters the world."

"It won't matter if it's a *bu* or a *maedel*." He cupped his hand to her cheek and smiled. "We'll be *froh* either way." He turned, retrieved the glasses from the table, and brought them to the counter.

"You don't have to help me, Josh. I can do the dishes."

"I don't mind." He set the glasses next to the platters before reaching for their utensils. "I enjoy helping you." He brought the rest of the dishes and the condiments to the counter, too, and then kissed her. "I'll be outside. The customers should be here soon."

Joshua went through the mudroom to the back door, and Carolyn smiled. She was thankful for her kind, thoughtful husband. God had certainly blessed her and Benjamin the day Joshua Glick came into their lives.

∽

Joshua playfully slapped Benjamin's arm while the customers loaded the two geldings onto their trailer. "*Danki* for your work today. We have two *froh* customers, and you are part of the reason those horses are trained so well."

"*Danki, Dat.*" Benjamin smiled.

Joshua's heart warmed at the word *Dat*. He enjoyed being someone's father, and soon he'd have two children to call him dad. He could hardly wait to meet his new child.

"I appreciate all you've taught me," Benjamin added.

"You do fantastic work. I'm proud of you."

The customers closed and locked their horse trailer before turning back toward Joshua. "Thanks again!"

"You're welcome!" Joshua waved as the men hopped into the pickup truck and drove away, the trailer bumping and rattling down the rock driveway toward the road.

Joshua and Benjamin started toward the barn. Joshua had been hoping to get Benjamin alone at some point today so he could talk to him. Now seemed to be the perfect time.

"I was wondering if I could ask you a question," Joshua began. "It's about your *mamm*."

"Oh?" Benjamin raised an eyebrow. "What did you want to ask me?"

"I'm worried about her." Joshua stopped a few feet from the barn to keep their conversation private. While he trusted Daniel, he wanted to keep family matters within the family. "She was exhausted when she got home yesterday, and she burst into tears when I asked her to do the books for the farm. She's really overexerting herself."

Benjamin folded his arms over his slight frame. Although he was close to seventeen, he looked more like thirteen with his skinny arms and legs and short stature. "Well, she didn't seem like herself at supper last night. I asked her if she was okay, and she insisted she was fine. I could tell something was wrong, but she's not *gut* at expressing herself when something is wrong. She tends to shut down."

"I've noticed that." Joshua sighed. "It's apparent to me that she's overdoing it, but I don't know how to get her to admit it. Why do you think she's determined to keep working at the hotel when it's obvious that she's tired? The *boppli* is sapping her energy, and she really doesn't need to work there anymore. Business here at the farm is booming. We need her at home more than we need any income she brings in from working at the hotel."

Benjamin gnawed his lower lip before responding. "You know *mei mamm* is stubborn."

"*Ya*, I know that. Her tenacity was one of the qualities I admired about her when I first met her. I'd never met a *maedel* who was so determined to stand up for what she believed in. She was very out-spoken when you first came to work for me, and she wasn't afraid to tell me when she thought I wasn't treating you right."

"Exactly," Benjamin agreed. "*Mamm* was always determined to contribute. She once told me she didn't want to take handouts from her family even though she had me when she was so young. She felt she had to work and help pay for groceries and everything I needed."

"I understand how that made sense when you were little, but she's not living with her folks anymore." Joshua looked back toward the house and considered Benjamin's response. "Why would she still feel like she had to contribute when we're a team now?"

Benjamin shrugged. "I don't know. Maybe old habits and feel-ings are hard to break."

"Maybe," Joshua muttered as he stared at the house.

"I'm going to go see what Danny's doing." Benjamin continued toward the barn.

"All right." Joshua lifted his hat and raked his hand through his thick hair. Why did Carolyn feel she still had to bring in extra income even though they were married now and working the farm together? Was there something he wasn't giving her that she felt she needed? Why would she want to work at the hotel when she said she loved the farm so much?

None of it made sense. Was she stuck in the mind-set she'd been used to while living with her parents on her brother's farm? If so, then he needed to show her that she didn't have to keep living in the past. He was determined to find a way to show her that he would support her now.

Chapter Three

Carolyn moved her gardening stool over to another patch of weeds and then sank back down onto it. Determined to keep her garden pristine despite her protruding belly, she swiped her hand over her brow as the late-April sun warmed her skin, then leaned down and pulled more weeds before dropping them into a bucket.

She was still working that same patch when she noticed a shadow had dropped over her.

Glancing up, Carolyn found her mother-in-law staring at her, gripping a casserole dish in her pudgy hands.

"Carolyn," Barbie began. "What are you doing?"

"Hi, *Mamm*." Carolyn wiped her hands on her apron. She wondered why it wasn't perfectly obvious to Barbie what she was doing, but she decided to give the obvious answer. "I'm weeding."

"But why are you weeding in your condition?" Barbie asked. "You should be resting since you're close to your time."

"I still have two months before the *boppli* will come, and I need to get ready to plant tomatoes." She thought about Joshua's comment about her garden earlier. "And I enjoy working in my garden. It helps me relax. What brings you over here today?" she asked, hoping to move the focus of their conversation away from her.

"I brought supper for Josh and Ben. I made chicken and dumplings, which is one of Josh's favorites." Barbie held up the casserole dish and frowned. "With all of the hours you work at that hotel, I worry that they might starve if I don't bring them food. I'm certain my son will appreciate a nice, warm meal after working so hard all day long."

Carolyn's lips formed a thin line as she pushed to her feet. "You know I only work part-time. I always make sure my family is fed, and I always make sure my husband gets to eat his favorite, warm meals."

"I'm sure you think you do, but you should be home with your family." Barbie pointed toward Carolyn's middle. "Especially with the *boppli* coming. You have things to do to get prepared, but you already know that. This isn't your first *boppli*."

"No, this isn't my first, and I will be ready." Carolyn ran her fingers over her belly and studied her mother-in-law's steel-blue eyes. Why had Barbie felt the need to point out that this wasn't Carolyn's first child? Was she making a derogatory comment about her teen pregnancy? Everyone else in their families and most, if not all, in their community had forgiven her years ago for her transgression, and Benjamin was a special young man.

"I hope you're not considering going back to that job after the *boppli* is born."

"I probably will go back." Carolyn felt herself grow weary while the sun beat on her face. She didn't want to have this conversation with Barbie. After all, this was something she had to decide, not her husband's meddling mother.

"You shouldn't even consider going back to that hotel. That's no place for you or any other Plain woman."

"I enjoy working there," Carolyn said while massaging her abdomen.

"I will never understand why you would want to work there and be around those *Englischers* all day long when you belong here taking care of your family. Besides, there is plenty to do here on my son's farm." Barbie turned to where the men were working with horses in the pasture. She tented her free hand over her eyes, and her frown creased her chubby face as she abruptly changed the subject.

"Josh may have adopted Ben, but with Ben's blond hair, brown eyes, and slight frame, he'll never be mistaken for Josh's biological son."

Carolyn gritted her teeth and bit back the sharp retort that bubbled up from her throat. *And that is precisely why I won't quit my job at the hotel.*

Barbie turned toward Carolyn and held up the casserole dish once again. "I'll put the chicken and dumplings in the refrigerator for you. Do you need me to do the dishes or anything else inside? I have some time, so I can clean or start the laundry if you'd like."

"*Danki*, but everything is done. I finished the laundry earlier, and the *haus* is already clean."

"*Gut.*" Barbie started toward the porch, and Carolyn closed her eyes while trying to will her heart to stop beating so fast. Joshua's mother had a way of saying things that cut Carolyn to her bone, but her comment about Benjamin had sliced straight to her heart.

Carolyn had always assumed that Barbie wouldn't really accept Benjamin into the family, but she never imagined Barbie would express her unkind thoughts aloud and so offhandedly.

Carolyn propped herself up in bed with two pillows while she brushed her long, blond hair that was falling in waves to her waist. She loved this time of night when the work was done and she had some quiet time alone with her husband. She could feel the soreness in her muscles begin to release while she moved the brush through her hair. The tension in her neck and ache in her feet also subsided slightly.

Why had Barbie's words hurt her so deeply? She should be used to dealing with Barbie by now. It was because of Ben. If only she could let go of her worries about his future.

Joshua stepped into the room clad in his blue pajamas, his dark hair wet from the shower. "You've been quiet this evening. Are you all right?" He sank onto the edge of the bed beside her and began to stroke her feet. "Are your feet bothering you?"

"No, tonight it's not my feet really, although I do love when you massage them." She continued to move the brush through her thick hair, carefully choosing her words. "I've been wondering something."

"What is it?"

"Do you love Ben?" she asked. "Do you really love him as if he were your own son?" She held her breath as she waited for his response.

Joshua stopped massaging her feet and his eyes searched hers. "Of course I do. That's why I adopted him and gave him my name."

She could see the truth glistening in his eyes, but she had to press on to the question that had been echoing through her mind ever since Barbie's visit. Carolyn looked down at her baby bump. "Will you still love him after our *boppli* is born?" Her voice vibrated as her eyes filled with tears.

"Carolyn, look at me." Joshua quickly moved closer to her,

placed his fingers under her chin, and tilted her head so that she was looking into his confused eyes. "Of course I'll still love Ben. He's my son, and he even calls me *Dat*." He paused. "Why would you ask that? Have I ever done anything to make you doubt my feelings for Ben?"

"No, you haven't." She shrugged and wiped her eyes. "I suppose my crazy hormones have my feelings all jumbled up as if I ran them through the wringer washer."

He didn't smile despite her lame attempt at a joke.

An uncomfortable silence stretched between them, and she felt the need to flee his pained expression.

"I'm really tired. I better go to sleep." She placed the brush on her nightstand. *"Gut nacht."* She tucked her legs under her quilt and pulled it around her as if to shield her heart from the doubt assaulting her mind.

With her eyes closed, she felt the bed shift as Joshua stood and then heard his footsteps as he made his way around to his side of the bed. The frame creaked as he climbed in next to her. He reached over and drew circles with the light brush of his fingers over her cotton nightgown.

"Carolyn?" His voice was soft and gentle next to her ear. "I have something I want to ask you."

"Ya?" she asked, keeping her face toward the wall.

"Do you feel like you have to work at the hotel to contribute income toward the household?"

Carolyn shrugged. *"Ya,* I do. I've always worked to contribute toward the household and also to save money for Ben. I have an account where I put a little bit of money away for Ben every paycheck."

"You don't need to worry about that, Carolyn. You're not living with your parents on your *bruder's* farm anymore. We're a team, and I can support all of us."

Carolyn nodded. "I know. You're a *gut* provider." She said the words out loud, but her worries still echoed in her mind, and she didn't want to confess them to Josh. He said he loved Ben, and she believed him. But still, Ben was not his biological child like the baby she was carrying.

"You have nothing to worry about. We're fine financially. *Gut nacht, mei liewe.*" His voice was soft and tentative. "I hope you believe me when I say that I love you and Ben, and I always will." His fingers brushed across her shoulders.

"*Danki,*" Carolyn whispered. She held her breath as more tears threatened to give away her doubts.

CHAPTER FOUR

Joshua guided his horse down the main road toward his farm, and his parents' house came into view. All morning he had longed to talk to his father, who always gave Joshua the best advice. Today he needed to bend his father's ear and ask him for some of that coveted guidance.

He brought his horse and buggy to a stop in the driveway and hopped out of the driver seat. He made his way behind the house and found his father brushing a horse in the barn, just where he suspected he would be.

"Josh." *Dat* set the brush on the top of the stall. *"Wie geht's?"*

"Hi, *Dat*. How are you?" Josh leaned against the stall. "I was on my way home from the feed store, and I thought I'd stop by." He stroked the horse's neck. "How are you, Fred?" The horse nodded his head as if to respond.

"Would you like to come inside for a snack?"

"Oh, no, *danki*. I really need to get back to the farm. We have customers coming this afternoon."

"Is there something on your mind?"

Joshua sighed and nodded his head. It was time to get to the true reason for his visit. "Carolyn hasn't been herself lately. Last night she asked me if I really love Ben and if I'll still love him after the *boppli* is born."

Dat's brow furrowed. "Why would she ask you that?"

"I don't know," Joshua said, throwing his hands up as if to surrender. "That's what I've been trying to figure out. I keep telling her I love Ben like my own son and I will always love both her and him. I'm not sure what else I can do to make her believe that's never going to change. I feel like I'm doing something wrong. I do my best to compliment Ben's work, and I'm teaching him everything I can about the business. I don't know what else I'm supposed to do to show her I'm a *gut dat*. Do you have any advice?"

Dat fingered his graying beard. "From what I've seen, you are a *gut dat*. In fact, you remind me a lot of your *bruder* and how he was with his *kinner*."

Joshua's heart tightened as he thought of his older brother, Gideon, who had passed way from a heart attack nearly a decade ago. "*Danki*. I can't think of a higher compliment. Gideon was a *wunderbaar dat*."

"*Ya*," *Dat* said. "He was a *gut dat*, and you are too. That's why I don't think Carolyn's worries are your fault."

"What do you mean?"

"I think Carolyn is just going through a lot with getting ready to have the *boppli*. Women tend to change during this time." His father smiled. "Your *mamm* went through a lot. She changed a bit."

Joshua raised an eyebrow. "Was she more uptight?"

Dat nodded. "She was worried and nervous. Everything had to be perfect, and I tended to get things wrong." He paused and grinned. "I got them wrong often."

Joshua chuckled. "So *Mamm* was a handful while she was pregnant."

"Ya." *Dat* shrugged. "But it was worth it. I had two *wunderbaar* sons." He patted Joshua's arm. "Have patience and faith. I know things are changing quickly, and it's a scary but exciting time for both of you. Your lives are going to change completely, but it will be for the better. Everything will be fine."

"I hope so." Joshua could hear the uncertainty in his voice.

"I'm certain Carolyn is worried that something will go wrong, but God is *gut*. Keep telling her how much you love her and Ben. She'll eventually realize she has nothing to worry about."

Joshua adjusted the hat on his head and longed for his father's wise words to settle his worry. "I'll try."

Dat crossed his arms over his chest and tilted his head. "You don't seem convinced."

"It's not that I don't believe you." Joshua struggled to put his thoughts into words. "I can't really put my finger on it, but it's almost like there's something she's not telling me. Something more than whether I'll still love Ben after the *boppli* is born."

His father's face clouded with a frown. "What do you mean?"

"She tells me she loves the farm, and I know she's telling me the truth. She seems happier and more relaxed on the days she's home instead of at the hotel." Joshua ran his fingers over the stall wall. "But she still seems stressed out much of the time. I think it's because she's overdoing it, but she won't admit it. Why can't I convince her to quit that job? I just don't understand it. She seems to think she needs to contribute income to our household, but that's not true. I can support all of us."

"Hmm." *Dat* shook his head. "I don't know about that, but I imagine Carolyn is still adjusting to being married after being a single mother for so long. Give her love and support, and she will get through this."

"That sounds like a *gut* plan." Joshua nodded toward the barn door. "I better get back to the farm. It was *gut* seeing you."

During the ride back to his house, Joshua contemplated his father's words and prayed Carolyn would believe that he would always love Ben and that the farm would support them all.

Carolyn wiped her hands on a dish towel as the aroma of freshly baked apple pie wafted up from the oven beside her. She turned to her mother, who was pouring hot water from the percolator into coffee cups. "*Danki* for bringing the apples over. I think the *buwe* will enjoy the snack this afternoon."

"*Gern gschehne*," *Mamm* said. "I saw those apples at the market and thought of you." She dropped tea bags into the cups and held them up. "You look like you could use this cup of tea. Let's sit and talk."

Carolyn tossed the dish towel onto the counter and then sat across from her mother at the table. She sipped the tea and curled her fingers around the warm cup.

"You look positively exhausted, *mei liewe*." *Mamm* reached across the table and touched Carolyn's hand. "Are you sleeping well?"

Carolyn shrugged and cleared her throat where a lump swelled. "*Ya*, I guess I'm sleeping okay."

"Are you certain?" *Mamm* studied her. "I had a difficult time in my last trimester when I was pregnant with your *bruder*. My back hurt so badly that some days it was all I could do not to break down in tears. Does your back hurt?"

Carolyn tried to smile as a tear trickled down her cheek. "Today I think everything hurts."

"Oh, Carolyn." *Mamm* scooted her chair around the table and pulled Carolyn into her arms.

Carolyn rested her cheek on her mother's shoulder as tears flowed from her eyes. She felt like a child who had fallen and scraped her knee. Why was she acting so childish today? It was so unlike her!

"*Was iss letz?*" *Mamm* moved her hand over Carolyn's back. "Talk to me."

"I'm just so tired." Carolyn wiped her eyes with a paper napkin. "I wake up during the night when the *boppli* kicks, and I worry about everything."

Mamm's brow knitted above her brown eyes. "What are you worried about?"

"Everything." Carolyn sniffed and wiped her nose. "Will the *boppli* be healthy? Will I be a *gut mamm*? Where will Ben fit into our family?"

Mamm smiled and pushed a lock of Carolyn's hair under her prayer covering. "*Ach*, Carolyn. You worry too much. The *boppli* will be fine, and you already are a *gut mamm*. Ben will always fit into your family. He'll be a *wunderbaar* big *bruder*. What is there to worry about?"

Carolyn shook her head. "When I close my eyes at night, I feel stuck in a well of worries. I know I need to give my worry over to God, but I struggle daily."

"The Lord has control, and He will take care of you and your family, Carolyn." *Mamm's* eyes glistened as she squeezed Carolyn's hand. "You're blessed beyond measure. You have a wonderful family already, and soon it will blossom. Give thanks for all you have, and don't let doubt ruin these last few weeks of your pregnancy. You remember how much life changed when Ben was born. You'll need your rest now."

"*Ya*, I do, but I was a *kind*. It will be different this time."

"True, but it will still be overwhelming." *Mamm* tapped the table for emphasis. "You should listen to your body. If you're that tired, then Sarah Ann and I can come over and help you more. Do you want us to come and clean for you next week?"

"No." Carolyn shook her head. "I can handle it, but *danki*."

"I think it's time you quit working at the hotel. You need your strength for the *boppli*."

Carolyn bit her lower lip. "I'm not sure." Her mother would never understand why she wanted to earn money. She hadn't made the same mistakes Carolyn had made when she was a teenager.

"Well, you need to think about quitting soon. You look like you could use more time preparing for the *boppli*." *Mamm's* expression brightened. "Is Josh working on the cradle?"

"*Ya*, he is, and it's going well." Carolyn lifted her cup. "Ben loved the idea of fixing up his old cradle. They've been working together on it."

"That's so nice. I'm certain Ben loves the time he spends with Josh."

"*Ya*." Carolyn sipped her tea. "I just pray that doesn't change, that Josh will still have time for Ben when the baby comes."

"Oh, I'm certain it won't." *Mamm* patted her hand. "Everything will be fine. Stop putting so much pressure on yourself. God is in control."

"*Ya*, He is." Carolyn nodded and prayed that she could share her mother's confidence that everything would be okay.

CHAPTER FIVE

Six weeks later Carolyn took a deep breath and sank into a chair in the hotel room she'd been cleaning. She hadn't felt right all day. Not only did her feet and legs ache, but her lower back also felt as if someone had been kicking it with steel-toed boots since she'd awoken early that morning. The discomfort began intermittently and increased as the day wore on.

When a sharp pain radiated through her lower back, Carolyn sucked in a breath.

"Carolyn?" Linda Zook, a petite brunette in her early thirties, appeared in the doorway. "I was coming up to check on you since you said you didn't feel well earlier." Her eyes rounded. "*Ach*, no. Are you all right?"

Carolyn looked at her coworker and shook her head. "No, I'm not feeling well. I'm actually feeling worse. I didn't feel right when I woke up this morning, but the pain in my back was bearable. I told Josh I didn't feel like myself, and he suggested I go back to bed. I guess I should've listened to him and called in sick today. He said I was pushing myself too hard, but I thought I would feel better once I got moving."

Another pang hit her, and she took deep breaths until the pain stopped. "I just need a minute to rest."

Linda grimaced. "You don't look well."

Carolyn swiped her hand over her sweaty forehead. "I'll be fine. I just need a moment."

"*Ya*, we need to get you home. I think you should rest there." She lifted the receiver on the hotel room phone. "Hi, Stacey. This is Linda. Carolyn isn't feeling well, and I think we need to get her home. Would you please tell Gregg? We need to get her a ride right away."

Carolyn gripped the arms of the chair as more pain drenched her like a wave. "Maybe you're right," she gasped. She gritted her teeth through the wave of pressure radiating from her lower back through her abdomen.

"Oh no. It's getting worse."

Linda was still listening to Stacey on the phone. "Thank you. I'll bring her right down." She hung up and frowned at Carolyn. "You look terrible. Let's get you home. We'll need to call your midwife so she can take a look at you too."

"Okay." Carolyn balanced her weight on the chair arms and slowly hefted herself up. As she stood, she felt liquid trickle down her legs, and she gasped again.

"Carolyn?" Linda's eyes widened. "*Was iss letz?*"

"My water just broke." She blinked. "*Ach*, no. Why is this happening now? It's too early."

"No, apparently it's the right time." Linda grasped Carolyn's hand. "We have to get downstairs. I'll call Josh so he can alert the midwife, and we'll get you home."

"But it's not time yet." Carolyn stood frozen to the carpet while the liquid continued to seep down her legs. "I still have two weeks."

"No, you don't have two weeks. Apparently God has chosen this day for your *boppli* to be born, so we have to get you home as soon as possible." Linda gently nudged Carolyn to the door. "Let's go. Stacey said Gregg will take us to your house. Everything will be just fine."

Carolyn continued to hold Linda's hand as they made their way down to the lobby where their supervisor, Gregg, was waiting for them.

Stacey, who worked at the front desk, rushed over to them. "What can I do?"

"Please call Carolyn's husband—they have a phone in their barn—and tell him that he needs to call Carolyn's midwife," Linda said. "Tell him we're on our way to his house, and they need to get ready to have this baby."

"I will." Stacey gave Carolyn a concerned expression. "Everything will be just fine. I'll call him right away."

Carolyn nodded as another contraction rose up, and she tried to breathe.

Linda guided Carolyn to Gregg's sedan, which he'd already moved to just outside the front door. As Gregg drove to the farm, Carolyn sat in his backseat, gripping Linda's hand as the contractions came like fire shooting through her lower back to her abdomen.

"It will be okay," Linda whispered in Carolyn's ear. "Stacey is going to call Josh, and I'm certain your midwife will be waiting for you at the *haus*. It will be fine."

Carolyn swiped her hands across her hot cheeks and stared at her apron while trying to control her breathing. The pain was almost too much to bear. Everyone kept telling her everything would be fine. Would it?

Gregg stopped his car in front of the farmhouse, and Linda helped Carolyn climb out. Carolyn leaned on Linda's arm for support as she headed toward the porch steps.

"Carolyn!" Joshua's handsome face emerged as he stepped out through the back door. "How are you?" His eyes flickered.

She shook her head, unable to speak through the pain.

"Let's get you inside." Joshua took her arm and gently led her up the steps. "You're going to be just fine. Everything's fine. Just breathe through the pain."

Carolyn gasped as another contraction gripped her. She opened her eyes and found Joshua studying her. He smiled, and Carolyn's stress eased slightly. If Josh thought everything would be fine, then maybe it would be.

"We're going to bring our *boppli* into the world," she whispered. "It's time."

"*Ya*, it is time, and I love you," he said as he squeezed her hand.

❧

Joshua's eyes filled with tears as he held his newborn baby in his arms. He smiled over at Carolyn, who was propped up on the bed while studying him. She was breathtakingly beautiful with her blond hair peeking out from under her prayer covering and her coffee-brown eyes glistening in the low light of the propane lamp on the bedside table. He thought his heart might burst with love for both her and their new baby.

"She's perfect," he whispered, his voice quaking.

Carolyn reached over and squeezed his arm. "*Ya*, she is. God has blessed us."

He stared down into the baby's face. "She looks like you."

Carolyn chuckled. "I think it's too early to tell."

"No, she's too *schee* to look like me." He grinned over at her. "*Danki.*"

Carolyn tilted her head. "Why are you thanking me?"

"*Danki* for making me the happiest man on the planet."

"*Gern gschehne.*" She paused for a moment. "What do you think of the name Sadie Liz after our two favorite aunts?"

"Sadie Liz?" Joshua smiled. "Sadie Liz Glick. *Ya,* I like it." He tilted his head in question. "Why did you change your mind? I thought we had agreed on Rachel Elizabeth."

She shrugged. "I can't explain it, really. I just looked on her *schee* face and thought of Sadie Liz. We can stick with Rachel Elizabeth if you'd like."

"No." He studied the baby's face. "I agree that Sadie Liz fits her."

"*Gut.*" Her eyes slowly closed. "Sadie Liz is her name."

"You should rest." He caressed her arm with his free hand. "I'll take care of things from here."

"Okay." Carolyn yawned and closed her eyes.

As he held his baby girl, memorizing her tiny nose and pink skin, Josh was certain he must be dreaming. Here he stood in their bedroom with his beautiful wife and his healthy baby girl. It wasn't too long ago that Joshua was convinced he'd spend his life alone running Glick's Belgian and Dutch Harness Horses, the horse farm he had built with his brother so many years ago. Now he had everything he'd always wanted—a family, a real family. He had Carolyn and a daughter and a son he could call his own.

He settled into the rocking chair, and Sadie Liz nuzzled against his arm. Soon she was asleep. She was like a tiny doll, so content and fragile, wrapped in a blanket and wearing a tiny pink crocheted hat. Time seemed to pass slowly while Carolyn slept in their bed and he held Sadie Liz. The midwife came to check on him twice, and each time he told her they were just fine.

After a while, a soft knock sounded on the bedroom door. Joshua opened the door and found his in-laws, Titus and Miriam Lapp, standing in the hallway with Benjamin.

"May we come in?" Miriam asked, craning her neck to look into the room. "Is Carolyn okay with having visitors?"

"*Ya*, of course," Joshua said. "Please come in."

"We got here as soon as we could," Titus said. "I'm so glad you called and left a message."

"I knew you'd want to be here. This is Sadie Liz." Joshua tipped the baby slightly so his in-laws and Benjamin could see her little face peeking out from beneath the light-blue-and-pink blanket Carolyn had made for the baby. "Sadie, this is your *mammi*, *daadi*, and *bruder*."

"Oh!" Miriam took Sadie Liz's tiny hand. "Look at her, Titus! She's so *schee*."

Titus smiled and nodded. "*Ya*. Just like our little Carolyn was when she was born."

"Come in." Joshua nodded toward the inside of the room. "Don't be shy."

Carolyn opened her eyes. "*Mamm. Dat*. I'm glad you're here."

Miriam and Titus stepped into the bedroom, but Benjamin lingered in the doorway. He looked at the baby with his eyebrows knitted together.

"Can I hold her?" he finally asked.

"Of course you can." Joshua turned toward the rocking chair. "Would you like to sit first?"

"*Ya*," Benjamin said. "That's a *gut* idea." He sank into the chair by Carolyn's bed, and Joshua placed Sadie Liz into his arms.

"Just hold her like this. Support her head with your arm." Joshua squatted beside the chair as the baby squirmed and then settled down again. "Are you okay?"

Benjamin looked at his little sister still swaddled in the blanket, and his brow remained furrowed. "*Ya*, I'm *gut*." He looked up at Joshua, and his serious expression melted into a wide smile. "I like this."

"That's *gut*." Joshua grinned.

Joshua stood and walked over to the side of the bed where Carolyn's parents spoke to their daughter. As he placed his hand on his wife's shoulder, he silently thanked God for giving him his precious family. At that very moment, he had everything he'd ever dreamt of, and his heart overflowed with joy.

CHAPTER SIX

Carolyn settled into the rocking chair in her bedroom and hummed while Sadie Liz suckled on a bottle. She both nursed her baby and supplemented with formula. It was difficult to believe her newborn was already three days old. A peace had immediately settled over Carolyn when Sadie Liz was born, and she still felt that peace. After waiting and planning, her baby was here. She couldn't be more thankful for the blessings in her life.

Although Sadie Liz had her days and nights mixed up, she was eating well. She seemed to be as healthy and perfect as she could be, but a worry still reverberated at the back of Carolyn's mind: Why had her baby been born two weeks early?

Carolyn had spent most of last night staring into the basinet and watching Sadie Liz as she snuggled under a blanket. She watched her newborn move and tried to ignore the questions that buzzed around in her mind. Was Sadie Liz breathing right? Were her little lungs fully formed? Was she truly ready to be born, or had

Carolyn been working too hard, which caused her precious baby to come early?

Sadie Liz grunted and groaned while her little lips smacked against the bottle's nipple. Maybe the worries were just part of the hormones that were still surging through her. From what Carolyn could remember, she'd been emotional after Benjamin had entered the world as well. Perhaps this was just a part of giving birth.

"Carolyn?" Her mother's voice sounded from the hallway.

"I'm in the bedroom, *Mamm*." Carolyn balanced Sadie Liz on her shoulder and patted her back.

Mamm and Carolyn's sister-in-law, Sarah Ann, appeared in the doorway.

"Oh, there she is!" Sarah Ann rushed over with her arms stretched out. "May I hold her?"

"Of course." Carolyn stood and handed Sadie Liz to Sarah Ann. "I was just trying to burp her. Maybe you'll have more success than I did. She doesn't seem to want to burp this morning."

"Oh, hello there." Sarah Ann kissed Sadie Liz's pink, bald head. "Aren't you the sweetest thing? I'm your *aenti* Sarah Ann." She sat in the rocker, hoisted Sadie Liz onto her shoulder, and continued to whisper to the baby while trying to coax a burp.

"How are you feeling?" *Mamm* asked Carolyn.

"I'm sore, but I'm fine."

Mamm touched Carolyn's hand. "Let's go into the kitchen. I want to show you what we brought for you."

"You didn't need to bring anything." Carolyn followed her mother into the kitchen.

"Sarah Ann and I want to help you." *Mamm* moved to the refrigerator and pulled out two casserole dishes. "I made macaroni and cheese, and Sarah Ann sliced up some roast beef with gravy."

"Oh, *Mamm*." Carolyn inhaled the sweet aroma of the meal. "This is wonderful. *Danki*. The *buwe* will love it."

"We're *froh* to help." *Mamm* placed the dishes back in the refrigerator. "What else can I do to help?" She peered toward the sink. "Why don't you sit, and I'll do the dishes."

"Oh, no. You don't need to do that. I was going to take care of them later." Carolyn waved off the offer.

"Don't be *gegisch*." *Mamm* turned on the faucet and squirted in the dishwashing liquid. "Sarah Ann and I came here to help. You sit down and get some rest. You look exhausted."

Carolyn lowered herself gingerly into a kitchen chair.

"Would you like a cup of tea?" *Mamm* began to fill the teakettle with water.

"*Ya*, that would be perfect." With one elbow on the table, Carolyn rested her head on her palm. Like Josh, her mother always seemed to know exactly what she needed, and Carolyn hoped she was just as intuitive with her own children.

"How is everything going?" *Mamm* asked as she prepared to wash the breakfast dishes. "Josh seems to be positively glowing."

"*Ya*, he's *froh*." Carolyn smiled. "I really enjoyed watching Joshua talk to Sadie Liz while I dressed her this morning. The little moments between the *boppli* and Josh warm my heart. I was a little concerned when Joshua kept calling Sadie Liz a *bu* instead of a *maedel* before she was born. I was hoping he wouldn't be disappointed when we had a *maedel*, but he's not disappointed at all. I can see it in his eyes every time he looks at her. Josh is definitely in love with his *dochder*."

"Of course he is." *Mamm* glanced over her shoulder at Carolyn. "Did you really think he wouldn't be in love with his child?"

Carolyn shrugged. "No, not really. I just didn't want him to be disappointed in me if I didn't give him a son."

"Even if you had any control over that, I don't think Josh could ever be disappointed in you, Carolyn. He's a *gut* man, and he loves you. Besides, Ben is his son now, so he has a *bu*." *Mamm* placed a dish in the drain board. "How is Ben doing with Sadie Liz?"

"He's fine." Carolyn nodded, putting aside her fears for Ben. "He fed her last night, and he seemed to enjoy it. I caught him whispering to her and telling her all about his favorite horses. It was really sweet."

"I knew he'd be good with a younger sibling." *Mamm* rinsed off a glass. "Your *dat* is outside talking to Josh and Ben. He wanted to come by to visit too."

"Oh, that's nice. I like it when Josh spends time with *Dat*."

"I do too." *Mamm* talked about Carolyn's niece and nephews while she continued washing the dishes. When the water in the teakettle was ready, she brought mugs, tea bags, and creamer to the table and sat down. Carolyn sipped the tea and closed her eyes, enjoying the sweet taste of her favorite drink. "I always enjoy my cup of tea."

"You should go take a nap after you finish it." *Mamm* cradled her mug in her hands. "Sarah Ann and I will take care of things here."

"Are you certain?" Carolyn asked. "I imagine Sarah Ann has things to do at the dairy farm."

"Neither of us has a certain time we have to be home. Sarah Ann told Amos that she planned to help you today, and he said he understood. He sent his love. We're here to do whatever you need. We can bring the bassinet out to the kitchen and take care of Sadie Liz while you sleep. You need your rest." *Mamm* glanced around the kitchen. "Just let me know what you want us to do. We can sweep or even start on the laundry for you."

Carolyn cupped her hand over her mouth to stifle a yawn. "I think I might take you up on your offer. I want to keep Sadie Liz up this evening, so she might sleep for longer periods tonight. I know she's very young, but I'd like to try to help her get her days and nights straight as soon as possible." Carolyn didn't want to admit that the sooner she could get her rest at night, the sooner she could go back to work at the hotel. Thoughts about her job were already trying to disturb the peace she'd been feeling since Sadie Liz was born.

"If that's the case, then you definitely need a nap." *Mamm* drank more tea. "I remember when you had your days and nights mixed up. I worried I'd never sleep again, but babies do make that change eventually."

"How long did it take me?"

"I think it was a few weeks. Maybe even a couple of months."

Carolyn grimaced. "Oh dear." She was certain she might pass out from lack of sleep, and there was no way she could return to work at the hotel without more sleep.

"It will be fine. You did a great job with Ben. You'll survive."

Carolyn drank more tea while thinking about the worries that had gripped her last night as she fed Sadie Liz. "*Mamm*, why do you think Sadie Liz came two weeks early?"

Her mother raised her eyebrows. "What do you mean?"

"Sadie didn't make it to my due date, but Ben went a little past his." Carolyn ran her fingers over the warm mug. "Why do you think she was early?"

Mamm shrugged. "I don't know. Some babies are early. Don't you remember your friend Mary's baby? He was nearly a month early."

Carolyn nodded. "*Ya*, baby Jake was so tiny. He looked like a doll."

"That's true, but he was just fine." *Mamm's* gaze remained on her. "Why are you asking about that? Is something wrong with Sadie Liz?"

"No, nothing is wrong. She seems just as healthy as can be. I was just wondering if there was a reason she came so unexpectedly. It's a *gut* thing Josh had finished the cradle and gotten the bassinet together for me."

"The Lord has His own timing. It's not our place to question that."

"I know." Carolyn cupped her hand to her mouth as another yawn overtook her.

"You need some sleep. I'll help Sarah Ann bring Sadie Liz and her supplies out here." Her mother stood. "Let's get you to bed."

As Carolyn followed her mother to her bedroom, she wondered again if the stress from working at the hotel and also at home had caused her baby to come into the world early. Her eyes widened and her heart pounded. Had she caused her baby to come too soon? Was it all due to her stubbornness? She prayed she hadn't caused her baby any undue stress.

⚭

Carolyn's eyes flew open, and her vision focused on a thin line of early-morning sunlight reflecting off the white ceiling. She yawned and stretched as the fog of sleep lifted from her mind. When she rolled to her side and saw that the bassinet was missing, she sat up with a start. Glancing around the room, she didn't see it anywhere. Her heart thumped in her chest and its beat accelerated.

Where's Sadie Liz?

Carolyn leapt from the bed, pulled on her robe and slippers, and rushed out of the bedroom.

"Josh?" She hurried through the family room to the kitchen where she found Joshua leaning against the counter and giving Sadie Liz a bottle. She stood in the doorway as he leaned down and nuzzled his nose against the baby's cheek.

Carolyn hugged her arms to her middle as her heartbeat gradually returned to a normal pace. Joshua looked so handsome as he gazed down at his baby girl. She could feel the love shining in his powder-blue eyes, and she was thankful for her wonderful husband.

Joshua looked toward the doorway and smiled. "*Gude mariye.* Did we wake you?"

"No, which is why I'm confused." She crossed the kitchen. "I never heard you get up."

"*Gut.* That was the plan." He lifted the baby onto his shoulder and patted her back. "Sadie Liz and I decided to let you sleep this morning." He looked down at the little body on his shoulder. "Right, Sadie?"

"You did?" Carolyn shook her head and looked at the clock on the wall. She couldn't remember a time when she'd slept past nine. "But it's so late, Josh. Why didn't you wake me up so you could go out to work while I took care of the *boppli*?"

"Sadie and I talked about it, and we both agreed that you needed your rest today. You've been working so hard, and we wanted to do our best to help you. Right, Sadie?" The baby responded with a soft belch and Josh grinned. "She already sounds like her *bruder*." He cradled Sadie Liz in his arms and returned the bottle's nipple to her little mouth.

Carolyn touched Sadie Liz's cheek. "But you have work to do today. Didn't you tell me that you had more customers coming to visit this afternoon?"

"Ben and Danny have it under control. Ben made breakfast while I held Sadie Liz, and we took turns eating. We did really well this morning. You'd be proud."

"Oh." Carolyn tried to imagine Joshua and Benjamin caring for the baby while she slept. She was thankful for their efforts, but she had to do her part. What self-respecting woman would sleep all day while her husband cared for their children? "*Danki* for letting me sleep, but I'm certain you want to get outside now. Just give me a minute to get dressed. I'll hurry."

Joshua met her gaze. "You can take all the time you need. I'm enjoying my *dochder*." He nodded toward the doorway. "You go ahead and get dressed, and Sadie and I will put on your eggs for breakfast."

Carolyn studied him. "How are you going to do that?"

He pointed to the seat on the floor. "Remember the baby seat your *mamm* brought over for you?"

"Oh, right." Carolyn smiled. "I had forgotten about that." She kissed his cheek and touched his shoulder. "*Danki.*" She didn't know what she'd done to deserve such a wonderful husband and family.

CHAPTER SEVEN

Carolyn was sitting on the porch and holding Sadie Liz when she spotted a horse and buggy making its way up the rock driveway past the Glick's Belgian and Dutch Harness Horses sign and toward her house. The horse came to a stop near the barn, and her mother and her eighteen-year-old niece, Rosemary, climbed out. They waved to Benjamin in the pasture before making their way to the house.

"*Aenti* Carolyn!" Rosemary rushed to the porch and sat beside her. "Hello, Sadie Liz. How are you?"

"She's doing fine. It's so *gut* to see you." Carolyn handed the baby over to her. "Sadie Liz, do you remember your cousin Rosemary?"

The baby grunted as Rosemary took her in her arms.

Mamm climbed the porch steps. "How are you feeling, Carolyn?"

"I'm fine." Carolyn tented her hand over her eyes. "I didn't expect to see you today."

"I told you we would come and help you as much as we could."

131

Mamm sat down beside her. "What can we do today? We're ready to do whatever you need—housework or laundry. We can also do your grocery shopping if you need us to. I can call a driver and head out to the market if that will help you. We're at your disposal."

"I think Sadie Liz needs a change. May I do it for you?" Rosemary lifted the baby to her shoulder. "You can trust me. I've been baby-sitting since I was twelve."

Carolyn smiled. "I know you can handle it. Everything is set up in my bedroom."

"I'll take care of it. Sadie Liz and I will be inside if you need us." Rosemary stood and headed into the house.

"So, how are you sleeping?" *Mamm* asked.

"I'm sleeping a little bit better. I'm trying to keep Sadie Liz up as late as I can so she sleeps longer periods during the night. She slept for a few hours in one stretch last night, which was a big improvement." Carolyn looked toward the garden. "I've been sitting here staring at the weeds and thinking about those tomato seeds I really need to plant. I'm just not certain I have the strength to do it on only a few hours of sleep."

"How about we work in the garden together?" *Mamm* offered. "I can get the seeds and help you plant. I'll do the heavy bending, and you can sit on a stool to do the rest."

Carolyn smiled. "That sounds fun." She retrieved the seeds from the kitchen while her mother headed to the barn for the gardening tools.

Carolyn met her mother in the garden and took her place on her favorite stool. She was so thankful when Joshua bought her the stool as a surprise last year. Sitting helped relieve some of the pain when the baby began to put pressure on her back.

Carolyn began pulling weeds and dropping them into a bucket

while her mother tilled the ground and planted the seeds. The warm May sun caressed Carolyn's cheeks as they worked together, and she smiled. Her eyes moved toward the pasture where she found Joshua, Benjamin, and Daniel training horses, and her smile deepened. She felt as if she were truly home. This was where she belonged.

"It's so *gut* to see you so *froh*," Mamm said while planting the seeds at the far end of the garden.

"What do you mean?" Carolyn stopped weeding and looked at her mother.

"You've been smiling so much lately." *Mamm* wiped her hands on her apron. "I can't remember a time when I've seen you this *froh*. You positively glow when you hold Sadie Liz, and I've been watching you work in the garden today. You smile without realizing it. I'm so thankful you've found this much happiness. I know you had a hard time when you were younger, but God had the perfect plan for you. You've found your joy."

Carolyn's lip quivered. *"Danki, Mamm."*

"God is *gut*." *Mamm* went back to her planting.

Carolyn looked toward the pasture as a tear trickled down her cheek. She was thankful for all the blessings in her life, especially her family. Her mother was right that she'd never been happier, but a dark, ominous cloud lurked at the back of her mind—she'd have to return to work at the hotel in a little over a month since her boss expected her to take only six weeks of maternity leave.

"Carolyn?" Rosemary called from the porch. "I put Sadie Liz down for a nap. Is it okay if I make lunch?"

Carolyn looked toward the porch. *"Ya,* that would be *wunderbaar. Danki,* Ro."

She turned back toward the pasture to where the men worked. She enjoyed being home to have lunch with her children and husband every day. Oh, how she wanted to stay home with her family, but she knew she had to go back to work, for Benjamin. She was his mother, and she had to make sure his future was secure. He was her responsibility, not Joshua's. She would do what was right for him.

After all, her parents supported her when she went astray and became a teen mother. She would give her children all the support she could, but especially Ben. It was the right thing to do. She felt sure no one else would understand, but she couldn't risk being unprepared if Joshua did not invest in Ben's future the way she knew he would for his own flesh and blood.

⁂

"Supper was *appeditlich*," Benjamin said as he brought his dish to the counter. "*Danki, Mamm.*"

"*Gern gschehne.*" Carolyn dropped the dish into the soapy water in her sink.

Sadie Liz began to fuss in her seat by the table, and Carolyn wiped her hands on a towel before starting to reach for her.

"Would it be all right if I got her?" Benjamin asked. "I haven't had a chance to hold her today. Ro hogged her most of the day."

Carolyn raised her eyebrows. "You want to hold her?"

"Of course I do." Benjamin shrugged. "Why not? She is my baby *schweschder*. We're going to be stuck with each other, so I might as well get to know her." He grinned, and Carolyn knew he was joking.

"All right," she said. "But she needs to be changed and fed."

"I can do that. Ro showed me earlier. She gave me a lesson on everything I wanted to know so I could help you."

"She gave you a lesson?" Carolyn asked as she lifted the baby and handed her to Benjamin.

"*Ya*, I asked her to show me. I told her I wanted to learn so I could take my turn too."

"Oh." Carolyn watched him, surprised that he wanted to learn how to care for a baby.

"I'll go change her and then warm up a bottle. I'll feed her in the *schtupp*."

Carolyn's heart warmed as she heard Benjamin whispering to Sadie Liz on their way out of the kitchen.

"Are you all right?" Joshua appeared behind her and placed a stack of books on the end of the table. He gently massaged her neck, and she felt tension release in response to his tender touch.

"*Ya*." She looked back at him. "I was just surprised that Ben wanted to take care of Sadie Liz."

"Why are you surprised? You once told me Ben was a very sensitive *bu*. You were right." He stopped stroking her neck and began retrieving dishes and utensils from the table. He brought them to the sink and dropped them in the water. Carolyn never had to worry about scraping food off their dishes before washing them. The men never left a trace on their plates—unless there were bones to contend with.

Josh started washing the dishes without a word.

"What are you doing?" Carolyn tried to take the dishcloth from him, and he moved it away from her.

"What does it look like I'm doing?"

"I can do the dishes, Josh." She reached again, but he took a step to the side, blocking her move. "Why are you being so stubborn?"

He nodded toward the stack of books on a chair next to the table. "I'd rather you look at the books. You told me earlier that you'd look at them."

"Oh." Carolyn looked at the books and at the sink, where he

was now scrubbing a pot. "I can do the dishes and then look at the books."

"I can do the dishes before I go check on the animals." He peered over at her. "Why won't you ever let me help you? You let your *mamm* help you in the garden earlier, and you let Ro and now Ben take care of Sadie Liz. Why can't I do the dishes for you?"

He had a point. She had let other members of the family help her. There was no use in arguing with Joshua. Instead, she settled in a seat at the end of the table and began looking over the books. She was reconciling the bills for the farm when Joshua sat down beside her.

"I've told you this before, but I love having you home," he said. "The *haus* is complete when everyone is here, especially you."

Carolyn looked up at his warm smile, and her heart thumped in her chest. *"Danki."*

"This is how it should be. We have our meals together every day, and our *kinner* are here with us too. Before you know it, Sadie Liz will be helping you in the kitchen while Ben and I are working with the horses." He leaned over and brushed his lips against her cheek. "I'm going to go check on the animals. I'll be in soon."

He headed out through the mudroom, and Carolyn sighed. If everything was as it should be, then why did she feel the need to return to work at the hotel? Josh just wouldn't understand.

CHAPTER EIGHT

Joshua pushed the rocking chair back and forth on the back porch the following morning and smiled down at his newborn baby girl in his arms as she suckled on the bottle he held for her. She was even more beautiful than he remembered from the day before. Her little nose and dark eyes reminded him of Carolyn. He thought his heart might explode with all the love he felt for the tiny child. Even though he loved Ben very much, he had no idea parental love could be such a consuming emotion with an infant. His love seemed to grow each day, with each gaze into her eyes.

"Did you see the horses?" he asked her while she stared up at him. "Your *bruder* and I raise and sell horses. When you're bigger, we'll show you how to train them, and you can help us if you'd like."

As Sadie Liz continued to stare, he thought about how blessed he was to have this perfect little being in his arms. He was so thankful for all the blessings in his life.

"So many people in our community love you," Joshua continued. "I'm eager for you to come to church and meet all of your cousins and friends. They will be so *froh* to see you, Sadie Liz." He moved his finger over her tiny hand, examining her perfect little fingernails. "They will say that you're so *schee*. They will all want to hold you and talk to you."

"Why aren't you working?"

Joshua looked up to where his mother stood staring at him from the porch steps.

"*Mamm?*" he asked. "I didn't hear your buggy." He looked past her to where her horse and buggy sat by the barn. He'd been so distracted by his daughter that he hadn't noticed a visitor approaching the farmhouse.

"I've been standing here for nearly two minutes." She smiled toward the baby in his arms. "May I hold her?"

"Of course." He stood and handed Sadie Liz and the bottle over to her. "What are you doing here so early on a Thursday?"

"I wanted to come by and check on you. I thought Carolyn might need some help today, and I wanted to see my newest *grosskind*." *Mamm* kept her eyes on Sadie Liz while feeding her. "Where's your *fraa*? Is she cooking breakfast?"

"No, she's still sleeping."

"Sleeping?" His mother gave him a look of disgust. "Why is she still sleeping? It's well after eight. She should be up and caring for the *boppli* so you can work." *Mamm* looked toward the barns. "Doesn't she realize you have to keep this farm running so you can support your family?"

"*Ya*, she know what it takes to keep the farm running." Joshua's shoulders tightened in defense. "She's been up late every night, trying to help Sadie Liz figure out her days and nights. I let her sleep this morning so she could rest up some. She's still recovering from giving birth."

Mamm grunted while studying Sadie Liz.

"I don't mind taking care of my *dochder*. In fact, I'm enjoying our time together." He gently touched Sadie Liz's head. "If I let Carolyn sleep, then I get some quiet time with Sadie Liz before I start my day. I guess I'm even a little selfish by letting Carolyn sleep so I can have Sadie Liz to myself. Besides, Danny and Ben know what they're doing out there. I have complete faith in them."

Mamm lifted Sadie Liz up to her shoulder and began to pat her back. "Is Carolyn really sleeping in and recovering so she can return to that hotel?"

Joshua blinked and studied his mother's snide expression before responding. "We haven't talked about it since Sadie Liz was born, but I am assuming she won't go back to work. Why would she want to?"

"I don't know, but she didn't seem to be in any rush to quit working before the baby was born. And she told me she probably would go back. I have a hard time believing it too. Is she going to expect you to take care of Sadie Liz on the days she works?"

Joshua's lips formed a thin line, but then his face relaxed. He wasn't going to allow his mother's disparaging comments to ruin his good mood. "I don't think she expects that, *Mamm*."

"I have a feeling she will go back to work. If she does, then you'll definitely need my help. I'll come over and care for Sadie Liz while she's at the hotel."

"You really think she's going to leave the *boppli* for that job?"

His mother shrugged. "*Ya*, I do. She seems to want to keep that job, though I have no idea why."

"I hope you're wrong." He pointed toward the front door. "It's getting hot out here even if it is only May. Would you like to come inside?"

"*Ya,* that sounds *gut.*"

Joshua opened the door, and his mother headed in through the mudroom to the kitchen, then sat at the table.

"Would you like some coffee?" he offered, heading to the counter.

"*Ya, danki.*"

He poured two cups of coffee and brought them to the table. He sat beside her and sipped his drink while he watched his mother continue to feed Sadie Liz.

"I could stare at her for hours," Joshua said. "Of course, then no work would get done, and we'd starve."

His mother chuckled. "It is an amazing thing to hold your own *kind.*" She smiled up at him. "It's even more *wunderbaar* to hold your *grosskinner.* I'm so *froh* to have more *grosskinner* in my life. You and Carolyn have blessed your *dat* and me. We had worried we wouldn't have any more *grosskinner* after Gideon died. You didn't seem interested in marriage. But the Lord has blessed us many times over, and maybe you and Carolyn will bless us again."

"I hope so, but I couldn't be happier now." Joshua sipped his coffee.

The floor creaked at the far end of the kitchen, and Joshua looked across the room to where Carolyn stood in the doorway. She was clad in a blue dress and black apron with her hair hidden by her prayer covering. Her eyes were wide as she looked at him and then his mother. The dark circles he'd seen under her eyes last night had faded, evidence that she'd slept better last night than she had the night before.

"*Gude mariye, mei liewe,*" he said. "You look well rested."

"*Gude mariye.*" Carolyn looked again from him to his mother. "*Gude mariye, Barbie.*"

"Nice to see you, Carolyn." His mother kept her eyes on Sadie Liz. "I was wondering if you were going to sleep all day."

Carolyn's pretty face clouded with a frown.

"Would you like me to make you breakfast?" Joshua hopped up from the table and walked over to her, hoping to distract her from his mother's comment. "I can fry some eggs and hash browns for you. How many eggs would you like? Two?"

"*Danki*, but I can make it." Her gaze seemed to search his. "I didn't expect you to let me sleep this morning. I told you last night that I could get up with you and make your breakfast. I'm feeling a lot stronger. I don't expect you to take care of me."

"It's fine." He touched her cheek. "I like taking care of you, and I don't mind letting you sleep. You looked exhausted last night after you finished the books. I'm sorry you stayed up so late working on that for me."

"I don't mind. It's my job to do the books for you." She looked toward his mother. "I didn't know you were planning to come over today, Barbie."

"I thought you could use some help." *Mamm* glanced back toward Carolyn. "But I didn't know Joshua would be caring for the baby while you slept."

Carolyn's frown deepened.

"It's fine," he whispered.

Carolyn's expression softened slightly. "Is there any coffee?"

"*Ya*, I'll pour you a cup." They walked to the counter, and he handed her a cup of coffee.

"*Danki.*" She took a long drink. "It's nice and strong, just the way I like it."

"That's why I made it that way." He smiled. "I better get outside."

"Okay." She smiled up at him, and he felt the tension in his shoulders release. "I'll think of something *gut* to make you for lunch."

"*Danki*." He kissed her forehead before heading out the back door. As he walked toward the barn, he prayed his mother wouldn't say anything else to upset Carolyn. He also hoped she was wrong when she said Carolyn would go back to work. He was thankful to see Carolyn finally looking rested. He'd been worried at how exhausted she'd been, both before and since Sadie Liz had been born. He wanted his wife happy and healthy, along with the rest of his precious family.

Carolyn pulled the frying pan out of the cabinet and cracked two eggs into a bowl. She hadn't expected to find her mother-in-law sitting in the kitchen this morning. While it was nice of Barbie to come over to help, Carolyn grew weary of her derisive comments. She silently prayed for strength and patience while she beat the eggs and then poured them into the pan.

"That's nice that Josh lets you sleep," Barbie commented behind her. "I think Eli did that for me a few times after each *bu* was born."

"*Ya*, it is nice," Carolyn said while the yolks fizzled and popped in the hot pan. "He's very thoughtful, and I appreciate it."

"Have you quit your job at the hotel yet?"

Carolyn moved the eggs around in the pan with a spatula. "I haven't spoken to my supervisor since Sadie Liz was born. I'm thinking about going to visit the hotel and taking her with me. I can talk to Gregg in person then."

"Why would you want to take the *boppli* to that hotel?"

Carolyn flipped the eggs in the pan while ignoring the disgust in Barbie's voice. "My friends will enjoy seeing Sadie Liz, and I want to visit them." She slipped the eggs onto a plate and sat across from Barbie at the table. After a silent prayer, she began to eat the eggs while Barbie burped Sadie Liz.

"You can just call your boss and resign from your job." Barbie rubbed Sadie Liz's back. "You don't need to take the *boppli* all the way to that hotel and tell him in person. He knows you had a baby. Didn't you say he stopped by to visit you last week?"

Carolyn nodded while she ate. "*Ya*, he did visit me, and he also sent flowers. But I want to go visit him and see how everyone is."

Barbie studied her for a moment. "Do you miss the job?"

Carolyn shrugged. Barbie would never understand how she felt about working at the hotel. She didn't miss the job, but she missed feeling as if she were working to secure Ben's future. Trying to explain it would be like speaking to Barbie in a foreign language. Her mother-in-law could never possibly understand what it felt like to be responsible for a child who didn't have a biological father to help support him.

"If you go back to work, I will have to come over to help Joshua with the *boppli*." Barbie kept rubbing Sadie Liz's back until she gave a little belch and hiccuped. "But you can't possibly want to be away from your *boppli* so you can clean hotel rooms."

Carolyn trained her eyes on her plate to avoid her mother-in-law's probing stare.

"My son makes a *gut* living here. Why would you want to work at a part-time job that you don't need? Everything you could possibly want is right here."

Carolyn sipped the coffee and tried to think of something to say that would change the subject.

"Do you think my son isn't a *gut* provider?" Barbie asked.

Carolyn's gaze snapped to Barbie's. How could her mother-in-law say something so negative and accusatory? "I never said Josh wasn't a *gut* provider."

"Then why do you need to work?" Barbie asked while feeding Sadie Liz the remainder of the bottle. "If you have everything you need, then you should be home with your *kinner* where you belong."

Carolyn gripped her cup to prevent herself from saying something disrespectful to the older woman. "I haven't decided if I'm going back to work or not."

"It doesn't seem like it's a difficult decision to me." Barbie smiled down at Sadie Liz. "Look at you. You look just like your *dat*."

"*Ya*, she does." Carolyn's expression relaxed. At least there was one topic they agreed on.

CHAPTER NINE

Carolyn was sweeping the kitchen early one morning a week later when her niece walked in from the mudroom.

"Hi, *Aenti* Carolyn," Rosemary said. "I wanted to come by to help you. I called *Onkel* Josh earlier, and he thought you might want to get away for a while today. That's why I have Aiden Monroe waiting outside in his van. Do you want to go shopping? We can take Sadie Liz with us."

"That sounds *wunderbaar*." Carolyn stowed the broom in the pantry. "I have a shopping list started. I was going to see if I could get a driver for tomorrow."

"We can go together." Rosemary turned her attention to the baby. "How are you, Sadie Liz? We're going shopping. Do you want to come with us?" Rosemary lifted her from the baby seat and looked at Carolyn. "Do you have a bag packed for her?"

"Let me put one together." Carolyn hurried to the bedroom and packed a diaper bag. When she returned to the kitchen, Rosemary was packing bottles. Carolyn added a few things to the shopping list, folded it, and placed it in her pocket with her wallet.

"Are we ready to take Sadie Liz out into the world?" Rosemary asked.

"I think so." Carolyn and Rosemary headed outside to the waiting van where Carolyn had already seen Joshua through the kitchen window helping the driver install the baby's car seat.

Carolyn smiled and greeted Aiden Monroe.

Joshua stepped back from the van. "Rosemary called earlier and asked if she could take you shopping. I told her I would pay for the driver so you could go out together."

"That's a great idea. How did you know I needed to get out of the house?"

He shrugged. "I guess I sensed your growing cabin fever."

"*Danki.*" It was just like him to know what she needed before she had figured it out herself.

"So, where are we headed?" Aiden asked. "I'm free all morning and then some, so you name the place."

"I have a list for the market," Carolyn said. "We're low on quite a few things."

"*Ya,* I had noticed that." Joshua touched Carolyn's arm. "You go on and take your time. After all, it's such a beautiful day."

Carolyn considered the idea she'd had since Barbie had visited. "I was thinking about stopping by the hotel first to see everyone and show them how big Sadie Liz is getting."

Joshua's smile faded. "You want to visit the hotel?"

"*Ya.*" She hesitated. "I just want to visit my friends. It will be a quick trip."

"I don't know if it's a *gut* idea for you to go there today," Joshua said. "You're going to be worn out just from grocery shopping, and

Sadie Liz may get cranky. What if you don't make it back in time for lunch? Are you certain you want to put you both through all that in one day?"

"It will be fine. Rosemary is here to help me." Carolyn turned to Rosemary, who was standing by the fence and talking to Danny while rocking Sadie Liz in her arms. "Rosemary?" she asked, and her niece turned to her. "Do you mind if we stop by the hotel to see my coworkers?"

Rosemary smiled. "That sounds like fun."

"Josh is worried that it will be too much for Sadie Liz along with shopping at the market," Carolyn said.

Rosemary shook her head. "Oh, no. We'll be fine, *Onkel* Josh. I've taken babies out before, and they just fall asleep after a while."

He nodded slowly. "All right, but don't overdo it."

"I promise I won't," Carolyn said. "And we'll be back in time for lunch."

Carolyn and Rosemary climbed into the van, and Carolyn secured Sadie Liz in the baby seat.

Aiden steered the van down the rock driveway toward the main road.

Rosemary leaned forward toward the driver seat. "Aiden, could we please head to the Lancaster Grand Hotel first?"

"Absolutely," Aiden said as he merged onto the highway.

"How are things at the farm?" Carolyn asked Rosemary.

"Oh, they're *gut*." Rosemary turned toward her in the seat while she spoke. "*Mei dat* bought a few more cows, and David and Robert have been busy helping him."

"And how are the youth gatherings going?"

Rosemary's cheeks blushed bright pink. "They're going really well. Danny has been coming to them."

"Oh?" Carolyn smiled. "Tell me more."

Rosemary spent the remainder of the drive telling Carolyn about her friends and who was dating whom. By the time they reached the Lancaster Grand Hotel, Carolyn knew about all the couples in Rosemary's youth group.

Joshua was working with a horse in the pasture when he spotted the van parking by the house. He jogged over, paid Aiden, and then helped Rosemary take the bags into the house while Carolyn carried Sadie Liz in her car seat.

"How was your visit at the hotel?" Joshua asked as he lined the bags up on the counter.

"It was *gut*." Carolyn placed the seat on the table. "We saw all of my coworkers and then went to the grocery store. Sadie Liz fell asleep in the van on the way to the store and slept through the shopping trip. I don't think I'm ever going to get her to sleep tonight. She was passed out, weren't you?" She leaned over the seat and touched the baby's cheek.

Rosemary pulled supplies out of the bags and began putting them in the cabinets. "I think your coworkers really enjoyed seeing the *boppli*. Even your supervisor was smiling while he talked to her. Everyone was so nice."

"*Ya*, they were *froh* that we stopped by." Carolyn smiled at Rosemary. "*Danki* for coming with me."

Joshua wanted to ask her if she'd finally resigned from her job, but he didn't want to risk upsetting Carolyn, especially in front of Rosemary. The subject of her going back to work was a sore spot for Carolyn, but he longed to hear her say she was going to quit.

Carolyn picked up Sadie Liz. "I'm going to go change her. Do you mind putting everything away, Ro?"

"I don't mind at all." Rosemary retrieved a pound of butter from the bag and slipped it into the refrigerator.

"*Danki.*"

"I'll come with you," Josh said. He followed her to the bedroom where she placed Sadie Liz on the changing table Sarah Ann had given her. "I'm glad you had a nice visit."

"We did have a nice time, but you were right, it was tiring for her." Carolyn slipped off Sadie Liz's dress. "It was *gut* for her to be out in the fresh air, though. And I think I did have a little bit of cabin fever. I enjoyed interacting with other people."

"Did you talk to your supervisor?" he asked, hoping to gently prod her to talk about her job. His heart would feel settled if he knew he had her at the farm full-time permanently. He didn't want to share her with the rest of the world when they had a family to raise now.

"I spoke to him briefly." She kept her gaze on the baby while changing her diaper. "He said it was *gut* to see me and the *boppli.*"

"That's all he said?" Joshua had a difficult time believing the subject of her return to work hadn't come up between them.

"He asked me to let him know if and when I'm coming back to work." He waited while she wiped Sadie Liz and applied diaper ointment, and then she went on. "He said he has someone filling in for me, and he's going to hire her on permanently if I don't return."

"And what did you say?" Joshua sank into a chair beside the bed.

"I told him I'll let him know." She pulled on a fresh diaper. "He said I should call him as soon as I decide."

She kept her eyes on their baby as she fastened the diaper and started to dress her again. *Why wouldn't she look at him? Was she avoiding his gaze? Was* Mamm *right when she said Carolyn would return to the hotel?*

"Why would you want to go back, Carolyn?" Joshua asked, praying she'd look at him. "Why aren't you *froh* here with me and the *kinner?*" He reached over and touched her arm.

"I am *froh*." Carolyn finally looked up at him. "I'm just not sure about quitting yet."

"Why aren't you certain?" Joshua searched her eyes.

"*Aenti* Carolyn?" Rosemary called from the kitchen. "Would you like me to start making lunch?"

"I need to go help Rosemary. We'll talk later, okay?" Carolyn's smile seemed forced. "I'll make you something nice for lunch."

Joshua nodded as Carolyn walked out of the room with Sadie Liz on her shoulder. He gritted his teeth and raked his hands through his hair. Why wouldn't she tell him what she was thinking? Had he done something wrong? His father had told him to be patient with Carolyn, but his patience was wearing thin. And his mother's prediction circled through his mind daily.

He would try to talk to Carolyn again later, when they were alone. Somehow he'd make her see that she belonged at the farm with their family.

CHAPTER TEN

Carolyn settled Sadie Liz in her cradle for her midmorning nap. Since the baby was sleeping soundly, she felt comfortable walking outside for a few minutes. She headed to the barn to check the phone messages, but first she stopped by her garden and noticed that the tomato seeds were finally starting to sprout. She loved watching the garden grow and flourish as the season wore on. Even as a little girl she enjoyed working in her garden with her mother and grandmother back on her brother's dairy farm.

With her hand tented over her eyes, Carolyn looked toward the pasture where she spotted Joshua, Benjamin, and Daniel repairing the far fence. She waved, and Joshua waved in response. Then she headed into the barn and checked the messages on voice mail. The first two were customers calling to inquire about horses. She listened to them and then hit the Save button for Joshua. The last message was for her.

"Hi, Carolyn. This is Linda. Last week when you stopped by the hotel, I mentioned I wanted to come by. I was wondering if tonight would be all right. I thought I could bring something for supper. I understand if it's not a *gut* day. Just let me know. Talk to you soon. Bye!"

Carolyn rubbed her hands together. She'd been thinking about making a ham loaf for supper, and tonight would be the perfect night. She dialed Linda's number and waited for the voice mail to pick up. "Hi, Linda. This is Carolyn. I would love for you to come for supper tonight. Please come anytime. I'm looking forward to seeing you. I'm going to make a ham loaf, so you can bring whatever you'd like to go with it. See you later."

Carolyn hurried back into the house and checked on Sadie Liz, who was still sleeping soundly. She then made her way to the laundry room to run another load of clothes through the wringer washer. She hummed to herself while she worked. She enjoyed being home and taking care of her household chores. Maybe Joshua was right—this was where she belonged. After the clothes were washed, she checked on Sadie Liz and found her stirring.

"Are you awake, little one?" Carolyn lifted the baby into her arms and carried her out to the back porch. "Do you want to watch me hang the clothes on the line? Pretty soon you'll be out here handing me the clothespins. I used to love helping my *mamm* with the laundry when I was little."

Sadie Liz cooed and gurgled, and Carolyn laughed.

"You're in an awfully *gut* mood today, Sadie Liz. I'm certain that's because you're sleeping more at night. I'm glad you're getting your rest. I'll set you in your seat, and you can watch me work. How does that sound?" Carolyn strapped the baby in the bouncy seat that was still on the porch from earlier that morning and continued humming while she hung the laundry on the line that extended to the barn. She moved the laundry down with a pulley that Joshua had installed for her.

First she hung Joshua's trousers and Benjamin's trousers, and next she hung their shirts. After her dresses and aprons were hung on the line, she added Sadie's diapers and onesies. Soon the line was full, and Carolyn admired how it looked with all of their clothes flapping in the warm breeze. It was a beautiful blend of colors—just like their family.

"I see you have help today." Joshua approached the porch. He lifted his hat and swiped his hand across his brow. "Are you teaching Sadie Liz about laundry?"

"I am." Carolyn smiled down at her husband. "I was just telling her how I used to hand my *mamm* clothespins. Soon she'll be handing them to me."

"I know she will." Joshua climbed the steps and leaned over the bouncy seat where Sadie Liz continued to coo. "Did she have a good morning nap?"

"*Ya*, she did. I thought she could use some more fresh air." Carolyn ran her finger over Joshua's arm. "We're going to have company for supper."

"Oh *ya*?" Joshua raised his eyebrows. "Who is going to join us?"

"Linda Zook wants to come by tonight. I thought I'd make ham loaf. Does that sound *gut*?"

"*Ya*." He picked up Sadie Liz and cradled her in his arms. "You know I love ham loaf." He turned his gaze to the baby. "Wait until you have ham loaf, Sadie Liz. You will love it. Trust me. Your *mamm* makes the best ham loaf in all of Lancaster County."

"Don't listen to him, Sadie Liz. My *mamm* is a much better cook than I am." Carolyn looked toward the back door. "Oh, I have so much to do before Linda gets here. I need to clean the *haus* and get all of the ingredients for supper together."

"The *haus* looks fine. Didn't you just clean yesterday? You've been cleaning nearly every day."

"*Ya*, I guess I have. I've been on a cleaning frenzy since Sadie Liz started sleeping more at night. I have more energy." She smoothed her hands over her apron. "I'm so glad Linda called. I had wanted to make an especially nice meal for us. Oh, this will be fun. It's been awhile since we've had someone over for supper."

Joshua kissed the baby's head. "It's *gut* to see you smiling again. I was beginning to worry about you, but now you're back to your former self." He kissed Carolyn's cheek. "You're my *froh fraa* again. *Ich liebe dich*." He whispered the words in her ear as if it were a secret kept between the two of them.

Carolyn felt as though her heart turned over in her chest. "I love you too."

"Josh!" Daniel called from the stable. "Can you come here and help us with something?"

"I better go." Joshua handed the baby to Carolyn. "I'll see you in a bit."

"Okay." Carolyn held Sadie Liz to her chest and sighed as Joshua loped down the steps and back toward the stable. She enjoyed every moment of her time at home with her family, and she dreaded the idea of going back to work at the hotel. She would miss mornings like this, out on the porch hanging laundry and talking to her baby.

Sadie Liz whimpered and began to cry.

Carolyn looked down at her. "Do you want a diaper change? Let's go get you fixed up and then we'll start on the cleaning."

Later, Joshua stepped into the stable and found evidence that Benjamin and Daniel were mucking the stalls. "How's it going?"

"It would go a lot faster if you lent us a hand," Daniel responded from somewhere near the back of the stable.

Joshua shook his head and smiled. Daniel and Benjamin were never afraid to speak their minds, and he appreciated their honesty. "I have *gut* news."

"What's that?" Daniel stepped out into his line of sight.

"It's noon." Joshua pointed in the direction of the farmhouse. "That means Carolyn has an *appeditlich* lunch waiting for us in the *haus*."

"Oh *gut*." Daniel started toward the front of the stable. "I'm ready for a break. It's hot in here today. It feels more like August than June."

"Make sure you wash up at the pump today," Joshua said as Daniel moved past him. "You're a mess."

"You're not so clean yourself." Daniel smirked as he headed for the house.

Joshua lingered behind and waited for Benjamin, who emerged from a stall near the far end of the stable. "Are you hungry?"

"I'm always hungry." Benjamin met him at the door. "Is everything all right?"

"*Ya*, I just meant are you too hungry to wait up a few minutes. I want to talk to you."

Benjamin frowned. "Did I do something wrong?"

"No, no." Joshua shook his head as they walked toward the house. "I want to ask you something. Have you noticed something different about your *mamm* lately?"

Benjamin stopped walking and looked up at Joshua. "No, I haven't. What's going on?"

"She seems so *froh* these days." Joshua pointed toward the laundry swaying in the wind. "Earlier today I watched her hang out the clothes, and she was humming and talking to Sadie Liz. She was actually glowing because she seemed so content."

Benjamin nodded. "*Ya*, I have seen that. She was singing to Sadie Liz last night when she gave her a bath. I haven't seen her so relaxed in a long time."

Joshua smiled. "I was wondering if you had noticed it too."

Benjamin's stomach growled. "I'm really hungry. Can we talk about this more later?" He started toward the house.

"Wait." Joshua caught up with him. "I want to ask you something else before we go into the *haus*. Has she said anything to you about going back to work at the hotel?"

Benjamin shrugged. "No, she hasn't. Why?"

"Well, I wanted to talk about it after she took Sadie Liz to visit her coworkers, but she either won't give me a straight answer about whether or not she's going back or she changes the subject when I bring it up. I tried pushing her to talk to me, and she gets defensive. I don't want to argue with her and ruin her good mood. I wanted to get your opinion about it. I'm wondering if maybe she won't go back to the hotel now since she seems so content to be here at the farm with us. Do you think she finally feels like she can quit?"

"I really don't know." Benjamin climbed the steps to the porch. "She hasn't said anything to me about it."

"Will you let me know if she says anything to you?" Joshua asked.

"*Ya*, I will."

After washing up at the pump, Joshua followed Benjamin into the mudroom where they shucked their boots. The aroma of freshly baked cookies and bread assaulted Joshua's senses as he stepped into the kitchen. He found Carolyn standing by the table, which was clogged with platters of food.

She made a sweeping gesture. "I hope you're all hungry. I had some fun making lunch."

Joshua couldn't believe his eyes. He hadn't seen so much food since the last barn raising he'd attended.

"*Danki, Mamm.*" Benjamin washed his hands at the sink and then sat at his usual spot at the table.

"Everything looks fantastic." Joshua washed his hands, too, and sat next to Benjamin. After a prayer, he filled his plate with lunch meat, bread, pickles, pretzels, and potato salad. He glanced over at Sadie Liz in her seat and smiled. "Has she had her lunch?"

"*Ya,* she finished a bottle just before I set everything out. She'll be ready for her afternoon nap soon, but I thought she might enjoy having lunch with you first." Carolyn sat across from him and placed a spoonful of potato salad on her plate.

While they ate, Benjamin and Daniel fell into a conversation about one of the horses. They continued talking, seemingly oblivious to Carolyn's and Joshua's presence.

"There are fresh chocolate chip and peanut butter *kichlin* and also carrot bread for dessert, so be sure to save some room. I just had time to put them in the oven before Sadie needed that bottle," Carolyn said while putting two pieces of turkey on a piece of fresh bread.

"You made *kichlin* and carrot bread too?" Joshua studied his wife. "You've been busy."

"*Ya,* I have." Carolyn shrugged. "I swept and picked up in the *schtupp.* The *haus* is all ready for when Linda arrives." Her cheeks flushed. "You're staring at me."

"I was just admiring you. You're glowing." He picked up a pretzel from his plate. "You seem to be really settled in our new life."

"What do you mean?" She added mustard and mayonnaise to her sandwich. "I've been settled in at the farm since we were married."

"I don't mean that. I mean you seem happy to be here all the time and not working part-time at the hotel."

Her smile faded slightly. Why did he have to bring up the subject? She had looked so happy and now he had ruined it.

"I am enjoying being home." She cut the sandwich in half. "I was thinking of making a pie for dessert tonight. Do you have a preference?"

"How about crumbly peach pie?" he asked, hoping to lighten her mood again. "You haven't made one of those in a long time."

Her smile was back. "That's a *gut* idea. I'll make that for Linda."

"I thought you would make it for me." He winked at her, and she laughed. Her sweet laughter was a melody to his ears. He hoped to hear her laugh more often.

CHAPTER ELEVEN

Carolyn put the ham loaf in the oven and began setting the table for supper. Sadie Liz sat nearby in her seat and cooed while Carolyn worked. She lined up the plates and pulled out the utensils.

"Dinner is going to smell *wunderbaar* tonight," she told the baby. "You won't believe how *gut* until you smell it."

Carolyn heard a knock on the back door and went to open it.

"Hi, Carolyn!"

"Linda!" Carolyn hugged her friend. "I'm so glad you came. I just put the ham loaf in the oven."

"That sounds fantastic." Linda pointed toward the bag she had in her other hand. "I brought a seven-layer salad."

"Thank you. I am sure it will be delicious."

Linda followed Carolyn into the kitchen, where she took her casserole dish out of the bag.

After cooing over the baby for a few moments, Linda looked at Carolyn. "How are you? You seem different."

"What do you mean?" Carolyn asked.

"You look younger, if that's possible." Linda paused, tapping her finger to her lip. "Well, that's not it exactly. You're radiant. You just seem more cheerful and more youthful. It's as if something's happened to you. You've been transformed."

Carolyn chuckled. "You could say I've been transformed. I did just have a *boppli*." She motioned toward Sadie Liz, still contented in her baby seat. "It's just part of having a *kind*."

"No, it's more than that. Something has changed for you. What is it?"

Carolyn shook her head as she took the salad to the refrigerator. "I'm not sure what it could be other than I had a really great day. I got a *gut* night's sleep because Sadie Liz is sleeping much more during the night lately. I did the laundry, cleaned, and baked. I made a special lunch for Josh, Ben, and Danny, and I got to plan this meal for you. I guess I spent the day doing all of my favorite things."

Linda snapped her fingers. "That's it. You're doing what you truly love. I think you've been craving this family life for a long time. You told me you thought you'd never find someone to love you completely because of Benjamin. You not only found and married Josh, but now that you have Sadie Liz, you feel as if your life is complete, right?"

"Maybe it is that." Carolyn leaned back against the counter and folded her hands over her apron. "I do feel complete now. I have my family, my husband, and my two *kinner*. We have this wonderful home. I didn't think I deserved a life like this after I became a mother when I was sixteen. Now I see that I have everything I ever wanted. I'm so thankful for all that I have now. Today I felt like I couldn't stop smiling."

She gazed at Sadie Liz, who cooed from her bouncy seat.

"*Ya*, I know you went through a hard time before you met Josh, but God had the perfect timing for you both. He answers our prayers." Linda tapped her finger on the counter. "It's like those Scripture verses in First Thessalonians say. 'Rejoice always, pray continually, give thanks in all circumstances; for this is God's will for you in Christ Jesus.' We always have to keep praying and thanking God. Even when we think things won't work out for us, God is in control. He will never abandon us. In the end, He's with us, protecting us and loving us."

"That's very true."

"Now, what can I do to help you get ready for supper?" Linda asked.

Carolyn scanned the table. "We need glasses."

Linda turned to the cabinet and pulled out four glasses. "Gregg asked about you yesterday. He wanted to know if I'd heard from you."

Carolyn's shoulders tensed. "What did you tell him?"

"I told him we hadn't talked about it, but I promised to let you know he asked."

"He hasn't offered my job to the other woman yet, has he?"

"No, but I heard her asking him about it. She said she really needs to find a stable part-time job. She's very nice. She's *English*, and she lives over in Bird-in-Hand." Linda retrieved a pitcher of water from the refrigerator. "You're not still considering coming back to the hotel, are you?"

Carolyn hesitated but decided to be forthcoming with her friend. "I don't want to go back, but I know I need to."

"Why would you have to come back?" Linda filled the glasses. "You just finished telling me how happy you are here. Why would you want to leave this?"

"I need to work for Ben." Relief flooded Carolyn as she said the words out loud. "I have to make sure he has everything he needs."

"What do you mean?" Linda shook her head.

"Ben isn't Josh's biological son."

"I know that."

"That means Josh may not feel like he has to help Ben when he's ready to buy his own farm or build his first *haus*. If I keep working part-time at the hotel, I can put money away for Ben to secure his future. I have an obligation to my son, and I have a savings account where I put a little bit of money away for him every time I get paid."

Carolyn pulled out a stack of paper napkins and started folding them. "I want him to have the same opportunities Sadie Liz will have when she's older. I'm certain Joshua will make sure Sadie Liz has everything she needs when she's ready to move out and have her own *haus*. I don't want Ben to resent Sadie Liz or any of his other future siblings if they get more than he did. It wouldn't be right for him to feel as though he's not as important as they are."

"Carolyn." Linda placed her hand on Carolyn's arm. "Josh loves you, and he loves Ben. I'm certain he wouldn't give more to Sadie Liz than he'd give to Ben. Why aren't you certain?"

"I don't think he would do it deliberately." Carolyn started setting the folded napkins under the utensils. "I think it might be subconscious. He may not even realize it if he favors his biological *kinner* over Ben. I can't run the risk of Ben resenting his other siblings or not having as much as they have. It's not Ben's fault that he came into the world the way he did."

"You need to stop punishing yourself for having Ben when you were sixteen. You're a great *mamm*, and Josh is a great *dat*," Linda said while placing the water pitcher back in the refrigerator. "I've noticed how Josh and Ben interact at church service, and it's obviously they have a great mutual respect for one another. I don't think Ben is missing out on not having his biological *dat*."

Carolyn nodded, but she couldn't stop the doubt from filling her mind.

"Carolyn, please look at me."

She turned to her friend.

"You told me Josh adopted Ben, and he calls Josh *Dat*, right?" Linda asked. Carolyn nodded. "What else does he need to do to prove to you that he considers Ben his son?"

The question was simple, but Carolyn answered, "I honestly don't know."

"Carolyn, I don't think you need to work at the hotel to try to prove anything else. I think you're already doing everything the best you can, without that extra income." She paused. "And I don't think the problem is Josh. I get the feeling you're still blaming yourself for becoming a *mamm* at such a young age. You've been forgiven, and you can trust God to provide for you and also for Ben's needs. Stop punishing yourself for your mistake. God has forgiven you, so now you need to forgive yourself, once and for all."

Carolyn sighed. "*Danki* for trying to help me sort out my feelings, Linda. I appreciate it."

Linda's words circled her mind. She needed to let them settle in her soul. Was Linda right? Did she still need to forgive herself, once and for all? Is that why she was so concerned about Ben and whether Josh would truly treat him as a son?

She had a lot to contemplate, and she was thankful for her friend's honest conversation.

Linda's words were still echoing through her mind while she rocked Sadie Liz later that evening. She held her baby close to her chest while she nursed. Was she overcompensating by trying to go back to work at the hotel? She still felt responsible for Benjamin, that she had to be the one to ensure his future, and she couldn't earn money for him staying at home. Some women like her mother and Sarah Ann earned some money sewing or quilting, but she didn't think her skills were as good or marketable as theirs. And neither of them had small children to care for now, so they had more flexibility.

No, working at the hotel still made sense, even though she despised the thought of going back and she felt more confused about making a decision than ever.

"Dinner was *wunderbaar* tonight." Joshua sat on the edge of the bed, which creaked under his weight. "I think Linda had a nice time."

"*Ya*, she did." Carolyn looked up at him. "I think she liked her crumbly peach pie."

"I still say it was my pie." Joshua smiled at her, and then his eyes seemed to question hers. "You look like you have something on your mind. Do you want to talk about it?"

"No, I'm fine. I'm just tired." She cupped her free hand over her mouth to cover a yawn. "It's been a long day."

"You stayed busy all day long." His gaze moved to Sadie Liz. "She seems *froh* there. Are you going to try to keep her up for a little bit?"

"*Ya*, I am. I'm hoping to get even more sleep tonight than I did last night."

"As hard as you worked today, I'm certain you need it." He watched Sadie Liz for a moment, and she wished she could read his thoughts. "But you've seemed happy. Even Ben has noticed how happy you've seemed lately."

"He has?" she asked, and he nodded. "Ben hasn't said anything to me."

"He's a teenage *bu*. What do you expect him to say?"

"You're right." She looked down at Sadie Liz. "You can go to bed. You don't need to sit up with us."

"I don't mind. I can wait for you."

They sat in silence while Sadie Liz finished nursing and then burped. Joshua leaned over and touched Carolyn's knee while keeping his eyes on the baby. Carolyn enjoyed having his company while she cared for Sadie Liz. She felt safe with Joshua near her side. Joy filled her as she enjoyed the quiet, intimate moment with her newborn and her husband.

Once Sadie Liz began snoring quietly, Carolyn gently placed her in the cradle and tucked her in. Then she climbed into bed beside Joshua, and he snuffed out the lantern.

"*Gut nacht*," he whispered before kissing her cheek and resting his hand on her arm.

"*Gut nacht*," she repeated. As she rolled onto her side, she opened her heart to God.

Lord, please guide me in my decision about returning to work at the hotel. I'm so confused by all of my feelings. While I still believe I need to build up a nest egg for Ben, I'm beginning to wonder if Linda is right. Do I need to trust that Josh will provide for all of our kinner, including Ben? And am I not seeing that I deserve complete forgiveness for my mistakes? Please guide my heart to the right decision. In Jesus' holy name. Amen.

CHAPTER TWELVE

Carolyn held Sadie Liz while she stood in Barbie's kitchen the following Sunday afternoon after service. Sadie Liz cooed and grunted while Carolyn gently patted her back. Lillian Glick, Joshua's niece, moved through the knot of women serving the noon meal and sidled up to her.

"She is getting so big, *Aenti* Carolyn." Lillian held up her hands. "I just washed my hands. May I hold her?"

"Of course." Carolyn handed her the baby. "I just finished nursing her, so she's *froh* and full."

Lillian smiled down at Sadie Liz. "Isn't it amazing how quickly babies grow? It seems like only yesterday that we were waiting for her to come into the world."

"*Ya*, I know." Carolyn sighed. "I can't believe she's a month old already. It feels like she was born only a few days ago."

"Carolyn." Her mother came up behind her. "How is my Sadie Liz?"

"She's doing great," Carolyn said. "She's enjoying her cousin right now."

Mamm touched Sadie Liz's hand. "Look at you. You're so big. Is she sleeping better at night?"

"Oh, *ya*. She slept a four-hour stretch last night. It was *wunderbaar.*" Carolyn nodded at her mother and then spotted a tray of peanut butter spread in her hands. "Do you need help serving the meal? Lily can hold Sadie Liz, and I'll help you."

Her mother pointed to a coffeepot on the counter. "You can fill coffee cups if you want."

"Okay." Carolyn turned to Lillian. "Do you mind holding her awhile longer?"

"Oh, no, not at all. I'd love to," Lillian said. "I'll take *gut* care of her."

Carolyn fetched the coffeepot and walked outside with her mother.

"The service was nice today," *Mamm* said as they walked toward the large barn where the benches were set up for the noon meal.

"It *was* nice," Carolyn agreed. "I missed part of it while I was walking with Sadie, but I enjoyed the parts I was able to hear."

"You seem completely relaxed today." Her mother studied her. "You didn't even hesitate when you asked Lillian to hold Sadie Liz."

Carolyn shrugged. "I know Lily is great with *kinner*. I've seen her with other babies, and she does a *wunderbaar* job. I know I don't have to worry when she watches Sadie Liz."

"No, that's not it." *Mamm* stopped walking and faced her. "You're different, Carolyn. You've changed since you've had Sadie Liz."

"I keep hearing that." Carolyn held the coffeepot by her side. "Even Ben and Josh have said I'm different, and I don't understand. I still feel like the same person, but everyone has been telling me I'm not. How am I different?"

"You were so worried before Sadie Liz was born, but you don't seem to be as worried anymore. You're almost always relaxed and positive about things. Every time I look at you, you smile. I'm so relieved to see you like this. I was concerned about you."

"You were?" Carolyn asked. "I'm sorry I worried you."

"Oh, no. You don't need to apologize. It's my job as your *mamm* to be concerned about you and your *bruder*. You were just so exhausted, and you didn't seem ready for Sadie Liz."

"I have my strength back, and that has made a big difference in how I feel."

Mamm tapped her chin with her free hand as she balanced the tray with the other. "But something was bothering you. You told me you were anxious about how Ben would fit into the family after Sadie Liz was born, but now you don't seem to be apprehensive about that anymore."

Carolyn shook her head. "No, I'm not. Ben is adjusting fine, and he loves his baby sister." *But I don't want to go back to work at the hotel. I haven't figured that out yet.*

Mamm touched Carolyn's arm. "I'm glad you're feeling better. And I'm proud of you. You're a *wunderbaar mamm*."

"*Danki.*" Carolyn's eyes misted over. "We'd better take in this food before the men start asking for the peanut butter spread. They also won't be happy if I fill their cups with cold coffee."

Carolyn and her mother entered the barn where the men were sitting at the benches to eat lunch before the women and children. While her mother delivered the bowls of peanut butter spread, Carolyn filled cups at several tables before she arrived where Joshua sat with her father and Benjamin.

"*Danki*, Carolyn," *Dat* said with a smile as she filled their cups as well.

"Where's Sadie Liz?" Joshua asked.

"Lily is holding her," Carolyn said. "I thought I'd help serve today."

"*Danki.*" Joshua winked at her.

Once the coffeepot was empty, Carolyn started back toward the house.

"Carolyn." Barbie walked beside her. "*Danki* for helping with the coffee."

"*Gern gschehne.*" Carolyn smiled at her mother-in-law. "I enjoy helping the other ladies serve the meal. It gives me a chance to say hello to everyone."

"I saw Lily rocking Sadie Liz on the porch. They both looked content." Barbie pointed to where the pair sat. "Josh told me you've got Sadie Liz in a *gut* routine, and she's sleeping longer at night. You're doing a great job with her."

Carolyn stopped walking and swallowed a gasp as she looked at Barbie. "*Danki.*"

Barbie gave her a stiff nod and continued toward the house.

Carolyn gripped the coffeepot in her hand and wondered if that was a sign from God for what she should do. If even her censorious mother-in-law thought she was a good mother, was she meant to stay at home with the children full-time, no matter her fears about Ben's future?

⋐∾⋑

Joshua and his father leaned on the pasture fence and watched as a line of buggies drove toward the main road. The noon meal was over, and families were headed back toward their homes.

"It was a *gut* day," *Dat* said while wiping his hand across his brow. "It sure is warm today. I enjoy hosting church, but it is a lot of work. *Danki* for helping us get the barn ready yesterday. I appreciate your help."

"You're welcome. *Ya*, it is a lot of work." Joshua took a long drink of water from a paper cup. "Do you need help with anything else before I go? I can help you take care of the animals."

"No, it's fine." His father waved off the question. "I'll check on them later. I'm going to go sit on the porch and enjoy this *schee* summer day."

"That sounds like a *gut* plan." Joshua and his father walked together toward the porch, where Josh thought he would find his family so they could head home.

"Josh," *Dat* said. "I've been meaning to ask you something. Right before Sadie Liz was born, you were concerned about Carolyn. You said she was worried about how Ben would fit into the family after the *boppli* was born. Is she still worried about that?"

Joshua shook his head and smiled. "No, she's been more relaxed than I've ever seen her. She walks around humming, and she seems to have boundless energy. She hasn't asked me anything like that again."

"*Gut.*" *Dat* nodded. "I'm glad to hear that. I know you're relieved that things are back to normal. Well, as normal as anything can be when you have a newborn."

Joshua chuckled. "It's amazing, *Dat*. God is so *gut*. I've never been more grateful."

"That's *gut*. I told you just to be patient with Carolyn."

"*Ya.*" Joshua tugged on the brim of his hat as his thoughts returned to a conversation he had with his mother shortly after Sadie Liz was born. "I'm a little concerned, though. Carolyn still hasn't told me that she's quitting her job at the hotel. I'm not certain she's going to quit."

"What do you mean?"

"She hasn't told her boss that she isn't going back."

"Why would she go back to work?" *Dat* crossed his arms over his chest. "You've told me the farm is secure, so why would she have to work?"

"That's what I can't figure out. *Mamm* told me she thought Carolyn would return to the hotel. I'm hoping *Mamm* was wrong. I'm hoping Carolyn will realize she doesn't need that job. Today during the service I prayed and asked God to help guide her heart to the farm. I'm hoping she will finally see that the *kinner* and I need her home full-time."

"I'm certain she will." *Dat* patted Joshua's arm. "You're a *gut* man, Josh. She'll figure it out."

"*Danki.*" Joshua spotted Carolyn sitting on the porch with Lillian and his mother. She looked toward him and waved, and his heart seemed to flutter. He hoped Carolyn was as content as he was.

⚭

The following morning Carolyn rocked Sadie Liz in her bedroom and hummed softly. She enjoyed hearing the quiet rhythm of her baby's snores, and she didn't want to put her down in her cradle. Not just yet.

Closing her eyes, she allowed her thoughts to focus completely on the sounds coming from her daughter. Her thoughts moved to the prayer she'd sent up to God a little over a week ago. She still hadn't felt the answer to her most heartfelt question. She didn't want to leave her baby and go back to work, but she still felt the need to go. What did God want her to do? Where did she belong?

She longed to spend the entire day just watching Sadie Liz

sleep, but there was work to be done. She needed to clean up the kitchen, sweep the porch, and check on her garden.

Carolyn gingerly lowered Sadie Liz into her cradle and then walked to the kitchen. She would have about two hours before Sadie Liz was awake again. After the breakfast dishes were washed and put away, she headed out to the porch with her broom in her hand. She was sweeping when her gaze moved to the stables. She wondered what Joshua and Benjamin were doing. She was surprised they weren't already out in the pasture working with horses.

Carolyn leaned the broom against the railing and walked back into the house. After lifting Sadie Liz from the cradle, she held the sleeping baby close to her chest, slipped back outside, and headed down the path toward the stables. She stood in the doorway and peeked into the stable.

"So, I've been thinking about something, Ben." Joshua's voice sounded from the stalls near the far end of the stable. "And I'm ready to discuss it with you."

"What's that?" Benjamin asked.

"In five years, you'll be ready to officially be my business partner, if that's what you want," Joshua said, stepping out into the main area of the stable with his back to Carolyn. "We can build a house for you beyond the pasture. You just let me know how many acres you want, and your *mamm* and I will sign them over to you. We can even change the name of the business to Glick and Son if you'd like. Of course, if your *mamm* and I have another *bu*, then we'll have to call it Glick and Sons."

"You want me to be your partner?" Benjamin's expression brightened with excitement and surprise. "That would be *wunderbaar, Dat*! I don't know how to thank you. I'd be honored to be your partner. I love working with you, and I love the horses so much. I never felt like I fit in at my *onkel's* dairy farm, but I feel like I belong here. I want to work here with you for the rest of my life. This is a dream come true for me."

"*Gut, gut,*" Joshua said with a nod. "I'm glad to hear you say that, Benjamin. That's what I'd hoped you'd say. We'll tell your *mamm* together. I wanted to be sure the farm was prospering long term and that partnering with me was what you wanted before I said anything to her about this plan."

Carolyn gasped and cupped her hand to her mouth. God had answered her prayer! She knew at that moment where she should be, and it was with her family, not at the hotel three mornings each week.

And it seemed as if the answer had been right in front of her all along. Just as Linda and her mother had said, when Joshua adopted Benjamin, he truly made the boy his son. It was more than just a legal formality; it was a true declaration of his love.

By asking Benjamin to be his business partner, Joshua was declaring Benjamin a part of the family she had built with Joshua, and that meant he would support the boy in every way he would support their biological children. Benjamin was just as important to Joshua as their new baby girl was to him.

"Thank You, God, for showing me that I need to stay home," she whispered as tears spilled from her eyes. "I can hear Your voice, God, and I understand now. I'm sorry I didn't trust You." She hugged the sleeping baby closer to her body.

Joshua turned toward the door, and his eyes rounded. "Carolyn? I didn't know you were standing there. Is everything all right?" He rushed over to her and stroked her arm. "Is something wrong with Sadie Liz?"

"No. Everything is fine." She wiped an errant tear from her cheek. "Actually, everything couldn't be any better."

"I don't understand." He shook his head while studying her.

"Let's walk outside so we can talk in private." She led him out of the stable and back toward the house where they climbed the porch steps and sat beside each other on the swing. "I've made a decision. I'm ready to call Gregg and tell him that I quit. I belong here at the farm with you and the *kinner*."

"Oh, Carolyn." His smile was wide. "I'm so thankful to hear you finally say that." His smiled faded slightly. "But what made you realize that you belong here? And why are you crying?"

"I've been worried that you might not feel you could support Benjamin financially like you would support your biological *kinner*." Carolyn wiped her wet cheeks with one hand as she settled Sadie Liz in her lap. "I had convinced myself that I needed to work and save money so I could be the one to help Benjamin when it came time to help him get his own home. I felt responsible for his future. I think my insecurities go all the way back to when Benjamin's father rejected me. I was afraid you'd, in a way, reject Ben."

"Carolyn—" Joshua began.

"Please let me finish." She touched her finger to his lips to stop him from talking. "I had convinced myself I had to work no matter what, even though you've been trying to tell me all along that you love Ben and will always love him. I prayed and asked God to show me clear direction for whether I should work or stay home with the family. He provided that for me just a few moments ago."

She nodded toward the stalls. "I heard what you said to Ben about making him your partner and giving him land to build a home. That was the sign I needed to realize how much you love Ben and how you will also support him because you do consider him your son." She kept a hand on Sadie Liz's tummy while she spoke.

"That's exactly right." Joshua's eyes were warm and tender. "I told you that when I adopted Ben, he became my son. I meant it, and I will always mean it."

"I know." Carolyn reached up and touched his cheek. "I see that now. I'm sorry for doubting you. You've been trying to show me how much you love Ben and me all along. I'm sorry I was too stubborn and scared to see it. Linda told me God has already forgiven me for how Ben came into the world and that I need to finally forgive myself. She was right. I had to let myself believe that I've moved past my mistakes and that I'm worthy of love."

Josh took her hand in his and kissed it. "Of course you're forgiven and worthy of love. I promise you that I will always take care of you, Ben, and the rest of our *kinner*, no matter how many we have. *Ich liebe dich.*"

"*Danki*, Josh." Carolyn smiled as fresh tears splattered her cheeks. "I love you too."

Joshua draped his arm around Carolyn, and she rested her head on his shoulder as she pushed the swing into motion with her foot. At that moment, she knew without a doubt that she and Joshua would always keep their children safe and provide for their future, together.

Reading Group Guide

1. Carolyn feels it's her obligation to plan for Benjamin's financial future without Joshua's help. She worries that Joshua won't love and support Benjamin as much as he will love and support his biological children. Do you think her feelings are justified? Take a walk in her shoes. How would you have handled this situation if you were Carolyn? Share this with the group.

2. Linda finds encouragement in 1 Thessalonians 5:16–18. (Write out the passage.) What do these verses mean to you?

3. Barbie has criticized Carolyn since before she married Joshua. By the end of the story, however, Barbie finally admits that Carolyn is a good mother. Have you ever been criticized by a close family member? If so, how did you handle the criticism? Share this with the group.

4. Joshua doesn't understand why Carolyn feels she has to continue working at the hotel to help the family financially

since the horse farm provides everything that they need. He is determined to convince Carolyn that he wants her on the farm with him. Joshua feels lost as to how he can help Carolyn realize that she doesn't need to work. What, if anything, do you think Joshua should have done differently?

5. Carolyn is irritated by Barbie's constant remarks about Benjamin not being Joshua's biological son. Due to a mistake she made when she was sixteen, Carolyn feels she's been judged much of her life by her community that is supposed to be Christlike. Do we do this in our own church communities—judge and gossip about our fellow Christians without considering the consequences?

6. Which character can you identify with the most? Which character seemed to carry the most emotional stake in the story? Was it Joshua, Carolyn, Benjamin, or someone else?

7. Before Joshua met Carolyn, he was certain he would never get married and have a family. He feels that God gave him a second chance when he fell in love with Carolyn, and he is delighted that they are going to be blessed with a family. Have you ever experienced a second chance?

8. What did you know about the Amish before reading this book? What did you learn?

ACKNOWLEDGMENTS

As always, I'm thankful for my loving family. Special thanks to my special Amish friends who patiently answer my endless stream of questions. You're a blessing in my life. I'm grateful to Stacey Barbalace for her help with the recipe and research.

To my agent, Sue Brower—you are my own personal superhero! I can't thank you enough for your guidance, advice, and friendship. I'm thankful that our paths have crossed and our partnership will continue long into the future. You are a tremendous blessing in my life.

Thank you to my amazing editor, Becky Philpott, for your friendship and guidance. I'm so grateful to Jean Bloom for her help polishing this novella. I also would like to thank Laura Dickerson for tirelessly working to promote my books. I'm grateful to each and every person at HarperCollins Christian Publishing who helped make this book a reality.

To God—thank You most of all for giving me the inspiration and the words to glorify You. I'm grateful and humbled You've chosen this path for me.

Author Bio

Photograph by

Amy Clipston is the award-winning and bestselling author of the Kauffman Amish Bakery series. Her novels have hit multiple bestseller lists including CBD, CBA, and ECPA. Amy holds a degree in communications from Virginia Wesleyan College and works fulltime for the City of Charlotte, NC. Amy lives in North Carolina with her husband, two sons, and four spoiled rotten cats. Visit her online at www.amyclipston.com Facebook: AmyClipstonBooks Twitter: @AmyClipston

A Heart Full of Love

KATHLEEN FULLER

To James—I love you

Glossary

ab im kopp—crazy

aenti—aunt

Amisch—Amish

appeditlich—delicious

boppli(s)—baby, babies

daed/vatter—dad/father

daag—day

danki—thank you

dochder—daughter

familye—family

frau—wife

garten—garden

geh—go

granddochder—granddaughter

grossmutter—grandmother

grossvatter—grandfather

gut—good

haus—house

hungerich—hungry

kapp—woman's head covering, prayer cap

kinner—children

kumme—come

maed—girls

maedel—girl

mamm/mudder/mutter—mom, mother

mei—my

nee—no

nix—nothing

onkel—uncle

perfekt—perfect

schee—pretty, handsome

schwester—sister

seltsam—weird

sohn—son

ya—yes

yer—your

yung—young

CHAPTER ONE

PARADISE, PENNSYLVANIA

"Are you ready for this?"

Ellie Miller turned her head toward her husband Christopher's, concerned voice. Their horse, Clyde, whinnied and pranced a bit in his buggy harness, signaling his eagerness to be on his way instead of waiting in their driveway. Ellie put her hand over her swollen abdomen. "Do I have a choice?"

She felt Chris take her hand. "We could wait and let it be a surprise."

"I don't think *Mamm* would appreciate that. She wasn't exactly thrilled when we told her we were expecting."

"That's because she worries too much."

"And you don't think she'll be worried about this?" She touched her belly again. She remembered her mother's tone of voice when she'd announced that she and Chris were having a baby. *How on earth will you manage?* Those were the first words out of her mouth. Not "I'm so happy for you," or "I'm going to be a *grossmutter!*" Had she even congratulated them on the pregnancy? Ellie couldn't remember.

Chris squeezed her hand before releasing it. "We can't control how your *mamm* reacts." He kissed her cheek, the softness of his beard tickling her skin. "But we can show her how happy and blessed we are."

She smiled. "*Danki* for reminding me."

During their buggy ride to her parents' house, Ellie's mind wandered. Despite her husband's reassurance, she couldn't stem her growing anxiety. She and Chris had been married for two years now, and they had fallen into a comfortable routine, with Chris working construction jobs in and around Paradise while she had continued her jelly-making business, Ellie's Jellies, which she had put on hold recently. She had never been so happy. When she discovered she was expecting, she could barely contain her joy.

Then she had given *Mamm* the news. Ellie had expected some reservations from her. Since the car accident that had taken Ellie's sight eight years ago, she'd had to prove to her mother that she was capable. She created her own business. She married the most wonderful man in Paradise. She was going to be a mother. Yet with a few words, her *mamm* could make her feel like that inept young woman who wondered if she would ever deal with her blindness, much less accept it.

Ellie clasped her hands together, tamping down her nervousness. Chris was right. She wasn't in control of her mother's reactions or feelings. She wasn't in control of anything. God was.

A short time later they arrived at her parents' house. Ellie stayed in the buggy as Chris settled Clyde in the barn, and then she heard the familiar crunch of his boots on the gravel drive as he came back to assist her. When his hand touched hers, she gripped it as he helped her step down to the ground.

She entwined her fingers with his, the strength of his nearness giving her the courage she needed to walk to the house. Ellie knew her father would be supportive when they told him the news. Maybe *Mamm* would surprise her and be excited too.

"You're cutting off my circulation," Chris said to her, his tone half joking.

"Sorry." She loosened her grip on his hand as they ascended the porch steps. Before they reached the top, Ellie heard the soft squeak of the screen door opening.

"Ellie!"

Her mother's shrill, worried voice made Ellie wince. She flinched when *Mamm* put her hands on her shoulders.

"You look tired. I knew we should have taken supper over to you instead of Chris bringing you here," she said.

"Hello to you, too, *Mamm*." After the accident her mother had been overly protective. Ellie had resented it at first, wanting her independence and working to achieve it. Eventually *Mamm* had realized Ellie could be independent. But now it was as if they were going back in time, when her mother was filled with doubts and worry. When she didn't believe Ellie was capable of anything.

"Let them get in the *haus*, Edna, before you start hovering." Her father's voice came from the direction of the doorway.

Mamm released Ellie's shoulders and stepped aside. Chris still held Ellie's hand as they walked through the front door. The tangy scent of stuffed cabbage mingled with the buttery aroma of fresh, cooked corn made her stomach rumble. Lately she'd been constantly hungry. As Chris liked to remind her, she was eating for two.

Not anymore . . .

"Smells *appeditlich*, Edna." Chris released Ellie's hand.

"Ellie, you have dark circles under your eyes." Ignoring Chris's compliment, *Mamm* stood in front of her so close that Ellie could feel her warm breath against her face. "Christopher, you need to make sure she's getting her rest."

"He is," Ellie said.

"And she shouldn't be out this late at night."

"It's not even seven o'clock." Ellie searched for her mother's hand and took it. "Everything is fine. You don't need to worry."

"That's what I've been trying to tell her," *Daed* said. "Edna, she looks healthy to me. Stop borrowing trouble."

Her mother didn't say anything, and Ellie could feel her intense gaze. "A mother knows her *dochder*," she said. "Something is going on."

"Ellie, didn't you say you were *hungerich*?" Chris said quickly.

"Starving," she said with a nod, grateful for her husband's ability to step in when she needed him to.

"But—"

"You heard them, Edna." *Daed* came up on the other side of Ellie. "They're hungry and so am I. Let's eat."

They all went to the kitchen, but Ellie could still sense her mother's scrutiny, imagining the mix of concern and frustration on her face as she tried to puzzle out what was going on. She should have known her mother would suspect something.

As she sat down at the table, she felt a movement in her belly. "Oh," she blurted, the strong kick taking her off guard.

"What?" Her mother was immediately at her side. "What happened?"

"Just the baby . . ." She felt Chris squeeze her shoulder. She took a deep breath. "Or the other one."

The room grew silent. After a long pause, her mother finally spoke. "What did you say?"

Ellie turned her face toward *Mamm*. "Christopher and I are having twins."

Neither of her parents said anything. As the silence lengthened, she felt a tightening in her chest. She expected her mother to be upset, but her father's silence surprised her. She covered Chris's hands with hers.

"Twins?" her father said at last.

Ellie swallowed and nodded.

He burst into laughter. "Two *bopplis*? That's wonderful news!"

"Ephraim, how can you say that?" Ellie heard the creak of a kitchen chair as her mother plopped down on it. "Twins? How will she ever manage?"

Ellie couldn't help but frown, her mother's words echoing her own thoughts when her midwife, Barbara, had told her she suspected Ellie was carrying twins. Yet when Ellie had told Chris, he'd been ecstatic, his enthusiasm and confidence bolstering hers. But as usual, her mother's words nicked at her, and those feelings of doubt crept back in.

"She'll be fine," *Daed* said, chuckling again. "Twins. Who would have thought?" Ellie heard him slap Chris on the back. "Congratulations, *sohn*. Now let's eat."

"Ephraim—"

"It's time to eat." Her father's tone had turned stern.

Ellie heard her mother rise and mumble something unintelligible under her breath. Chris patted Ellie's shoulder and sat down next to her. "See," he whispered, "that wasn't so bad."

She nodded, even though she disagreed with him. During the meal her mother didn't say anything, letting Chris and her father do most of the talking. Ellie tried to focus on the delicious food, but her earlier, ravenous appetite had disappeared. Why couldn't her mother be happy for them? They should be celebrating. Instead, Ellie just wanted to go home.

After supper, she halfheartedly offered to help with the dishes, knowing her mother would refuse. Would she have to prove herself all over again? How could she fight both her doubts and her mother's?

When Ellie and Chris reached home, he pulled the buggy to a stop but didn't get out. "Don't let your mother get to you."

"I'm not." She frowned. "Well, I'm trying not to."

"You're going to be a great mother. I truly believe that. Your *mamm* will see that too." He patted her knee and jumped out of the buggy.

Ellie touched her belly as the twins moved around inside. She'd already come to notice that one of the babies was more active than the other. "From your mouth to God's ears," she whispered, then said a silent prayer, asking the Lord to help her get through the next few weeks.

◌

Three weeks later Ellie and her mother were spending the early afternoon in Ellie's garden. She couldn't have asked for a prettier spring day. She listened to the soft rustling of the oak leaves as the tree branches swayed in the gentle wind. Her skin soaked up the warmth of the sun, her mind drawing peace from the calm, quiet surroundings.

A spasm went through her, making her catch her breath. She paused, waiting to see if her mother would notice. She'd had a few of them since they had started working in the garden an hour ago, but she'd kept them hidden from *Mamm*. Barbara had told her she would experience pre-labor contractions the closer she came to her due date, so she wasn't too worried. She wasn't supposed to have the babies until June, another two weeks away.

Ellie sat on the ground with her knees bent and her legs to one side, supporting her weight slightly on one hip and one hand flat on the soil as she worked with her other hand to pull weeds. She smiled as she shifted her weight and moved her legs to the other side. She could hardly believe that soon she and Christopher would be parents. Even her mother had seemed to settle down a little bit since they had told her about the twins, although she had insisted on coming over every day this week to help Ellie prepare for their arrival.

She and Chris already had everything ready, though—a cradle for the boppli to share until they were ready to transfer to separate cribs, plenty of clothing, cloth diapers, pins, even a few baby spoons, although it would be awhile before the babies would eat solid food. Ellie thought she had everything under control and taken care of, but her mother kept finding things to do, as if she couldn't keep still for more than a minute. Ellie insisted on being involved in the running of her own household, despite being tired. Her house had never been cleaner, her garden was almost weed free, and it seemed as soon as she and Chris put on fresh clothes for the day, the ones from the day before were washed and hung on the line before breakfast. Her mother seemed to have an endless supply of nervous energy.

Another contraction went through her, catching her off guard. She took in a sharp breath.

"Ellie?" *Mamm* scurried to her from the opposite end of the garden. "What's wrong?"

She clenched her teeth, weary at the panic she heard in her mother's tone. Just when she thought *Mamm* had gotten a handle on her stress, she overreacted once again. "I'm fine," she said, moving her hand from her side.

"Are you sure? There isn't something wrong with the babies, is there?"

"They're fine too." She moved to a kneeling position, not an easy feat considering her belly seemed to have doubled in size in the past month.

"Maybe you should *geh* inside," *Mamm* said. "I can finish up the weeding."

Ellie shook her head. "The *bopplis* are just active today, that's all." She discerned the weeds from the plants in front of her by lightly touching each one. She was near the tomato plants at the edge of the garden. A few minutes earlier her mother had placed wooden stakes next to each tender plant, in anticipation for when they would need to be tied to the stakes for support. She pulled a small tuft of grass that had invaded the tomato row, one of the few weeds she could still find.

"I'd like to finish taking care of this, *Mamm*. It won't take long. Then I'll *geh* inside and start dinner for Chris and me." She searched for another weed, hoping her mother took the hint.

"Nonsense. I'll make supper tonight."

"You don't have to—"

"You've been looking so tired lately." From the direction of her mother's voice, Ellie could tell she'd walked to the other side of the garden. "Exhausted, actually."

Ellie couldn't deny that she'd been more tired lately. But she wouldn't say she was exhausted. She opened her mouth to tell her mother not to worry when another twinge assaulted her belly, this time on the other side, followed by a healthy kick that took her off guard again. *"Ach!"*

Her mother's footsteps came so fast Ellie was certain she'd trampled a few plants. "That's it. You're going inside and putting your feet up. Here's your cane."

Ellie stifled a groan. She knew exactly where her white cane was. She'd made sure to keep it less than a foot away from her, and she didn't appreciate when her mother—or anyone else—assumed she couldn't find it. But she held her tongue as she took the cane from her mother.

"Let me help you up," *Mamm* continued, putting her hands underneath Ellie's arms.

It was no use arguing with her, and this time Ellie accepted her help willingly. Getting up was a lot harder than sitting down, and that had nothing to do with her blindness. To reassure her mother that she was all right, Ellie gave her a smile before turning her face toward the sun, taking in one last sunbeam of warmth before she was banished inside.

At least Chris would be home soon. In his diplomatic way, he would tell her mother that he and Ellie were fine and she could go home, making sure to let her know how much he appreciated her help during the day while he was at work. Then her mother would be on her way. Ellie wished *Mamm* would listen to her the way she did Chris, but she was thankful for small miracles where her mother was concerned.

She angled her cane in front of her, running it lightly in a half arc and making sure the path to the back porch was clear. It usually was. She and Chris kept their house and property neat and organized out of necessity. "You're turning me into a tidy person," he'd joked a few weeks after they had moved into their home two years ago. "*Mei* whole *familye* is shocked."

Ellie smiled at the memory, only to immediately double over in intense pain. She gripped her cane with one hand and cradled her belly with the other while she gasped for breath. *Uh-oh. That wasn't a normal pain.*

Her mother's arm came around her shoulders, and Ellie leaned against her. She could barely hear her mother call her name as another wave of pain came over her.

"I think it's time, Ellie."

For once her mother's tone was calm, comforting, and breaking through the pain. With *Mamm's* support she continued toward the house, thankful her mother was by her side.

CHAPTER TWO

As Sarah Lynne pulled into the Millers' driveway, she saw her brother, Chris, pacing in front of his barn. When he noticed her approaching, he walked to her buggy. She stopped the horse and handed him the reins before climbing out. "What are you doing outside?" she asked him as he looped the reins over a tying post.

"Edna won't let me see Ellie. It's been seven hours since labor started."

Sarah Lynne saw the pain etched on her brother's tanned skin. Chris had always been dark, his hair nearly as black as the coal in her stove back home. But since he started working construction soon after he and Ellie married, he had a perpetual tan, even in the winter. She put her hand on his arm. "She will be okay. Barbara is a *gut* midwife. And you know Edna won't let anything happen to Ellie."

Chris nodded, but her words didn't seem to bring him much comfort. "I should be with her. Not out here, doing *nix*." He looked at Sarah Lynne. "She's in so much pain."

"But not lasting pain. Besides, she doesn't need to see that you're worried."

He leaned against the fence post. "You're right. I'm always the one telling Ellie not to worry. That everything's going to be okay. It wouldn't do for me to give her pause now."

Sarah Lynne tilted her head. "Chris . . . she will be all right. The *bopplis* too. You believe that, *ya?*"

"*Ya.*" He ran his hand over his face, weariness seeping into his brown eyes. "Although I've had a time convincing Edna of that. Don't get me wrong. I am glad she's been here while I'm at work, especially today. If Ellie had been alone when she'd gone into labor . . ." A look of panic entered his eyes.

"But she wasn't."

"Thank God." Chris hung his hat on the corner of the tying post. "Still, Edna continues to drive me *ab im kopp* sometimes. I don't know how Ellie keeps her patience. I've been trying to keep her fretting from affecting Ellie, but it's been difficult."

Confused, Sarah Lynne frowned. "Is there a reason Edna is so worried?"

He shrugged. "I'm not sure. I haven't brought it up with Ellie, but I've noticed how her *mamm* is even more overprotective than usual. She's concerned Ellie can't handle the babies, or that something is going to be wrong with one of them . . . or both. We all know how strong Ellie is, and Barbara has given us only *gut* reports about the pregnancy. Yet Edna can't seem to let her fear *geh.*"

"Have you mentioned it to Ephraim?"

"I don't have to. He sees it too." Chris sighed. "Hopefully after her grandbabies are born she'll be able to relax and enjoy them." He looked at Sarah Lynne, giving her a half smile. "I'm glad you're here. We haven't seen much of you since Ellie started to show."

"I wish I could have visited more. But I've been helping with the farm now that Isaiah has had to take on extra work." She had married Ellie's cousin a year before Chris and Ellie had married. Isaiah had wanted to make a go of the farm, and he had. But they couldn't ignore the economic realities, and Isaiah had found work at a local factory. They were saving every penny for the day they started their family . . . whenever that would be.

Chris began to pace, and Sarah Lynne could see he'd only partly heard her. She put her hand on his shoulder, stilling him. "Why don't we check on Ellie?"

He nodded eagerly and grabbed his hat. As they neared the house, Sarah Lynne's excitement grew. "Twins," she said glancing at Chris. "I can't wait to meet them. Will they be girls or boys? Maybe one of each?"

"I just hope they're healthy." He shot a look at Sarah Lynne. "And maybe one of each."

Sarah Lynne chuckled. "I knew it."

As soon as they entered the house, the midwife came out of Ellie and Chris's bedroom, a large grin on her small, round face. "She did it," Barbara said.

"Is she all right?" Chris asked, his tanned face suddenly growing pale. Sarah Lynne realized that for all his talk about being calm and steady for his wife and mother-in-law, he had been holding a lot inside. "The *bopplis* . . ."

Barbara put her hand on Chris's shoulder and smiled. "Ellie and the *bopplis* are fine. Two *maed*, as sweet as can be. And *yer frau*, she is incredible. There were no complications, although she is very tired. I expected her to be in labor longer, but those *bopplis* were ready to be born." She motioned to the bedroom. "*Kumme* and see *yer dochders.*"

Sarah Lynne stayed back as Chris left with the midwife. She briefly touched her own flat stomach. Would she and Isaiah ever have a family of their own? After three years of trying, she was starting to doubt.

She clasped her hands together and forced the thoughts away. Today was her brother and sister-in-law's day to celebrate the miracle of life. Two lives, strong and healthy. She thanked God for the tiny blessings.

Despite the residual pain coursing through her body, Ellie was eager to hold her daughters. When she first heard one tiny cry, then two, she had laughed through the tears pouring down her cheeks. She was exhausted and ecstatic at the same time.

"Where are the *bopplis*?" Ellie asked, her voice sounding weak with weariness.

"Here is the first one." *Mamm* placed a tiny bundle in the crook of Ellie's arm. The baby was clean and wrapped in a soft flannel blanket.

"What does she look like?" Ellie asked, running her fingers over the top of her daughter's downy head.

"Beautiful, like her mother."

Ellie smiled at Chris's voice, turning her head in his direction. "You're a little biased."

"Maybe." She felt the springs of the bed give as he gently sat down next to her. "I'm holding the other one, and they're both *per-fekt*." His hand brushed away her damp hair, allowing the breeze from the nearby window, now open, to cool her forehead. "How are you?"

She leaned her cheek against the baby's head and smiled. "Happy," she said. "I'm so happy."

He continued to stroke her hair. "I wanted to be here, by your side," he said, his voice almost a whisper. "But *yer mamm*—"

"It's okay, Chris." Ellie lifted her face. "Tell me what they look like. Are they identical?"

"They look like babies to me." Chris chuckled. "Barbara said they're fraternal. Both have dark hair. The one I'm holding has a little more than the other. She's also got a tiny dimple in her chin."

"I suppose we should name them, *ya*?"

They had discussed many names over the past few weeks, but hadn't come to a conclusion for either boys or girls. "This one is Irene," she said, sliding her finger down the baby's tender cheek and over her tiny chin.

He paused. "After *mei grossmutter*? I thought we had decided not to name either one after members of our families."

"*Ya*. But the name feels right for her, don't you think so?"

"She looks exactly like an Irene."

"What should we name our other daughter?" Ellie said, her eyelids growing heavier.

"Julia," he said.

"After *mei grossmutter*." She smiled. "Can I hold Julia too?"

"Of course."

Ellie opened her other arm and Chris nestled Julia in the crook. She tilted her head toward Chris and smiled. "They're finally here," she whispered, fighting off the weariness that threatened to take over.

"*Ya*," he said, brushing her cheek with the back of his knuckles. "They finally are."

"All right, that's enough."

Ellie's eyes flew open at her mother's voice slicing through the precious moment.

"Ellie needs rest," *Mamm* said, taking Irene from her.

But Ellie wasn't ready to let go. "Christopher?" she cried as Julia was also lifted from her arms. She didn't want to rest. She wanted to hold her babies.

"*Yer mamm's* right," Barbara said. "You do need to rest. Your body has been through a lot. Don't worry, you'll get to spend plenty of time with them soon enough."

Ellie could hear a soft cry from one of the babies. "But they need me now."

Chris rose from the bed and kissed her temple. "I'll bring them to you later. Sleep now, Ellie. You've earned it."

She nodded, her eyes already drifting closed as she heard everyone leave the room. Then silence. After the excitement and pain of giving birth, being able to hold her precious babies, to spend a brief but special moment with her husband and their twins . . . now all she felt was emptiness. And alone.

"Why did you take them away so soon?" she mumbled, her eyes stinging with tears as she closed them, drifting off into a fitful sleep.

Sometime later Ellie's eyes opened. She had no idea how long she'd slept, and she didn't feel refreshed. If anything, she was agitated. She shifted slightly in the bed, ignoring the throbbing in her body. She stilled when she heard low voices right outside her doorway.

"I don't know how she'll handle the babies, Barbara."

Ellie frowned and then sighed. Of course her mother was still worried about how she'd manage. But how was she supposed to figure out how to be a mother when she couldn't hold her own babies for more than a second?

"I'm sure she'll be fine, Edna. Ellie is a smart woman. She does very well considering she's . . ."

"Blind. You can say it. And you're not telling the truth, Barbara. I can see it on your face. You're as concerned as I am."

"I wouldn't say concerned, but realistic, ya," Barbara admitted. "There will be some challenges. There always are with twins."

"And when the mother is blind? Ellie doesn't know anything about taking care of a baby. Now she has two. She and Christopher should have waited until they were more prepared."

"Edna, listen to me. All this worry is going to affect your *dochder*—and the babies. They can pick up on the tension."

Ellie struggled to sit up. Her babies could sense stress?

"Ellie will be a *gut mudder*," Barbara continued. "But she will definitely need help. Has she made arrangements?"

"I don't know." Her mother sounded hurt. "Anytime I tried to talk to her about helping out, she changed the subject."

Ellie's face heated. That was true. But her mother had always made it sound like Ellie wouldn't be able to do anything to care for her own babies. And she didn't want to be a burden to anyone— especially her mother.

"She'll have to talk about it soon. But not now. You and Christopher are here—that will be enough for the time being. I'm going to check on Ellie. She's been asleep for two hours."

Two hours? What about the twins? They had to be hungry by now. When she heard Barbara walk into the room, she asked, "Where are my babies?"

"They're fine." Barbara's voice was soothing, but that didn't keep Ellie from wanting her children. "They're in the cradle in the extra bedroom." Ellie sensed Barbara nearing the bed, and within a few seconds, she felt the woman's hand on her arm. "How are you feeling?"

"I want to see them."

"Are you in a lot of pain? I can get you some herbal tea. That will take the edge off."

"I want to see my babies!" Ellie didn't understand the utter panic going through her, the whirlwind of emotions that churned like a storm inside. She only knew that she needed her twins with her.

"Ellie, listen to Barbara." Now her mother had come in and was walking toward her. "She said the twins are fine."

"They have to be hungry." Ellie's breasts ached to feed them.

"They've already eaten."

"What? How?"

"Barbara and I gave them formula. We thought that was best."

"You thought that was best, Edna," Barbara said quietly.

"You made that decision without me?" Ellie pushed off the covers and felt for her cane. "Where's Christopher?"

"He's outside taking care of the animals," Edna said, her calm infuriating Ellie.

"I need to talk to him." Surely Chris didn't know what had happened. How could her mother have decided how the babies were to be fed without even consulting her?

"Barbara," *Mamm* said evenly. "I think Ellie could use that tea now."

"I don't want any tea!"

"Ellie. Enough." Her mother sat down on the bed near her. "Barbara, please bring the tea."

Once Ellie heard Barbara's footsteps disappear, Ellie said, her voice growing sharp, "Why are you keeping the *bopplis* from me?"

"Because they're sleeping, Ellie. You shouldn't disturb them."

"I'm their mother—don't tell me what to do!" Sobs choked her, a mix of anger and something else she couldn't define. She shouldn't be crying like this. She shouldn't be so weak. Yet she was powerless in the face of the emotions overtaking her.

"You're being irrational." Her mother's voice was stern but soft. "Now listen to me. I talked it over with Christopher while you were sleeping. He agreed with me that it would be easier for you to bottle-feed the babies. They both need to be on the same feeding schedule, and someone else can feed one while you feed the other."

Ellie wiped her eyes, unable to speak. It sounded logical, but she wanted to be consulted. "Where did you get the formula?"

"I bought it awhile ago."

"And you never said anything to me?"

"Ellie, anytime I brought up making a plan for the babies, you didn't want to talk about it."

"That's because you always tell me what to do. It wouldn't be my plan. It would be yours!"

Her mother didn't say anything for a moment. Ellie crossed her arms, tears streaming down her cheeks. Was this how she was supposed to feel as a new mother? Her emotions out of control? Her resentment growing toward her own mother—even her husband? This wasn't how she imagined it would be after the babies were born.

"Here's the tea," Barbara said when she returned. "I already had it steeped and ready for when you woke up."

Ellie paused before uncrossing her arms. "Set it on the side table. Please," she added, realizing she had sounded rude.

The soft thud of the ceramic mug touching the wood echoed in the room. Her mother stood. "I'll get supper started. I imagine Christopher is hungry."

Ellie ignored her mother, still resenting how she had taken over. But once she was sure *Mamm* was gone, Ellie slumped and put her head in her hands. "I'm sorry, Barbara. I don't know what's wrong with me."

Barbara sat down on the bed and rubbed Ellie's back, the rounding motions feeling soothing underneath Ellie's thin gown. "It's all right, Ellie. I understand."

Turning her head toward Barbara, Ellie shook her head. "My relationship with my mother is . . . complicated."

"I know. And right now your emotions are fragile. It's the hormones from giving birth. You'll be more settled in a few days. Please drink the tea. It will help you feel better."

"I hope so." Ellie felt for the tea, then cupped her hands around the warm mug. She took a sip, not recognizing the blend of herbs in the lightly flavored tea. "Right now I feel helpless."

"Trust me, Ellie, you're not. But you are tired, and I'm sure in some pain."

Ellie nodded.

"I know you don't want to, but you do need to get as much rest as you can. The *bopplis* will sleep a lot at least during the first week or so, and you need to take advantage of that. Soon enough they'll be keeping you up at all hours." She patted Ellie's hand.

"I know you're upset with your mother right now, but she is here to help. And she's partly right about the bottle-feeding. The twins do need to be on the same feeding schedule. It will be easier on all three of you that way. If not, you'll be feeding one or the other the whole day and you won't have time for anything else."

"You don't think I could manage breastfeeding them."

"I never said that. But you need to do what's best for you and the twins. There will be times when bottle-feeding will be easier."

"Because I'm blind?" Ellie sounded snappish, but she didn't care.

"Because they'll be hungry at the same time. Two babies are hard for anyone to handle. But you can also breastfeed them."

She felt a glimmer of hope. "I can?"

"*Ya.* I'll show you before I leave. I'll also show you how to use the hand breast pump for when you're unable to breastfeed. But regardless of how you feed the *bopplis,* don't be afraid to ask for or accept help." The sheets rustled as Barbara stood and smoothed the bedclothes back over Ellie's legs. "That's not a sign of weakness."

Ellie nodded, but she didn't completely believe Barbara's words. If she could see, would everyone be treating her this way? Would she feel this way, growing more and more doubtful that she could take care of her own children?

"Is it all right to come in?" Chris's voice sounded tentative near the doorway.

"Of course, Chris," Barbara said as she placed pillows behind Ellie's back. "I'll check on the babies. If they're awake, I'll bring them to you, Ellie, and you can try feeding them. They ate a couple of hours ago, so they might be hungry again."

"*Danki,* Barbara." Ellie set down the mug and leaned back against the stack of pillows. Chris sat down beside her. She felt him take her hand, but she turned away from him.

"Ellie?"

Tears stung her eyes, then slid down her cheeks. She didn't understand. This was supposed to be a happy day, one of the happiest of her life. Instead, she couldn't even face her husband, not wanting him to see her tears . . . her weakness.

He didn't say anything else, only stroked her hand. She felt the familiar roughness of his skin from the past two years of working construction. Her eyelids fluttered as the tea began to take effect, and she shifted her body down so that her head was against the pillows.

"You look sleepy," he said.

"I am. Must be the tea."

"It's also past ten."

"Then you should get to bed," she said, mumbling.

"I love you," he said, his voice sounding far away.

"I'm sorry."

"What?"

But that was all she could bring herself to say.

CHAPTER THREE

Chris slid his hand from Ellie's as she drifted off to sleep. He stared at her, worry filling him. This wasn't his Ellie. She thought she'd hid her tears from him. But he knew her well. Those were not tears of joy, but of pain.

He rose from her side. Something had happened while he had been outside finishing up the chores. He left their bedroom, walked to the other side of the house, and found Barbara coming out of the spare bedroom. "What's going on with Ellie?"

Barbara put a finger to her lips and closed the bedroom door. "The babies are still sleeping. Edna is in there keeping an eye on them."

"Why? Is there something wrong with the *bopplis*?"

She shook her head and led him to the living room. "They're fine. She insisted on being in there with them."

"Did she say something to Ellie?"

"*Nee.*" She gave him an odd look. "Why do you ask?"

"Ellie's upset."

207

"She's tired. And she's apprehensive. New mothers always are."
She smirked. "So are new fathers." Then she smiled, her eyes filled
with wisdom and understanding. "She's going to be fine. You both
are. Keep encouraging her, Christopher." Her smile slipped a little.
"Is Edna the only one available to help?"

"*Mei schwester* and *mamm* offered."

"*Gut.*" She paused. "Edna seems very attached to the *maed* already."

He nodded, not adding that he thought Edna might be too
attached. But what did he know about any of this? When Edna
had insisted the twins be bottle-fed, he agreed. Her argument had
made sense. He wanted what was best for his daughters—and his
wife. But he wasn't sure what that was anymore.

"Christopher," Barbara said, putting her hand on his arm. "Set
aside your worry. Enjoy your new *familye.*"

He took in a deep breath as she walked toward the kitchen. Of
course she was right. So many times he had told Ellie not to worry,
and now he was doing the same thing. He closed his eyes and
prayed for peace in his soul and the strength and wisdom to be the
husband and father God wanted him to be. When he opened his
eyes, calm had replaced the stress. God was in control. He needed
to remember that.

Edna stared at her precious granddaughters as they lay in the cradle
next to the bed. They were so beautiful, so perfect. They both had
plump cheeks and long fingers, just like Ellie had when she was
born. Julia's left hand formed a tight fist while Irene's right hand
was similarly closed as they both slept. Edna watched the slight
rise and fall of their tiny chests.

She turned at the sound of the door opening. Barbara walked in and motioned for Edna to come into the hall. Edna paused, looked at the babies for a long moment, then reluctantly left their side.

Barbara closed the door behind them. "Edna," she whispered, "are you okay?"

Edna lifted her chin. "Of course I am."

"Just making sure."

"You should be taking care of Ellie, not checking on me." Edna put her hand on the doorknob. "I won't let anything happen to the *bopplis*."

"I didn't think you would." Barbara tilted her head. "You're hanging on to these babies too tightly, Edna."

Edna scowled. "You're telling me how I should handle *mei* grandchildren?"

"I'm only pointing out what I see."

"Are you finished?"

Barbara folded her arms across her chest. "*Ya.*"

"Then let me get back to the *bopplis*." Edna opened the door and shut it behind her, a little too loudly. One of the babies started to stir. She tiptoed to the cradle and smiled when she saw they were still asleep.

Barbara didn't understand. She didn't have a blind daughter. Her grandchildren weren't at risk.

Deep inside, Edna knew she wasn't being fair to Ellie. But two little lives were at stake here. She would make sure nothing happened to Julia and Irene, just as she had protected Ellie and her son, Wally, when they were infants. She would be as diligent now as she had been back then. Even more so, considering Ellie's disability.

She couldn't—and wouldn't—let history repeat itself.

Three days later Ellie snuggled Julia in the crook of her arm. She searched for her baby's mouth, and once she found it, slipped the nipple of a three-ounce bottle inside. The now-familiar sounds of a baby taking her bottle reached Ellie's ears. She'd only had a chance to breastfeed the babies a couple of times, and she didn't feel confident doing it discretely in front of company. She sat back in the rocking chair and turned her head toward Chris's mother, who was sitting on the couch opposite her, feeding Irene.

"They are just precious, Ellie." Bertha Miller cooed at Irene. "Absolutely *perfekt*." She paused for a moment. "Irene looks like you."

"She does? Chris thinks she looks like him."

"She has his dark hair, but this round little face and clear blue eyes are all you."

Ellie grinned. "What about Julia?"

Bertha chuckled. "She looks like me, of course."

Ellie laughed. "Obviously."

Sarah Lynne walked into the room. "I brought some sandwiches and iced tea," she said.

"*Danki*." Ellie felt the bottle slip from Julia's mouth. She leaned close to her daughter and listened for her soft, steady breathing. After a few moments, she realized the baby had fallen asleep. "Is Irene still awake?" she asked Bertha.

"*Nee*. They both fell asleep at the same time. Imagine that."

"I'll take them to their cradle," Sarah Lynne said.

"I can do it." Ellie set the bottle down on the small table next to the rocker. She gripped Julia and started to get up.

"I'd like to, if you don't mind."

Ellie caught something in her sister-in-law's tone. "*Danki*, Sarah Lynne."

After Sarah Lynne left with the twins, Ellie turned toward Bertha. "Is Sarah Lynne okay?"

Bertha sighed. "She's fine. But you know *mei dochder*. She's impatient to start her own family."

"Oh. I should have realized—"

"Don't apologize. Sarah Lynne and Isaiah will have children in the Lord's time. Like you and Christopher."

Ellie leaned back in the chair. "I'm glad you're happy about the twins."

"Why wouldn't I be?"

"Not everyone is." She ran her hand along the smooth, curved arm of the hickory chair.

"If you're talking about Edna, you're wrong. She's happy. She just has an unusual way of showing it. Here, let me get you a sandwich. Sarah Lynne made your favorite, chicken salad."

"I'm not really hungry." Ellie's mind was on her mother. She had left earlier when Bertha and Sarah Lynne had arrived, saying she was going home to pick up a few things and would be back in a couple of hours. Ellie dreaded her return. Her mother was so efficient, she never gave the babies a chance to cry. Or Ellie a chance to tend to them, saying that Ellie needed to "heal." But she was healing just fine. What she wasn't doing was taking care of her daughters.

"Are you sure?"

"*Ya.* But you go ahead. I know you like chicken salad too." Ellie rose. "I'll be right back."

"Okay." A few minutes later Bertha said, "Mm, I think Sarah Lynne outdid herself with this chicken salad."

Ellie made her way down the hall to the spare bedroom where her mother was staying. Her mother had also insisted on keeping the cradle in that room, explaining that she could take care of the babies at night while Ellie and Christopher slept. For the first two nights, Ellie didn't argue. Her emotions were still rocky, and doubt about her ability to care for the twins had lingered. To add to that, Chris had been working extra hours and came home the last couple of nights exhausted. But Ellie ached for her babies, and each time she heard them cry, she wanted to rush to them. But with the spare bedroom at the opposite end of the house, she couldn't reach them in time.

She heard Sarah Lynne's sweet, soft singing as she entered the room. Her sister-in-law's voice was just above a whisper as she sang one of the church's popular hymns. Instead of singing it in the chanting voice usually used during church, she had added a lovely melody to the words. Ellie touched the doorjamb before entering the room, then walked toward Sarah Lynne's voice.

The singing stopped. "They're still asleep," Sarah Lynne whispered.

"*Gut.*" Ellie moved to stand beside her. She ran her fingers along the edge of the cradle.

"You are so blessed," Sarah Lynne said quietly. "Such *schee bopplis.*"

Ellie took Sarah Lynne's hand. "Your time will come."

She sighed and squeezed Ellie's fingers. "I know. That's what Isaiah says. I had just thought . . . hoped . . ." She let go of Ellie's hand.

"I'll pray," Ellie said.

"*Danki.*"

Ellie heard the back door slam shut. She tensed. "*Mamm's* back."

Hurried footsteps sounded down the hall. "Ellie, I have a surprise. I brought your bibs from when you were a *boppli.*" Her mother entered the room.

"Shh," Sarah Lynne said.

"They're sleeping," Ellie added.

"Oh, let me see *mei* precious ones." Her mother sandwiched herself between Ellie and Sarah Lynne. "Are you sure they're all right?"

"Sarah Lynne just put them down."

"*Gut.* I wouldn't want you to have to—"

Ellie turned toward her mother. "Have to what?"

"Never mind." Her mother walked away. "We must leave now. We don't want to wake the *bopplis.*"

Sarah Lynne threaded her arm through Ellie's as they left the room. When they were several steps away from the bedroom, she leaned over and whispered, "Has she been this way the whole time?"

Ellie nodded. "Sometimes worse."

Ellie could sense Sarah Lynne shaking her head. "Ellie, I'll be praying for *you.*"

CHAPTER FOUR

"And just look at what *mei* friend Linda made for you."

Ellie gripped the back of the chair at the kitchen table. When her mother didn't say anything right away, Ellie snapped, "Do you want me to guess?"

"Of course not. You didn't give me a chance to explain it." Her mother sighed. "Honestly, Ellie. Have I ever made light of your blindness?"

"*Nee*. I'm sorry." The knot in her stomach had tightened since Bertha and Sarah Lynne had left a few minutes ago. She remembered what Barbara had said about the babies sensing tension. Ellie took a deep breath and tried to smile.

"Feel this." *Mamm* took Ellie's hand and ran it over something pliable and pillowy. "Isn't it wonderfully soft?"

"*Ya*." She ran her hands over the object, trying to detect what it was. Some kind of cushion, she guessed. She'd never felt anything like it before.

"It's quilted with pink-and-white cotton fabric," her mother added. "*Perfekt* for the *maed*."

"What is it?"

"A specially shaped pillow that will help with feeding the twins. You can lay them on each side of the pillow and have them face you. See how the edges are raised and firm? That keeps them from falling off."

Ellie continued to check out the pillow. Her smile grew as the strain between her and *Mamm* eased a bit. "This is nice."

"It will make feeding them at the same time much easier." *Mamm* took the pillow. "I'll *geh* put this in *mei* room."

So much for relaxing around her mother. "*Mamm*, I think it's time the *bopplis* moved to my and Chris's room."

She heard her mother's footsteps stop. "It's too soon."

"*Nee*, it's not—"

"I'll be back in a minute," she said, walking away again. "Then I'll get started on supper. I hope Christopher will be home on time today for once."

"He's had to work—"

Her mother disappeared out of the room.

"—late." Ellie scratched the top of her head through the kerchief she'd taken to wearing since having the twins. When she was ready to leave the house, she would wear her *kapp*, but right now the kerchief would do. She reached in front of her and touched a paper bag with handles on it. Pulling it closer to her, she searched inside.

A thick stack of diapers, which could also be used as burp cloths. Four small baby bottles, plastic and still attached to the cardboard. A couple of cans of formula. Despite being irritated with her mother, Ellie was glad she had brought the supplies. And of course the pillow. That would be a lifesaver. She'd have to dictate a thank-you note to Chris and send it to Linda to express how much she appreciated the wonderful gift.

She found another big bag and started riffling through it. She frowned. The clothing inside wasn't baby clothes, but her mother's. At least a week's worth. How long was she planning on staying?

Ellie heard one of the babies crying. She turned and made her way down the hall, passing her bedroom to reach the spare room. By the time she arrived, both babies were fussing, but she could hear her mother making calm, cooing noises above the din.

"You're both a little wet, that's all," her mother said. One of the cries grew into a screech. "Now, Irene, is that the way a *yung maedel* should behave?"

Ellie approached her. "I'll change Julia," she said.

"Already done."

"That fast? They just started crying."

"Julia was making a bit of noise right before that." Ellie heard the snap of a safety pin. "There you *geh*, all clean and dry."

"Where's Julia?"

"In the cradle. I thought I'd rock them for a little while."

"But you said you were going to start on supper."

The creak from the rocker sounded when her mother sat down. "Why don't you make it tonight?"

Ellie put her hands on her hips. "I have a better idea. How about I rock my *dochders* while you cook?"

"But they're already settled. You don't want to disturb them, do you?"

The rocking chair moved back and forth along with the different sound of the cradle being manipulated by her mother's foot. Ellie listened for the babies, but her mother was right. They did seem settled. She rubbed her forehead. There was no point in starting an argument. "All right. But I'll feed them next time." Ellie turned to go.

"We'll see," her mother murmured.

"What did you say?"

"*Nix*, Ellie. All the ingredients you need to make meat loaf and potatoes are in the bags on the table."

Ellie left the room, her nerves wound tight again. She couldn't go on like this. After supper she was determined to set some ground rules with *Mamm*.

A few hours later Ellie checked her Braille watch. Six thirty. Chris was late from work again. She finished washing the dishes, except for the plate of meat loaf and mashed potatoes that she would heat up for Chris when he got home. She covered that in foil and set it by the oven, which she had on the lowest warm setting.

She went to the spare bedroom to check on the babies. When she walked inside, her mother said, "Shh. They're almost asleep."

"You fed them again?"

"You were busy."

Ellie fisted her hands. "You could have told me they were awake and needed feeding." How was she going to be able to take care of her daughters if her mother wouldn't give her the chance? *Lord, give me the words to say to her.*

She moved toward the cradle. "*Mamm*, I want to spend some time with the twins right now. Just the *three* of us."

"Julia's already in the cradle and Irene's eyes are closing." Her mother's voice sounded tight, defensive. And her words, too overprotective.

"How can that be?" she asked, feeling like her mother was duping her. Were they really asleep, or was *Mamm* just saying that to keep Ellie away from them?

"They're newborns, Ellie. That's what wee ones do. I thought you knew that."

"I knew they slept a lot, just not this much," she admitted.

"In a couple of weeks they'll be up more often. You should enjoy the time you have to rest."

"I don't want to rest!" The words came out in a harsh rush. "I want to be with *mei bopplis.*"

A pause. "Don't you raise your voice with me, Ellie Chupp."

"It's Miller, *Mamm.* I've been married for two years." She made her way to the rocker, bumping her shin against the end of the bed. "Ow." One of the babies started to murmur. "Why can't you remember that?"

"Old habits die hard." The baby's murmuring grew into a soft wail. "Look, now you've woken Julia." Ellie heard her mother getting up from the rocker. They met at the cradle, Ellie's hand bumping her mother's as they both reached for the baby.

"*Mamm*, this is ridiculous. You're already holding Irene. Why won't you trust me to get Julia?"

"I do trust you." Her mother paused. "I just don't . . . ," she whispered.

Exasperated, Ellie raised her voice over Julia's louder cries. "Don't what? Don't want me to hurt them? Or drop them?"

"That's not what I said—"

"Ellie? Edna?"

Chris's voice sounded from the back of the house. Ellie heard the heavy tread of his feet as he made his way down the hall.

"Is everything all right?" Chris said as he entered the room.

"*Nee*—" Ellie said.

"*Ya*—" Mamm said at the same time.

"Doesn't seem like it." He neared the cradle. "What's wrong with Julia?"

"How did you know it was Julia?" *Mamm* asked.

"Easy. I'd recognize her little squalling anywhere." He inserted himself between the two women. Ellie heard him pick up their daughter. She instantly quieted.

"She's a daddy's girl." He chuckled. "Has she been fed?"

"*Ya*. Diaper changed too." *Mamm* moved away from the cradle and sat down in the rocking chair. "She was asleep until . . ."

Even though she couldn't see her mother's face, Ellie knew she was giving her the usual disapproving look. Her throat burned with the threat of tears. Both her mother and husband were better with the babies than she was. She turned and rushed out of the room, ending up in the kitchen. She grabbed on to the edge of the sink, forcing the tears at bay.

A few moments later Chris came up behind her, just as the tears she tried so hard to stop slipped down her face. Why couldn't she control her emotions anymore? She wiped at her face, retrieved his supper plate from the fridge, and put it in the already warmed-up oven. "Your dinner will be ready in a few minutes," she said, trying to keep tears of frustration from falling. She may be a terrible mother, but at least she could fix her husband a decent meal.

"Ellie." Chris put his hands on her shoulders. "Talk to me. What's going on?"

"*Nix*. I know you must be starving, and I want to get your dinner to you."

"Supper can wait." He turned her to face him. "The tension between you and your *mamm* is thicker than a slice of her sourdough bread."

Ellie shrugged, turning away from him. "It's nothing I can't handle." She didn't need him to think she wasn't capable of dealing with her mother. It was enough of a hit to her confidence that her mother didn't think she was able to take care of the babies. "She's been a lot of . . . help."

"Maybe too much?"

Ellie stood like a statue in front of the sink. Although she didn't need to, she washed her hands, letting the water get near to scalding. "She's doing what she thinks is right."

"And what about you?" He reached over, turned off the water, picked up a kitchen towel, and started to dry her hands. "What do you think is right? Having the babies sleep in the same room with her instead of us?"

She didn't realize he'd even thought about that.

"You've been working so hard lately. You need your sleep. *Mamm* said the babies would wake you up in the middle of the night."

"So? I'll fall back to sleep. Or I'll feed them with you." He ran the back of his hand over her damp cheek. "You've been crying. And I haven't seen you smile in days. Honey, I'm worried about you."

His kind words should have brought her comfort. Instead, they burst the brittle dam of emotion inside her. "You're worried I can't take care of the twins. That's what this is all about."

"*Nee.*" He sounded surprised. "That's not it at all."

"Then what?" She backed away from him, wishing she could see his expression. Since they'd been together, she'd touched every inch of his handsome face, and of course she remembered what he looked like as a teenager. But there were times when memories and touch weren't enough. Times when it wasn't fair. Although she tried to stop them, the tears flowed down her cheeks again.

"Ellie, please don't cry." He tried to take her in his arms. "I didn't mean to upset you."

She pulled away from him and threw open the oven door. She reached in to yank out his supper, only to burn her hand because she'd forgotten to use a potholder. "Ow," she yelped in pain, jumping back. *Stupid, stupid.* She couldn't do anything right.

"Let me see your hand," he said. "Did you burn it?"

She opened her mouth to speak but couldn't find the words to voice her frustration. She rushed out of the room, bumping into walls in the darkness of her world. When she reached her room her chest heaved with sobs. Her hand burned from her mistake with the oven and her self-assurance was in shambles, like it had been when she'd first been blinded.

Her hand throbbing, she went to the bathroom and found a jar of salve in the medicine cabinet. She rubbed the soothing cream on her burn, but it did little to relieve her turmoil. What was happening to her? She couldn't wait to be a mother. When she found out she was pregnant, she'd been thrilled. When the babies were born, she'd been ecstatic and filled with love for the tiny miracles God had blessed her and Chris with. But in only three days everything had changed. Now she was miserable.

Is this what motherhood was? Pain and self-doubt and endless, helpless tears? How could she overcome any of it?

CHAPTER FIVE

Edna rocked back and forth in the chair, both babies snug and asleep in her arms, resting peacefully. But turmoil ruled her heart. She'd heard Ellie's raised voice, the pain smothering her words, the frantic, familiar footsteps as she fled down the hall. Ellie wasn't the only one in this house with heightened senses.

She should put the babies in their cradle and go talk to her. But what could she say? Her daughter had been so stubborn, unwilling to see that all Edna wanted to do was help care for the twins. She straightened in the rocker. Ellie should be thrilled to have a mother who would drop everything in her life and make so many sacrifices for her granddaughters. But instead Ellie was resentful. Surly. Not appreciative . . . the way she should be.

Yet as Edna held the babies closer, she couldn't ignore the guilt her thoughts triggered. Ellie was capable, the most capable woman she knew. Her daughter had not only overcome a tragic accident and the loss of her best friend and her sight, but she had also become an independent woman who had her own business, one she'd given up in the third trimester of her pregnancy. There wasn't any reason to think she wouldn't be a wonderful mother.

Except that she was blind.

Every time she thought about leaving the tiny babies with Ellie, Edna panicked. So many things could go wrong with one baby, and that possibility doubled with two. She also couldn't be honest with Ellie. If she told her about her fears, about how she'd lain awake nights wondering if these precious babies would be safe with their own mother, Ellie would be deeply hurt. And her daughter had suffered enough.

A quiet voice sounded in her head. *Aren't you hurting her now? Can't you trust Me to watch over those you love?*

Edna breathed in the sweet, baby-powder scent of the babies, resisting what God was speaking to her heart. Yes, she'd heard all her life to let go and let Him be in control. But she couldn't do that . . . not yet.

"Edna?"

She glanced up at Christopher as he entered the room, blinking as she cleared her thoughts. He wasn't making things easier by working so late. If she wasn't here, Ellie would be alone with the babies even longer every day, and how would she manage?

Edna held a sigh. She'd been hard on Chris in the past as well. When he'd left the Amish after Ellie's accident, which had taken the life of his fiancée, she had thought him weak-minded and ill-suited for an Amish woman, especially her Ellie. But she hadn't understood the depth of his pain that drove him from Paradise. Her husband, Ephraim, always had to remind her not to judge others, and she had fought to curb that side of her spirit when she joined the church over fifty years ago. Yet despite her prayers and pleas, it reared itself at the worst times. Like now, when she believed he should be more available to his young family instead of working fourteen hours a day, six days a week.

"*Ya?*" she finally said, forcing an even tone. She pulled the babies even closer to her.

Chris raked his hand through his hair. The dirt from work still clung to his clothes. Outside the light had dimmed with dusk approaching. He looked weary. No, he looked plain tired. Still, she didn't move from the chair.

"We need to talk," he said.

"The babies are asleep," she whispered. "I don't want to disturb them."

"Put them in the cradle, Edna."

She lifted her chin. How dare he speak to her like that? Yet he was the head of this home, and she had to respect that.

"Once they're settled," he added, "meet me in the living room."

"I'll be there in a moment."

As Chris turned and left, she stood, balancing the twins, her arms aching from their slight weight. Truth was, she was tired too. Taking care of these two was the hardest job she'd ever done. Raising children was so much easier when she was younger. She carefully laid the babies in the cradle, taking a few seconds to touch Julia's soft hair and stroke Irene's plump cheek before leaving to join her son-in-law.

When she entered the living room, Christopher sat down on a chair. He gestured to the couch across from him. When she sat down, he said, "Ellie's upset."

"She's tired—"

"It's more than that." He scrubbed his hand over his face,

stopping to tug at his thick, black beard. "There's a problem between you two, and I aim to find out what it is."

Edna touched her chest, offended by his tone. "I'm only trying to help her with the babies."

"I don't think Ellie sees it that way."

Edna crossed her arms. "Then how does she see it?"

"I'm not sure. She won't talk to me. I just know that when I came home today she was crying, and you seemed very . . . protective."

"I am protective of *mei dochder*. I won't apologize for that."

"I wasn't talking about Ellie. I'm talking about the twins. Edna, I'm sure Ellie appreciates your help. I know I do. But I'm concerned she's not getting a chance to spend enough time with the babies. You feed them at night. You're up with them in the morning. Tonight when I came home you were taking care of them again. When does Ellie . . . you know . . . what's the word? Get close with the babies?"

"You mean bond with them?"

He nodded. "It's like you don't trust her to take care of our *dochders*. Is that true?"

Edna looked away. "You have *nee* idea how difficult it is to manage twins."

"You're right. I don't. I'm gone a lot, and the timing couldn't be worse. I wish things were different, but I have to take the work when it comes. But that doesn't answer *mei* question." He blew out a breath. "Do you trust her to take care of our *kinner*?"

"Of course I do." But she couldn't face him when she spoke.

"If that's the case . . . Then prove it." He took a deep breath.

She looked at him. "What?"

"I think it's time you went back home."

The muscles in her jaw tightened. "You want me to leave Ellie alone?"

"Not completely. But you don't have to spend the night anymore. Give Ellie and me a chance to take care of the twins at night. And *mei schwester* and *mamm* can help out during the day too. They've been wanting to spend more time with Julia and Irene."

Hurt coursed through her. "I see how it is. You'd rather have your family here than me."

"That's not true." The weariness in his eyes seemed to increase. He sighed. "I'm letting you know that Ellie has plenty of help. You don't need to take on the whole job yourself." He leaned forward. "Ellie needs the chance to be a mother. I know you're worried about her and the babies. But you have to trust us, and trust her. With God's help, we will make this work."

His words made sense, but they didn't override the rejection she felt. "So you don't need me. Fine. I'll leave right now."

"Edna, I meant in the morning—"

"Oh *nee*. I don't want to upset you and Ellie further." She shot up off the couch. "And I don't want to be where I'm not wanted." She pulled back her shoulders. "Despite everything I've done, this is how you treat me."

He stood, shaking his head. "That's not what I meant."

"I know exactly what you meant. I'll pack my things and be out of your way in a few minutes. You won't have to worry about me being underfoot at night anymore." She turned to go.

"Edna."

She stopped and turned. Even though she recognized the regret on his face, her own pain wouldn't allow him any sympathy. "What?" she said sharply.

"I didn't mean to hurt your feelings. I think you misunderstood me."

She paused. Maybe she had. Perhaps he realized how important it was for her to remain with the babies as much as possible. "I have?"

Chris walked toward her. "Edna, I want you to know"—he paused to smile—"you're always welcome here during the day."

The day. So he was dictating the hours she could see her daughter and grandchildren. "How generous of you."

"I . . . never mind." He shook his head. "At least say good-bye to Ellie before you leave."

"I don't want to *bother* her." She squared her shoulders again and left her ungrateful son-in-law behind. She went to the spare bedroom, walking straight to the cradle. In the dim light of the gas lamp, she could see the twins tiny bodies pressed against each other, their delicate fists clenched as they usually were when they were sleeping. Irene's lips moved a bit, as if she were drinking from a bottle. Edna's heart ached. She loved them so much. And now she was being dismissed, as if she were hired help.

She couldn't move, her mind spinning with hurt and worry. When she thought of Ellie taking care of these precious little ones without her help, she remembered the fragile young woman who had discovered she would never see again. The anger that had nearly consumed Ellie in the months afterward. And how difficult it had been for her to learn and master the simplest of tasks, even after she had accepted her blindness.

How easy it would be for Ellie to trip while holding Irene, or for her to poke Julia with a diaper pin. Edna was willing to take care of those things for her. To take care of her babies and keep them safe. Yet Ellie and Christopher didn't want her help. They didn't want her around.

Finally, she was able to pull herself away from the cradle. She quickly packed her belongings and went out the back door.

Christopher had already harnessed her horse and was hitching it to the buggy. Obviously he couldn't see her leave fast enough.

He handed her the reins. "I wish it didn't have to be like this."

"You've made your wishes plain, Christopher." Edna climbed into the buggy, bypassing his offer of help. He said something else, but she ignored it as she tapped the reins on the back of the horse and guided him down the driveway.

Chapter Six

In her dreams Ellie heard her babies crying. But she couldn't reach them. They were too far away, and she couldn't find them. She held out her hands, seeking them but finding nothing. Their cries grew louder, feeding the rising panic in her chest.

Her eyes flew open, unseeing, yet she could still hear the twins. She'd struggled to bring herself out of the dream. Once she was completely awake, she realized her daughters' cries were real.

As their wails grew louder and more high-pitched, she reached out to feel for Chris. She touched his side, detecting the slow rise and fall of his chest. He was so deeply asleep, he didn't stir. The babies continued to cry. Confused, Ellie sat up. She'd never heard the twins this upset before.

She carefully got out of bed, not wanting to disturb her husband. She made her way to the spare bedroom. Julia's cry was especially piercing. She entered the room. *"Mamm?"* But there was no answer. She hurried to the bed, to find it was still made from this morning.

She moved to the cradle, alarm going through her. Why wasn't her mother here? She reached inside the cradle and felt one of the diapers. Soaked. She felt the other one, and it was also wet. "Shh," she said to the girls amid their screeching. "It will be all right." She wanted to look for her mother, but the twins needed tending first. She went to the dresser where *Mamm* had told her she put the extra diapers and cloths, but they weren't there when she opened the drawer.

The babies' cries echoed around the room. Had her mother moved the diapers and not told her? She called out for her again, and once again heard no response.

"Ellie." Chris's sleepy voice sounded behind her. She heard him snap on the battery-powered lamp. "What's wrong with the girls?"

"They need changing." She turned toward him. "Where's *Mamm*?"

"She . . . went home." He sounded alert now—and wary.

That didn't make any sense. "Why?"

"We can talk about it after we get the twins calmed down."

She held up her hands, frustrated. "I can't find the diapers. *Mamm* must have moved them." She heard Chris open a few of the drawers. Then he walked past her and opened the closet. "They're in here."

Ellie picked up one of the babies. She touched the *boppli's* right ear, searching for the tiny dent at the top. When she felt it, she knew she was holding Julia.

"Do you think they're hungry?" Chris asked.

"I'm sure they are."

"I laid the diapers and pins on the bed," he said. "You take care of changing them and I'll fix their bottles."

He sounded so tired. "I can do it," Ellie said. "You *geh* back to bed."

"*Nee*. I'm up now."

Ellie easily found the diapers. Chris never failed to give her the instructions she needed. Even when they were dating, he was always sure to verbalize everything so she didn't miss a single thing. She took the diapers to the cradle. She quickly changed Julia and Irene before Chris returned. She balanced both babies in her arms and sat down in the rocker just as Chris walked back into the room.

"Midnight snacks are ready," he said. She heard him move toward the rocker, and she knew he was about to take one of the babies.

"I can feed both of them," she said.

"How?"

"There should be a pink-and-white pillow-looking thing in the room somewhere. Maybe in the closet. When you find it, bring it to me."

A few minutes later she had both babies nestled in the pillow.

"Let me know when you're ready for the bottles," Chris said.

But Ellie didn't want the bottles. The urge to nurse was so strong, and it was the first time she'd had the opportunity to try to feed both of them at the same time. She adjusted her night-gown, and with very little effort both babies were feeding. Soon the cacophony of the babies' cries receded, replaced by soft suckling noises. Ellie leaned back in the chair, pleased that she was finally able to feed her babies on her own.

She heard Chris collapse on the bed. "That pillow is a life-saver," he said, sounding even more exhausted than before. "Where did you get it?"

"*Mamm's* friend Linda made it."

"Guess we didn't need the bottles after all."

She nodded. "Chris, why did *Mamm geh* home? Is she all right? And why didn't she say anything to me?"

He sighed. "You were so upset last night, I thought I should have a talk with her. I know things have been tense between you."

She couldn't deny that. "What did you say to her?"

"That she should leave. I told her we could take care of the babies at night."

"Oh *nee*." She cringed. "I guess she didn't take that very well."

"Not at all. I thought she'd *geh* home in the morning, but she was so mad she left right away, and I didn't tell you because you were already asleep when I came to bed." He paused. "I wish she would have waited until morning, but I still believe I did the right thing. We need to learn how to take care of them ourselves, Ellie. And she wasn't letting us—especially you."

Ellie closed her eyes, blinking back more tears. This time they came from a different place. Her husband did understand. She opened her eyes, unseeing but sensing he was looking at her, waiting for her to respond. "*Danki*," she said softly.

He let out a weary chuckle. "At least one woman isn't mad at me tonight."

"*Mamm* will be okay. She just needs some time. She's never taken to being told what to do."

"Sounds like someone else I know."

"Ha." Ellie shifted a little in the rocker but didn't disturb the babies. For the first time since they were born, it felt like she could handle being their mother. But that feeling was tempered by reality. "I can't do this alone," she said. "If you hadn't been here I wouldn't have even found the diapers without having to search too long."

"Sarah Lynne said she would come over during the day. *Mamm* too. And I told your *mudder* she was welcome here, just not at night. Although I probably could have handled that better."

"You handled it fine." Although Ellie could only imagine how upset her mother was right now. Still, she wanted to encourage her husband. "Don't worry about *Mamm*, Chris."

"I won't. I'm sure your father is glad to have her back home."

"I don't know. He might have welcomed the break."

Chris chuckled. She heard him get up from the bed. He kneeled next to her and kissed her forehead. "I love you, Ellie. Everything is going to be okay. God is watching over us."

She nodded. "I love you too." He was right. Everything would be okay. She'd have help during the day, and Chris would be here at night. She'd make sure tomorrow she knew where everything was so she didn't have to wake him unless she needed his help. She didn't like the idea of him getting up and losing sleep, but he didn't seem to mind. She smiled, enjoying the moment with her sweet babies and wonderful husband. And as long as she had him by her side, everything would be all right.

∞

"Things seem to be going well," Sarah Lynne said a week later. She was in Ellie and Chris's room, and Ellie had given her the task of folding small onesies freshly dried on the line. "How do you like the babies sleeping in the same room with you?"

"I was nervous about it at first," Ellie said. She held Irene while Sarah Lynne's mother was with Julia in the kitchen. "But after a couple of nights I figured out how to feed the babies without waking up Chris. Which is *gut*, because he's still working extra hours."

"Wonderful." Ellie could almost hear Sarah Lynne smiling. "I can hardly believe the change in you since the last time I was here. You seem so much more at ease with everything since . . ."

"*Mamm* left." Ellie rubbed Irene's back.

"I probably shouldn't have said anything."

"It's all right." Besides being related by marriage, the women were also friends.

"Has she been by to see the *bopplis*?"

Ellie paused. *"Nee."*

"Not even once?" Sarah Lynne sounded surprised.

"Nee."

"Ellie, I didn't realize you had been here alone during the day with the *bopplis*. I assumed *yer mamm* was coming by every day."

"Fortunately I've had lots of visitors, so I've had plenty of help during the day." Ellie held Irene against her shoulder as she rocked back and forth in the chair. "Of course, Chris is here with me at night. So we have everything under control."

"But what are you going to do about *yer mamm*?" Sarah Lynne asked.

"I'm not sure. I want to talk to her, but I haven't had time to go see her. I do miss her and wish she was here with me." She lifted her head toward Sarah Lynne. "I'm sure that sounds strange, considering we asked her to leave." Ellie lifted her chin, trying to keep her voice steady. "But if she can't be bothered to visit her grandchildren, that's not *mei* problem."

"Oh. I see."

Ellie didn't miss the note of disapproval in Sarah Lynne's voice. But Ellie didn't care . . . at least not that much. Sarah Lynne didn't understand. Neither did Chris, who had offered to take her and the *bopplis* to her parents more than once. Ellie had refused. She hadn't done anything wrong—she only wanted to have time with her own children. Her mother was being ridiculous. And stubborn.

Like mother, like daughter.

Her father's oft said words echoed in her mind, but did nothing to change it.

"Ellie, are you sure you're doing the right thing?" The floorboards creaked softly as Sarah Lynne stood up and padded across the room. "I know how important independence is to you. But so is family."

"I don't want to talk about it." Ellie knew she sounded childish, but there was nothing more to discuss. Obviously her mother cared more about nursing a grudge than seeing the twins.

"All right." A drawer shut, and Ellie assumed Sarah Lynne had put away the clothes. Sarah Lynne sat back down on the bed. "I'll change the subject. Have you and Chris figured out what you're going to do when the babies get older? Before you know it they'll be scooting around."

"*Ya*," she said, eager to discuss what she had recently learned about taking care of Irene and Julia. "I contacted my rehabilitation teacher, the one who helped me after my accident. She gave me a lot of ideas for what we can do through each stage of life. For example, when they're old enough to crawl I'll tie bells to their shoes—a different one for each *maed*." She put her lips against Irene's cheek.

"Has Barbara been by to check them?"

Ellie nodded. "She came earlier in the week. She said Irene and Julia are doing well. Everything is wonderful right now."

"Except you and *yer mamm*."

"Sarah Lynne—"

"You've got to talk to her, Ellie."

"I will. When she decides to talk to me. And even then, I'm going to have to lay down some ground rules when it comes to the twins. She can't take over like she did before. I know she doesn't think I'm capable of being a *gut mamm* . . ." She turned away, pain pricking at the admission.

"*Yer a gut mamm.* Anyone can see that."

"*Danki*, Sarah Lynne." She sighed. "Sometimes it's so overwhelming. But then I get some time to spend with one of the girls, or I'm feeding both of them and they fall asleep in my arms . . . it's so special." She stilled, her face heating as she remembered Sarah Lynne was trying to conceive. "I'm sorry. I wasn't thinking."

"It's okay."

When Sarah Lynne didn't say anything else, Ellie grimaced. How could she be so thoughtless? But Ellie had no idea what she could say to make her feel better.

"Can I hold Irene?" Sarah Lynne suddenly asked.

"Of course." Ellie held Irene out to her. "Do you want to sit down?"

"I can stand." Sarah Lynne took the baby from Ellie. She started to walk back and forth across the room. "I'll have to get used to holding a *boppli*," she said. Then she added, ". . . in about seven months."

Ellie gasped and jumped up from the chair. "Congratulations!" She smirked. "And here I was fretting about hurting your feelings."

Her sister-in-law laughed. "Gotcha."

"I'm so happy for you."

"Me too. And relieved." She lowered her voice. "You can't say anything to anyone, Ellie. Not even Chris. I haven't said anything to *Mamm* . . . or Isaiah."

Ellie nodded. "I won't say a word. But why haven't you told Isaiah?"

"I wasn't sure at first." She stopped in front of Ellie. "I'm seeing Barbara tomorrow. After I talk to her, then I'll tell him. Although he might suspect something since I've been sick for the past week. I didn't realize morning sickness lasted all day."

"You're feeling all right now?" Ellie asked.

"*Ya.* I make sure to keep crackers with me." She laughed again.

"I hope you don't mind me asking you to keep the news secret. But I had to tell someone. I was about to burst!"

"I don't mind at all." Ellie hugged her, mindful of Irene. Although she wished she could tell Chris the good news. He would be as thrilled for his sister and brother-in-law as Ellie was. "I'm so happy for you both."

☙

Five hours later happiness was the furthest thing from Ellie's mind. She was at her wit's end. Chris was late coming home from work again. It was well past suppertime, and the babies hadn't stopped crying for over an hour.

She was seated in the rocker, each baby secure on the nursing pillow. But Irene wouldn't nurse, and all Julia wanted to do was eat. She held Julia to her breast as she tried to calm Irene. "Shh," she said above her daughter's screeching. She cringed as Irene took a deep breath and began howling again.

"What do you want?" Ellie shouted, which caused Julia to startle, then join Irene in her cacophony of cries. When Ellie tried to feed her again, she refused.

Ellie adjusted her dress and picked up both babies, letting the pillow fall to the floor as she laid them in the cradle. They continued to cry. She brought her fingertips to her throbbing temples. She had no idea what they wanted. They were fed, changed, and bathed. "Why are you still crying?" she shrieked.

"Ellie?" Chris walked into the room, his tired voice filled with concern.

"I can't do this." Ellie turned her face toward him. "I've tried everything . . . They won't stop crying . . ."

Chris didn't say anything. She heard him walk to the cradle. Irene, who had a higher pitched cry than Julia, quieted. "What did you do?" When he paused, she yelled, "Answer me!"

"I fixed her diaper pin."

Ellie put her hand on her cheek. "It was sticking her?"

"*Ya.* But she's fine now. And Julia seems to be settling down too."

He was right. Now that Irene was quiet, Julia had stopped crying. Ellie walked to the bed and sat down, numb. She didn't even think to check the diaper pins. She'd changed Irene over an hour ago. Her daughter had been in pain that long, and Ellie didn't even know.

But Chris did. In mere seconds he was able to fix the problem. *Because he can see.*

"Ellie—"

"I'll fix your supper." She rose from the bed and walked out of the room, unable to face him. Her chest heaved with guilt. She'd hurt their daughter. Her heart ached as if it had been stabbed with a thousand pins.

She busied herself with warming up Chris's meal, but her mind was focused elsewhere. What other things would she overlook with her daughters because of her disability? How many times would she inadvertently hurt them or put them in danger?

She heard Chris's feet dragging on the floor as he entered the kitchen. He sat down on a chair, hard, not saying anything. Ellie swallowed as she placed a dish of baked chicken and black-eyed peas in front of him.

"I'm not hungry." He shoved his plate away.

Of course he was angry with her. She stood behind his chair, wringing her hands together.

"The *maed* are asleep," he said wearily. "Ellie, please sit down. We need to talk."

CHAPTER SEVEN

Ellie sat down next to her husband, noting the tired edge in his voice. "I'm sorry," she whispered, hanging her head.

"Sorry? For what?"

"For hurting Irene."

"Ellie," he murmured, reaching for her hand. "Is that why you're upset? Irene is fine. The pin barely poked her. I think she was more uncomfortable than anything else." He squeezed her hand. "It's not a big deal."

"But what if it had stuck her? What if she'd been bleeding? What if—"

"Then you and I would have handled it. We're both learning how to be parents. Next time you'll double-check the pins, that's all."

"I'll triple-check them."

He let out a tired chuckle. "That's *mei maedel*."

His calmness reassured her. And he was right—they were both

learning. Relieved not only by his logic but knowing that the babies were all right, she squeezed his hand back. "You sound exhausted."

"I am."

She searched for his plate on the table. When she touched the edge, she carefully moved it toward him. "Maybe you'll feel better after you eat."

"I'm too tired to eat."

"I'm sorry work has been so hard for you lately."

"It's not the work that's hard. It's the hours. But I'm grateful for it. So many are out of work right now. We're blessed that I have this job. Even though it threw me a curveball today."

"Did something bad happen?" she asked.

"*Nee.* Actually, I have some good news. Sort of." She felt his fingers entwine with hers. "I got a raise," he said.

She grinned, not expecting such a blessing. "That's wonderful."

"I also got a new position." He covered her hand with his other one. "In eastern Pennsylvania. Four hours away."

Ellie clutched his hand at his words. "What?"

"But it's only temporary," he said, the tone of his voice not showing any traces of its earlier weariness. "For three weeks they want me to help with a subdivision project. I don't have all the details about the job, but they're going to pay for room and board while I'm there."

"Three weeks?" she squeaked out.

His voice sped up as he talked. "It sounds like a long time, but you know how fast it will *geh.* It seems like yesterday that the *bopplis* were born."

"Then you already took the job?"

"*Ya.* I did."

Ellie yanked her hand from his. Three weeks might as well be three years.

"I didn't have time to talk to you about it or I would have. I didn't have much of a choice either. If I'd said no, they might have let me *geh* from the company. There are so many people who need work, Ellie. *Amisch* and *Englisch*. I—we—can't afford to lose this job."

Her brain knew he was right, but her panic overruled any logic. "You can't leave."

"Ellie, honey—"

"You can't *geh*." Her throat ached, as though a rock were lodged in it. "I can't do this without you."

"*Ya*, you can."

She shook her head as tears spilled down her cheeks. "I can't do this alone."

"You won't be. *Mei mamm* and *schwester* can help you with the twins during the day."

Ellie thought about Sarah Lynne. She couldn't count on her, now that she was expecting and was having a hard time with morning sickness. But she couldn't tell Chris about that.

"And I thought"—Chris cleared his throat—"well, if she would agree to it . . ."

She sucked in a breath. "You want *Mamm* to come back at night."

"More than that. I'm hoping she'll come and stay while I'm gone."

Ellie cringed and sat back in the chair. She knew Chris was right. She couldn't be here at home alone, and to ask anyone else to stay with her and the twins would be an extraordinary request. But her mother . . .

"We have to ask her tonight. I'm leaving tomorrow."

She clutched his hand, fresh panic washing over her. "So soon?"

"*Ya*." He took her face in his hands, rubbing his thumbs across her cheeks. "Ellie, I know this is hard on you. But it's hard on me too. I don't want to be gone from you or the girls."

"I know." She ran her fingers through his thick hair, setting aside her own fear for a moment. He was sacrificing a lot for the benefit of his family. She had to be strong for him and for their daughters. He didn't need to worry about them while he was gone. "We'll talk to *Mamm*," she said. Somehow she'd deal with the hurt and resentment.

He kissed her, then touched his forehead to hers. "Let's get the twins, then."

As she and Chris readied the girls for their first ride in the buggy, Ellie tried to steady her nerves. Maybe time had soothed her mother's hurt feelings. She doubted it, since time had had no effect on Ellie's emotions. But she had to set that aside and convince her mother that she not only wanted her to come and stay but that she needed her. She prayed that somehow her mother would understand.

Edna finished drying the last of the supper dishes and returned them to the cabinet. Ephraim was already in the living room, reading the paper, as was his habit in the evening. She looked out the kitchen window at the orange-and-pink-streaked sky. This window always allowed her a perfect view of gorgeous sunsets. It was her idea to put the window here when Ephraim built the house. But since Ellie's accident she didn't glean much pleasure from seeing the color-soaked skies at the end of the day. How could she, when her daughter would never see another sunset?

She clenched the damp kitchen towel. Ellie and the babies were never far from her thoughts. Neither was the hurt from the fact that they had sent her away. She'd thought they would have at least visited, but she hadn't seen Ellie since the night Christopher asked her leave. Ellie wasn't able to attend church yet, not until the babies were a little older. Last Sunday she'd had to field questions about the babies and Ellie, which only drove the pain further home. Of course she never let on that she hadn't seen them.

Never mind that Ephraim had offered to go with her to see the babies. He'd only seen them once since they were born, and he'd mentioned several times wanting to visit. But Edna refused. She hadn't shared the reason she'd come home that night, just telling her husband that Ellie and Christopher were able to take care of the babies by themselves. She couldn't even admit to her husband how deeply her daughter had hurt her.

She was about to join Ephraim in the living room when she noticed a buggy pulling into the driveway. As it neared she realized who it was. She brought her hand to her chest. Ellie and Christopher.

She attempted to steady her heartbeat by breathing slowly and promised herself she would watch her tongue. Even though she had stayed away, she had longed to see the babies, and now that they were here, she didn't want to say anything that would make Ellie leave. She wanted to be sure the twins were healthy. She had prayed for them constantly while she was away from them.

A sudden panic came over her. What if something was amiss and that's why Ellie and Christopher were here? She flew out of the kitchen and through the back door, meeting them just as Christopher brought the buggy to a halt.

"What's wrong?" she blurted. "What happened to the *bopplis*?"

Ellie's brow furrowed over her beautiful, unseeing eyes. "*Nix, Mamm.* They're fine."

"Oh, thank God." She saw them nestled in Ellie's arms. Immediately she took Julia from her. "I've missed you," she cooed to the baby. She glanced at Irene. They seemed to have grown while she was gone.

Christopher came over to the other side of the buggy and took Irene from Ellie, then helped her out of the buggy. But Edna hardly noticed their movements as she checked over Julia to make sure she was okay. When she glanced up, she saw Christopher giving her a hard look, but she didn't care. She had to make sure herself that that they were all right.

"*Mamm*," Ellie said, unfolding her white cane, "we need to talk."

Edna held Julia tightly. Something was wrong. She just knew it.

∞

"I thought you said the babies were fine."

Ellie heard the worry in her mother's voice, and the tension inside her tightened. Would her mother ever trust her with the babies? She hadn't even invited them into the house, instead jumping to the conclusion that something terrible had happened while she was gone. "*Mamm*, can we go inside?"

"Of course you can," her father said. She heard the screen door shut behind him, and seconds later felt his comforting hand on her shoulder. "I'm glad to see you, Ellie."

Her father's calmness soothed her. "I'm glad to see you too, *Daed*. I've missed you."

"Well, I told *yer mamm* we needed to visit earlier in the week but she—"

"Ephraim, we need to get the *bopplis* inside," *Mamm* said quickly. "We don't want them to catch cold."

"It's June, Edna. They're not going to catch cold."

The door slammed closed.

Daed let out a sigh. "Ellie, I don't know what's wrong with *yer mudder*. She's been acting *seltsam* since she came home last week."

"We know why," Chris said.

"*Gut*, because I need an explanation," *Daed* said. He paused. "Why do you have your cane out, Ellie? Nothing has changed here."

"I wasn't sure. *Mamm* moved a few things around at our house." She felt like she was tattling on her mother, but it was crucial that she was able to navigate any environment.

"Hmm. That's not like her either."

"Ephraim," Chris said. "We really need to talk to Edna—to both of you. Could we *geh* inside?"

"*Ya*. Sorry." Ellie felt her father take her hand and put it above the outside of his elbow, guiding her into the house the way her rehabilitation teacher had taught him. She smiled, and they all went inside and into the living room.

Ellie folded her cane and went to the chair near the door. She heard her mother speaking in hushed tones to Julia.

"Do you want to hold Irene too?" Chris asked *Mamm*.

"*Ya*." Ellie listened as Chris gave the baby to her mother, then joined her father on the couch. Her mother kept whispering to the babies over and over how much she missed them. How much she loved them. How she had prayed nothing had happened to them while she was gone. Her voice was nearly inaudible, and Chris and her father couldn't hear her.

But Ellie did. She gripped her cane.

"So what brings you here so late in the evening?" *Daed* asked.

Chris didn't say anything right away, and Ellie knew he was searching for the right words. She was tempted to speak, but waited until he was ready. Finally, he explained the job situation to her mother and father.

"You're abandoning your wife and babies?" *Mamm* said.

"That's not what he said, Edna. He has to work."

"He'll only be gone three weeks," Ellie added, trying to force a smile. She could barely do it in the face of her mother accusing Chris of neglecting his family.

"That's nearly a month." Ellie heard her mother shift in the rocking chair. "These babies are soaking wet, Ellie. Didn't you change them before you came here?"

"Ya—"

"It's a *gut* thing I have some diapers here at the *haus*." The back of the chair hit the wall as she rose. "I'll take care of them."

Ellie started to get up. "I can do it."

But her mother didn't reply as she walked out of the room. Ellie shrank back in her chair. The next three weeks were going to be torture.

"Ellie," Chris said gently, "*geh* with *yer mamm*."

"What's the use? She's got everything handled," Ellie said, unable to keep the bitterness from her voice.

"Ellie." This time her father spoke. "*Geh.*"

Cringing, Ellie stood and walked to the hallway. "*Mamm?*" she called, not sure where her mother had taken the twins. She had to follow her mother's voice as she walked down the hall to find her in her and her father's bedroom.

"Now it's Rachel's turn. Oh, how I've missed you," her mother said.

Ellie stood in the doorway. "*Mamm?* Are you all right? You just called one of the girls Rachel."

"I did no such thing. You are the two sweetest little girls," her mother continued.

"*Mamm*, I know what I heard."

A pause. "Ellie, *geh* back into the living room with your *daed* and Christopher. I'll take care of the twins."

Ellie flattened her lips. She was being treated like a child and her mother was acting oddly. "I'm not moving. Not until we get a few things straight between us."

"Like what?"

"You left without saying good-bye."

"Your husband threw me out."

She touched her temple. "He didn't throw you out. He said you didn't have to stay with us anymore. There's a big difference."

"Humph."

Ellie took a few steps into the room, feeling for the small chair she knew was next to her parents' dresser. She sat down. "*Mamm*, please. I'm sorry we hurt your feelings. We didn't mean to. But we needed time with the babies. I wish you could understand that."

"I do. And I've done what you wished. I stayed away."

"You didn't have to. Not for a whole week."

Irene, who was turning out to be the more vocal of the two girls, started to fuss. "You and Christopher seem to be just fine without me," *Mamm* said above the baby's noise.

Ellie stood up and then sat on the bed, searching for Irene and Julia. They were lying in the middle of the bed, side by side. She felt their ears, found Irene, and picked her up. The crying stopped. "I thought you'd be happy to know that we can take care of our *kinner, Mamm*."

"I . . . am."

"You don't sound like it." When her mother didn't respond, Ellie could see the conversation was going nowhere. There was nothing to do except ask her the question she was dreading all evening. "*Mamm*, Chris and I didn't come over here just to tell you about the job. We . . ."—she took a deep breath—"I need your help."

"Of course you do. Somebody has to be there for *mei gross-dochders*. It's not the babies' fault their father is leaving them."

"*Mamm*, stop it. You're not being fair to Chris."

But her mother continued to talk as if Ellie hadn't said anything. "I just need to pack a few things and I'll come with you."

"Right now?"

"There's *nee* sense in me driving the buggy over in the morning. I'm assuming Christopher is taking a taxi?"

"His boss is driving several of the Amish there himself."

"Then I can use your buggy when I need to." Ellie heard the snaps of her mother's suitcase open. The old hard-shell case had belonged to her grandmother.

"*Geh* get *yer daed*. I won't be able to carry my suitcase and the babies at the same time."

Ellie stood, ready to do what her mother ordered. Then she stopped, shocked at how easily she was about to let her mother take over. She couldn't live like this for three weeks. She would have to take a stand for herself now. She tucked Irene in the corner of one arm and picked up Julia with the other.

"What are you doing?" her mother asked.

"I'm taking Julia and Irene to the living room. We'll wait for you there. Please bring my cane when you leave."

"But, Ellie, what if—"

"I fall? I drop one of the babies? *Mamm*, I know this house as well as I know *mei* own. I won't fall. *Nix* will happen to *mei kinner*. I am their *mudder* and I will make sure of it." She thought about the diaper pin poking Irene earlier. Chris had been right. It was a mistake. And she would make them as she and Chris raised the girls. But she had to be given the chance to learn to be a parent.

"I wish you trusted me, *Mamm*," Ellie continued, trying to keep the pain out of her voice. "I'm blind, not helpless. Or useless."

"You've never talked to me like this before," *Mamm* muttered.

"I never had to." Ellie turned and left, her heart thumping in her chest. She probably ruined any chance of her mother staying with them while Chris was gone. Yet she didn't regret speaking her mind.

"Where's *yer mamm*?" her father asked as she entered the living room.

"Packing." At least Ellie hoped she still was. "Chris, would you mind taking Julia?"

He came to her and took the baby. As he did, he leaned closer to her. "What did you say to her?" he said in a low voice.

"Something I should have said a long time ago."

"So is she coming?"

Ellie swallowed. "I don't know."

"Let me *geh* talk to her," her father said. "Chris told me why you came. I'll tell her to get a move on."

They waited for several minutes, but neither her mother nor father appeared. The babies started fussing, ready for their nightly feeding. She and Chris needed to get them home. "I'll check to see what's going on," she said.

"*Danki*, Ellie."

She frowned. Her husband was so tired, the babies were hungry, and her mother clearly was rethinking staying with them. What a mess.

As she made her way down the hall, she heard the murmur of her parents' voices. Her father's serious tone made her stop just outside their bedroom. Although she knew she shouldn't eavesdrop, she couldn't force herself to leave.

CHAPTER EIGHT

Edna sat at the edge of the bed, stinging from Ellie's words. Is that what Ellie thought? That her mother considered her helpless? *Useless?* How could she believe that? All Edna wanted to do was help. To love her grandchildren and keep them safe. Yet her daughter had to twist it into something that wasn't true. She had to make it about *her.*

Edna crossed her arms, steaming with anger. If Ellie was so sure of herself, then why did she need her mother, whom she clearly didn't respect anymore?

"Edna? They're waiting on you."

She glanced up at Ephraim, who was now standing near the bed, but she didn't move. She stared straight ahead. It would take more than her husband's words to make her get up. It would take an apology from Ellie.

He frowned. "I know that face." He sat down next to her. "Don't be stubborn, Edna."

"Me? Stubborn?"

Her husband rolled his eyes. "I can see you're thinking about not helping them. And shame on you for those thoughts."

She cut her eyes at him. "You can't read *mei* mind."

"I've been married to you for forty years. I know exactly what you're thinking. I also know that you're hurt for some reason." He angled his body toward her. "Why don't you tell me what happened."

"You tell me," she said, getting up, "since you can read *mei* mind and all that."

He blew out a breath, a noise she recognized as his long-suffering sigh. Her lower lip trembled. It seemed like she was a burden to everyone.

"I can guess. But I'd rather hear it from you. Both you and Ellie have been out of sorts for a long time, ever since she was expecting."

"And of course that's *mei* fault."

"I never said that. Ellie is as stubborn as you." He came up behind her. "And as sensitive."

She whirled around and glared at him. "What do you mean by that?"

"You both feel very deeply, which is a *gut* thing." He smiled, the wrinkles around his eyes crinkling. "It's one reason I love both of you. But it can also cause you to have hurt feelings over little things."

"This is *not* a little thing. Do you know what she said to me? She thinks I don't trust her."

"You don't."

Her brow shot up. "How can you say that?"

"Because it's true. You don't trust anyone easily. Remember how long it took you to believe I loved you?"

Her lip trembled. "*Ya,*" she whispered.

He grabbed her hand. "*Nee* one knows more than I do the pain you've been through. Not just when Ellie lost her sight, but when you were young. But you have to put all that hurt behind you. Ellie and Christopher need you right now. Not just to help, but to support and respect their decisions. The *bopplis* need you, too, but the *kinner* are theirs, Edna, not yours." He gazed into her eyes. "Can you let *geh* and help them the way they need to be helped?"

She forced down the lump in her throat. She didn't want to admit it, but he was right, as he almost always was. But she didn't answer him right away.

"Edna . . ."

She nodded. "All right. I'll try." Then she paused at a shuffling sound near the bedroom door. "Did you hear something?"

"Like what?"

Edna stilled, much like Ellie did whenever she was listening carefully. She thought she heard someone outside their door. She walked to the doorway and peeked into the hall. But no one was there. "Must have been *mei* imagination," she said more to herself than to her husband.

"I'm glad you're willing to try. Now hurry and get packed. And *nee*, it's not because I want to see you leave."

"I never said—"

"You were thinking it." He winked at her and left.

Edna looked at the suitcase on the bed. She walked to the side table, picked up her Bible, and placed it on top of one of her light-blue dresses. If she was going to trust, to let go, she'd need God's help. She'd never been able to do it on her own.

She finished packing, closed the suitcase, and clicked the clasps shut. Straightening, she went to the living room. In the middle stood Ellie holding Irene, Christopher holding Julia, with Ephraim between them. Her daughter and son-in-law looked as tense as she felt. Then she met her husband's gaze. He gave her an encouraging smile.

"I'm ready," she said, managing a smile of her own. "Ephraim, carry *mei* suitcase while I take the *bop*—"

He cleared his throat.

"Um, never mind. I can carry the suitcase." She turned toward the door.

"Edna, wait." Christopher came up beside her. "If you'll hold Julia, I'll take the suitcase." He put the baby in her arms, picked up the case, and walked out of the house.

She glanced at Ellie. At least her daughter had stopped scowling. That was progress.

❧

That night, after the twins were asleep in the cradle and Ellie's mother was settled in the spare bedroom, Chris and Ellie were finally able to climb into bed. But Ellie was preoccupied with what she'd heard during her parents' conversation. What was her father talking about, her mother being hurt when she was young? Ellie had never heard either of them speak about that before.

Chris leaned over and kissed her cheek. "Everything okay?"

"Sure," Ellie said, forcing a cheery note in her voice. "Why wouldn't it be? *Mamm's* here now, so you don't have to worry about us while you're gone."

"I'll always worry about *mei maed*," he said, resting his chin on her shoulder.

"God will watch over us."

"I know. That doesn't mean I won't think about you all every single minute I'm gone." He traced her chin with his finger. "Are you sure everything is all right? When you came back from checking on your *mamm* at her *haus* you seemed . . . not upset exactly . . ."

She tilted her face toward his. "You are tired and imagining things." She couldn't burden him with this. Not now, not when he was leaving the next morning.

"Must be." He turned on his side, and she heard the click of the battery-operated lamp being turned off. Then he gently rolled her over and pressed her back against his chest. "Our last night for a while," he whispered in her ear. "I want to spend it with you in *mei* arms."

Despite her concern about her mother, Ellie smiled. She covered his hand with hers. Soon the sound of his heavy breathing in her ear let her know he was asleep.

Although she felt loved and secure in her husband's embrace, sleep eluded her. She was unable to get her mother out of her mind. She'd always thought *Mamm* was overprotective, even before Ellie was blind. She was less so with her older brother, Wally, but even when Ellie had her sight, *Mamm* had always peppered her with questions when she wanted to go to a friend's house, or when she started dating John, the young man who had left her after the car crash. But Ellie had thought that was simply her mother being guarded of her daughter, and now as a mother herself, she could understand that better.

Then the car accident and Ellie's losing her sight had thrown her mother over the edge, and it had taken a long time for her to let Ellie live her own life. Ellie thought about other major events in her life—her courtship with Chris, their marriage, and the birth of the twins. Each time her mother had reacted strongly. Ellie had assumed it was her personality.

But what if it was something else? Something so painful that no one, including her relatives, ever spoke of it? Whatever it was, she would have to tread carefully to find out.

CHAPTER NINE

"Is something going on with your *mamm*?" Chris asked.

Ellie paused as she folded a pair of his broadfall pants. Had he suspected something? She quickly packed them in his duffel bag. "What do you mean?"

"She didn't argue about the babies being in our room, she didn't insist on feeding them this morning, and she's actually been . . . pleasant."

"Chris, *mei* mother can be nice, you know."

"I'm joking. Sort of." He took the duffel from her and zipped it up. "Whatever your father said to her last night sure made a difference."

Ellie pressed her lips together. She had also noticed the change in her mother. She was making an effort to be helpful instead of controlling. But she couldn't connect how her father's words had made an impact on her mother. She was surprised they hadn't opened some old wound, making her mother more difficult than ever.

"Whatever caused the change," Chris continued, "I'm thankful.

It makes leaving you and the babies much easier knowing that you and Edna are getting along."

Ellie nodded, but she didn't see anything easy about Chris going away. She also wouldn't go so far as to say she and her mother were getting along. Cordial was a better description. She sighed. It would be a long three weeks.

The impact of Chris being gone for so long hit her full force. "I'm going to miss you so much," she whispered, nearly strangling on the words.

He dropped the duffel bag on the floor and took her in his arms. "Me too."

"I wish you didn't have to *geh*."

He held her more tightly. "Me either. But the time will *geh* by fast. I gave your *mamm* a number to call if there's an emergency. I left it there on the dresser for you too." When she opened her mouth to speak, he put his finger over her lips. "Not that I think there will be an emergency. But I want to be prepared."

She nodded, and he removed his finger. "I understand." She took his hand. "Will it be okay to call you every night, after the *bopplis* and *Mamm* have gone to bed? I can't bear the idea of not talking for almost a month. I know *Mamm* wouldn't approve, but writing letters would take too long."

"*Ya*. It will be our secret."

The windows were open, letting in the warm summer air. A honk sounded in the distance. "That's my ride," Chris said softly. Then he kissed her, deeply, longingly, until the horn honked again. "I have to *geh*."

"Be safe. I'll pray for you every day."

"Same here—for you and the babies. And *yer mamm*, of course."

Ellie chuckled thickly. "Of course."

Chris left, and she didn't follow. Instead, she sat on the edge of their bed and bowed her head, praying for his safety while he was gone. Although he would be only four hours away, that didn't offer much comfort. After she finished, she went to the living room. "*Mamm?*"

"I'm here. Irene is on a blanket on the floor. I'm holding Julia."

She appreciated her mother telling her where the babies were in the room. She wasn't surprised that her mother was holding one of them. Even though *Mamm* seemed more at peace, she still held them any chance she had.

"It's a *schee* day outside," her mother said. "Would you like to work in the garden?"

Ellie thought for a moment. She hadn't had much time to spend there, and surely there were plenty of weeds that needed to be pulled. Then she realized this was her mother's way of offering an olive branch. She nodded, and then as an afterthought said, "Would you like to join me? We can take the babies with us, put them on a blanket in the shade under the oak tree."

Her mother didn't say anything right away. Then she replied, "That sounds nice."

A short time later the babies were napping under the canopy of the oak tree, a place where Ellie and Chris would sometimes have picnics on Sunday afternoons after church. The girls were lying on a quilt Sarah Lynne had made for them. She had described it as a center-diamond quilt, with a large pale-pink diamond in the middle, surrounded by peach-colored fabric. Ellie and her mother were a couple of yards away, tending the garden, which had indeed become fairly weedy since the birth of the babies.

"I guess I should have weeded for you while I was here last time," *Mamm* said.

"It's okay," Ellie said, checking the size of the tomato flowers on the plants. Some were pretty big, and in a month or so would be producing pea-size orbs that would eventually grow into large, beefsteak tomatoes. "Everything has been hectic since the *bopplis* were born."

They continued to work in the garden in silence except for the twittering of birds. Ellie cocked her head to listen for the babies, but all she heard was the sound of the birds—robins, finches, with an occasional black bird squawk interrupting their delicate melodies.

But Ellie's mind wasn't on their sweet music. All she could think about was what her father had said last night. *Nee one knows more than I do the pain you've been through. Not just when Ellie lost her sight, but when you were young.*

She sat back on her heels. Her mother definitely seemed more even-keeled than she had been in a while, so this might be a good time to bring up the subject. "*Mamm,*" she said tentatively, "can I talk to you about something?"

"*Ya.*"

Though *Mamm's* answer was short, it wasn't curt. She took a deep breath. "I, uh . . . I overheard you and *Daed* talking last night." She waited for her mother to say something. After a long pause, Ellie asked, "Did you hear me?"

"I heard you." Her mother's voice was tight and strained.

Ellie grimaced. She should have known it was a mistake to mention this. "I'm sorry—"

"You shouldn't eavesdrop." She heard the rustle of the grass as her mother got up. "I brought you up better than that."

"I know, but I couldn't help it."

"Someone forced you to listen to my private conversation?"

Ellie also got to her feet. She brushed the dirt off her hands. "I was checking to see if you had decided to go home with us. When I got to your room, I heard you and *Daed*."

"And of course you couldn't walk away." *Mamm's* tone grew more tense, as if it were a tightly strung fishing line about to snap. "What did you hear?"

"I shouldn't have said anything—"

"What did you hear, Ellie?" Her *mamm's* footsteps came toward her.

She hesitated, not wanting to continue. She and her *mamm* had been getting along all morning, and she had to mess that up by bringing up an obviously hurtful subject. But she had flipped open the can of worms, so she should see it through. "*Daed* said you were hurt when you were *yung*. I don't remember you saying anything about that when we were growing up. What happened?"

"What happened is none of your business."

Mamm's voice slashed at her, making Ellie take a step back.

"That was a private conversation," *Mamm* continued. "One that you had no right to listen to. Do not bring it up again."

"But, *Mamm*, maybe if you talked about it, you would feel better—"

"Julia's fussing," *Mamm* said.

"I don't hear anything."

Her mother didn't respond, and Ellie knew the conversation was over. But her curiosity was more piqued than before. She had several relatives in Paradise, but her mother said very little about her own childhood. Ellie had never thought much about it before, not until now. Whatever *Mamm* was hiding, it had to be more painful than Ellie could imagine.

"Ellie!" Her mother called from a few feet away.

The panic Ellie heard in her mother's voice caused her to

quicken her steps and forget about her mother's secret. "What, *Mamm?*"

"There's something wrong with Julia."

"What? What is it?"

"She feels hot."

The alarm that had risen in Ellie when she first heard her mother say something was wrong with Julia subsided. "*Mamm*, she's probably warm from being outside. It's pretty hot today."

"She has a fever," *Mamm* said, her voice filled with absolute certainty.

"Are you holding her?"

"*Ya.*"

Ellie knelt by the edge of the blanket and felt for Irene. Her fingers found teeny toes, which were cool to the touch. She moved forward and scooped up her daughter. Irene didn't feel warm at all.

"We should get them in the house," Ellie said, knowing that would probably reassure her mother. When *Mamm* didn't answer, Ellie realized she had left without her.

Ellie scooped up Irene and went back to the house, finding the smooth, stone path Chris had laid when they first moved in the house. He had embedded the rocks in such a way that the edges were flush with the ground, preventing her from tripping. They led directly to the back porch steps.

"*Mamm!*" she called when she walked inside the house. Her yell startled Irene, who started to cry. "I'm sorry, little one," she whispered in her baby's ear, then cooed to her daughter until she calmed down. She cuddled Irene and listened for her mother or Julia. Finally, she heard Julia's piercing wails from the spare bedroom. When she walked into the bedroom, she heard her mother speaking in a low, almost childlike voice.

"It's okay, Rachel."

Ellie raised a brow. Rachel again? From the pain in her mother's voice it sounded like she was trying to hold back tears. Ellie's wrinkled her brow. She couldn't remember the last time she heard her mother cry.

"Julia's sick," *Mamm* said in a desperate voice. "We need to get her to the hospital right away."

Ellie walked to the bed, leaned over, and placed Irene in the middle of it. "Let me see Julia, *Mamm*. Maybe she needs to nurse in order to cool off."

But *Mamm* refused to let Julia go. "I won't let anything happen to you," her mother whispered to the baby. "You're not going to die."

A shiver passed through Ellie as she heard the chilling words.

CHAPTER TEN

Edna kissed Julia's forehead, feeling her hot skin beneath her lips. This couldn't be happening again. Not to her granddaughter. *Not to her Rachel.*

Ellie's voice faded as Edna's mind wandered to the past, a place she'd dared not think about for the past six decades. She thought she'd put it all behind her, had buried that agony so deep that it only came to the surface in her nightmares . . . and after Ellie's babies were born. She couldn't fail them. Not like she'd failed Rachel.

"*Mamm!*" Ellie's voice broke through the veil of memories. Julia's and Irene's cries chimed in. She looked up, her daughter's distraught face coming into focus. "Ellie?"

"Please give me Julia. I need to see if she's all right."

Dazed, Edna stood from the rocker and let Ellie sit. When she placed Julia in Ellie's arms, her mind had completely turned to the present. "I'll get the buggy ready."

"*Nee*," Ellie said. She used her forearm to check Julia's forehead. "She does feel warmer than Irene, though. Let me nurse her and see how she does."

How could Ellie be so calm at a time like this? "Ellie, listen to me. She has a fever—a very high one. If it doesn't come down she could . . ."

Ellie nestled Julia, and soon the baby started nursing. "She's okay, *Mamm*. She's nursing. If she was sick she wouldn't want to eat." But as soon as the words were out of Ellie's mouth, Julia pulled away and started crying. A sick, strangled cry.

"Ellie, please." Edna could feel the sobs rising in her throat, the helplessness in her heart. "I can't lose another *boppli*."

Her daughter's head snapped up, her blue eyes focusing off center. "What are you talking about?"

She knelt in front of Ellie. "She needs to *geh* to the hospital. She needs to see a doctor."

Julia latched onto Ellie again and started nursing. "*Mamm*," Ellie said softly. "She's okay. I promise. Look, she's eating again."

Edna saw Julia eagerly taking Ellie's milk. She stared, certain that at any moment the baby's mouth would drop away and her body would go limp. After several moments, neither happened.

"Feel her forehead now." Ellie grasped for Edna's hand. Edna let her guide the back of her hand to Julia's forehead, which was considerably cooler than before. "See? She's okay. She just got a little too warm outside."

Edna breathed out a long sigh of relief. Irene started to cry on the bed behind her.

"Would you mind giving her a bottle?" Ellie asked.

Standing, Edna nodded. Then remembering her daughter couldn't see, she said, "*Ya*. I'll get it." She left the room and went to the kitchen, only realizing how much her hands were shaking when she opened the cabinet door to get a bottle.

She leaned against the counter, trying to get her bearings. Julia was okay, she kept telling herself. She wasn't Rachel. She closed her eyes and prayed a prayer of thankfulness, only to stop when the bitterness of the past rose like bile in her throat.

She was glad Julia was all right. But why couldn't Rachel have been? Why had God taken a tiny, innocent baby away? Even after all these years, she couldn't let go of the hurt, the regret . . . and the shame.

But she had to follow her mother's example, the way she had in the years since then. Edna straightened her shoulders and made Irene's bottle. She walked into the bedroom, picked up her fussy granddaughter, and sat down on the edge of the bed, her back to Ellie. Although her daughter couldn't see her, Edna didn't want to face her right now and the barrage of questions that were sure to come.

To her surprise, Ellie didn't say anything. They fed the babies in silence, punctuated by a few strong burps, one so loud from Julia that it was clear her granddaughter was just fine. She didn't turn around when Ellie put Julia in the cradle. "Here, *Mamm*," Ellie said as she rounded the bed and stood in front of her. "Take the rocking chair."

"Irene's nearly done with her bottle."

"That's all right," Ellie said softly. "Take your time with her. I'll *geh* finish weeding in the *garten*."

"You sure?"

She nodded. "*Ya*. I'm sure."

After Ellie left, tears welled in Edna's eyes. Her daughter was a remarkable woman in so many ways. She stood, and then through clouded eyes sat down with Irene, rocking her until the baby fell asleep. But instead of putting her in the cradle with her sister, she looked at the infant, taking in her olive-colored skin and dark eyelashes, so much like her father's. She cuddled her granddaughter close, forcing away the past and basking in the love she felt for these two precious babies.

A week passed, and neither Ellie nor *Mamm* brought up the incident with Julia. Several times Ellie had been tempted to ask her mother about Rachel, wondering who the mysterious girl was. But she kept her thoughts to herself, respecting her mother's privacy. There was a reason she'd never talked about the past, and Ellie didn't want to force her to.

But that didn't mean her curiosity wasn't plaguing her. During the second week Chris was gone, Ellie told her mother, "I'd like to *geh* see *Daed*."

"All right," her mother said, placing a plate of what smelled like perfectly crisped bacon on the table. "We can *geh* after breakfast."

"I thought I would *geh* by myself—if you don't mind watching the twins for a little while." Ellie fiddled with the edge of her napkin.

"Oh?" *Mamm* asked, sounding a bit suspicious.

"I miss him. I mean, I know you miss him too, but that's not the only reason I want to see him." The words sounded lame to her ears.

"You two have always had a close relationship." *Mamm* sat down across from her and pushed the plate of bacon toward her. "And I don't blame you for wanting to get out of the house for a little bit. It's a beautiful *daag*."

She sighed. "So you don't mind watching the twins?"

"Of course not. That's why I'm here. And don't worry; they'll be fine."

Ellie smiled. "I'm not worried." She sniffed the air. "That bacon smells *gut*."

The plate slid even closer. "Help yourself," her mother said. But despite her mother's calm demeanor, there was an underlying current of tension since the episode with Julia. Maybe her father would have some answers.

After the breakfast dishes were done, Ellie said good-bye to her twins, which was harder than she thought. She'd never been away from them, and even though she was only going down the street, it still felt like a part of her was missing when she went outside. As she unfolded her cane, she could only imagine how hard it was on Chris, being so far away. She'd talked to him briefly on the phone last night, but still hadn't mentioned what happened with *Mamm*. He didn't sound as tired as he had been the past few weeks, but he was ready to come home. Ellie said a quick prayer for him and headed for her parents' house.

It was about a half hour's walk there, and as usual she was glad they lived on a road with very little traffic. She kept to the edge of the road, staying alert as she swept her cane in front of her in a wide arc. She had walked to her parents' house many times since she and Chris were married, and even though the path was familiar, she never let down her guard. Finally, she arrived at their driveway, the comforting sound of the cows lowing reaching her ears.

She walked down the long driveway toward the house and knocked on the door. When no one answered, she headed for the barn. *"Daed?"*

"Hold on," her father's voice sounded from inside the building. "I'll be right out."

Ellie wiped the perspiration from her face. Despite it being only midmorning, the day already promised to be another hot one.

"Hi, Ellie," her father said, his boots crunching on the gravel driveway. He paused. "Did you walk here by yourself?"

"*Ya.*"

"And *yer mudder* let you?"

Ellie nodded.

"And they say there's no such thing as miracles." He put his hand on her shoulder. "How are the *bopplis*?"

"Fine."

"*Gut, gut.*" He paused, dropping his hand. "And *yer mudder*? How are you two getting along?"

"Really well." Ellie rubbed her cane in between her forefinger and thumb. "Surprisingly well."

"So you just came by to say hi to *yer* old *daed*?"

"You're not old."

"That's not what *mei* knees have been telling me. Come on, we'll go inside and have some tea. I'll have to make it first. Haven't had tea since *yer mamm* left. Haven't had a decent meal either."

She took his arm. "You could have come over."

"Nah. I think it's *gut* for you and *yer mamm* to have this time together."

"You also like the peace and quiet."

He chuckled. "That too."

A short time later they were in the kitchen. Ellie heard the rumbling of the water in the kettle as it started to boil. "When was the last time you made tea?" she asked when the teakettle began to whistle.

"Can't remember. Possibly when you were a *boppli* yourself." Earlier he had brought some ice cubes from the cooler in the basement and put them in glasses. When he finished making the tea, it was more tepid than iced, but Ellie didn't mind. She heard her father sit down across from her.

"Now . . . tell me why you're really here," he said.

She tugged on one of her *kapp* strings. She could never put anything past him, and there was no reason for her not to be straightforward. "Who's Rachel?"

He sucked in a breath. "Where did you hear about her?"

Ellie explained about overhearing his and her mother's conversation, then about *Mamm's* strange behavior with Julia. "She called her Rachel. I had heard her do that before, but she insisted I was mistaken. I don't know what to think."

The drumming sound of her father's fingers against the wood table filled the silence of the room. "This isn't my story to tell, Ellie. Have you asked *yer mamm* these questions?"

"Once. She didn't want to talk about it."

"She never did." His chair legs scraped against the floor. Her father's boot heels echoed as he walked toward the sink. She imagined him standing there, looking out the window. Her mother used to do that, Ellie remembered. She liked to see the sun set. How many times had she stood there and thought of Rachel?

"Ellie . . ." From the direction of his voice she could tell he had turned to face her. "If I told you about Rachel, I would be betraying your *mudder.* I won't do that."

She let go of the *kapp* string, disappointed but not surprised. "I understand. I would feel the same way about Chris."

"But I do think Edna needs to let this *geh*. And she'll never do it if she continues to keep it all bottled up inside her."

"I've tried talking to her about it."

"So have I." Her father moved closer. "I think there's only one thing we can do."

"What?"

"Show her that no matter what, we love her." He put Ellie's cane in her hand. "Let's *geh*."

CHAPTER ELEVEN

Edna sat on Ellie and Christopher's front porch, enjoying the late-morning air. Despite the heat, there was a lovely breeze that made the rising temperature bearable. She had brought the cradle out with her and placed both babies inside. She used her foot to rock the cradle back and forth. They weren't asleep, but they weren't fussing either. She kept glancing at them, keeping them close to her, making sure neither was too warm or uncomfortable in any way.

She looked out at the yard in front of her. As she had over the past few days, she thought of her behavior with Julia. She'd foolishly overreacted. Fortunately Ellie hadn't brought it up, but that still didn't temper her embarrassment that she thought her *granddochder* was deathly ill when she wasn't.

A buggy turned into the driveway, and she immediately recognized it. She smiled. Although she was enjoying her time with the babies and Ellie, she missed Ephraim. He parked the buggy near the barn, and after several moments, he and Ellie appeared.

"I see you're enjoying the morning, Edna," he said, escorting Ellie up the steps.

"*Ya*. It's been a fine *daag*. What are you doing here?"

He bent over and picked up both babies in one swoop. Edna started. "Ephraim, what—"

"I think I deserve some quality time with these *bopplis*." He flashed her a grin and opened the screen door.

Edna shot up from the chair. "You don't know the first thing about taking care of twins."

"I took care of *mei* own two *kinner*," he said.

"Excuse me?" She put her hands on her hips, ignoring Ellie's laughter in the background. "*Who* took care of our *kinner*?"

"It was a dual effort. Well, we gotta *geh*. Time for Irene and Julia to hear all about my favorite fishing hole."

The door shut behind him before she could say anything else. She turned to Ellie, who was still smiling. "Are you going to let him take the girls like that?"

"He's their *grossvatter*." She carefully moved to the porch swing and sat down, still holding her cane. "Plus, it will give us a few minutes alone."

"What do we need that for?"

Ellie's expression grew serious. "So you can tell me about Rachel."

Ellie paused, waiting for her mother to respond. Instead, all she heard was the sound of horse's hooves on the road as a cart went by. She could tell the difference between a cart and a buggy by the sound the wheels made. When the cart and horse passed and her mother still didn't say anything, Ellie sat back in the swing. "I want to know what happened to her."

"It's not your business. Rachel is . . . personal."

"I know. *Daed* told me."

Her mother gasped. "What did he say? I can't believe Ephraim would do that to me."

"Wait," Ellie said. "He didn't tell me anything, other than he wants you to be free."

"I am." *Mamm* sat down. "Rachel is in the past."

"Not anymore." Ellie leaned forward. "I don't think she ever was. Please, *Mamm*. Tell me what happened."

She heard a sob catch in her mother's throat.

"She was . . ." *Mamm* sniffed. "She was *mei* sister. And I was supposed to take care of her. It was *mei* job to keep her safe." She choked on the next words. "She died because of me."

Ellie got up from the swing and sat at her mother's feet. She reached out until she found *Mamm's* hand. "How old was she?"

"Just a baby. Not even six months old. *Yer* grandmother had to take *yer aenti* Roberta to the emergency room—she'd fallen out of a tree and hit her head. *Vatter* was at work, and *Mutter* asked me to watch Rachel. But as soon as Roberta and *Mutter* left in the taxi, Rachel started to cry. She wouldn't stop."

"Oh, *Mamm*." Ellie stroked her mother's hand. *Mamm* squeezed her fingers, stilling Ellie's movements.

"She was very hot too. I didn't know it at the time, but she had a high fever. I tried to cool her off with a cold cloth. I gave her a bath. But she kept crying. She wouldn't stop . . ." *Mamm's* voice cracked. "I had to put her in the cradle. I closed the door because I couldn't take the crying anymore." *Mamm's* voice sounded soft. Young. As if she was reliving the nightmare at that moment. "Finally, she stopped crying. Then I went to *mei* room and played with *mei* dolls. I . . . forgot about her."

Ellie's heart filled with pain. "What happened?"

"*Mamm* and Roberta were gone for a long time. Hours. It was almost dark when I remembered I was supposed to be watching Rachel. I ran into the room. I looked in the cradle, and she wasn't moving. I touched her. She was cold. So very cold."

Tears streamed down Ellie's face. "How old were you?"

"Seven." She pulled out of Ellie's grasp. "Old enough to take care of a *boppli*."

"It wasn't *yer* fault she died."

"I forgot about her, Ellie. I should have taken her next door to the neighbors. They would have known what to do. But I forgot all about her. If I hadn't put her in the cradle . . . if I hadn't shut the door . . ."

Ellie rose and put her arms around her mother. "I'm so sorry."

Mamm stiffened. "*Mutter* never blamed me. Neither did *Vatter*. I remember them saying she died from the fever, but other than that we never spoke of it again, right up until the day they died. It was as if Rachel never existed."

"But she did, *Mamm*. And she still does. In *yer* heart. You can't keep blaming yourself. You have to know it wasn't your fault."

"It was God's will. That's what *mei onkel* said. But that was little comfort."

Ellie sat back down. "We don't always understand God's will. Remember, that's what you told me after the accident."

"*Ya*," she whispered. "I remember."

"And Rachel is in heaven. She has her angel wings. You need to let her *geh*." She laid her head in her mother's lap. "You can't keep worrying about the twins. Or about me. All this fretting is keeping you from enjoying your grandchildren."

"I realize that, Ellie." She stroked Ellie's back. "And I thought I had come to terms with it. When Wally and you were born, I wasn't afraid. Not like I am now."

"Because you kept us safe."

"*Ya*," she whispered. "I kept you safe."

Ellie lifted her head. "*Mamm*, don't you see? It's God who's in control. Even when we think we are, God's will is always done. We have to do our part, but we also have to accept when God's decisions aren't ours."

Mamm touched Ellie's cheek. "Like with your blindness."

"Like with your Rachel."

"Ellie, I . . . I'm not sure how I can forgive myself for what happened to her."

"Let's take the first step." She reached out and touched her mother's cheek. "Let's pray."

CHAPTER TWELVE

Ellie paced the front porch, her stomach in knots. *Mamm*, sitting in a chair, her knitting needles clacking away, cleared her throat.

"You're going to wear down the porch boards," she said. "Be patient. He'll be here soon."

Ellie checked her Braille watch. "He's half an hour late. What if their van got into an accident?" An ache formed in her chest, close to panic as her own car accident flashed in front of her. Almost instantly she felt her mother standing beside her.

"What did you tell me about worrying?" *Mamm* said.

"That it doesn't change anything." Ellie sat down in the swing. Why couldn't she take her own advice? Chris's three weeks had turned to four, and he was finally due home. Unfortunately, he was late. She had talked to him almost every day, but the phone was a poor substitute for him being here.

Mamm sat back down in the chair, picked up her needles, and started knitting again. She was making two dark-blue sweaters for the girls. The sound of her foot rocking the cradle back and forth against the porch boards was in perfect rhythm with her flying needles. Since their talk on the front porch that day, Ellie and her mother had grown closer. *Mamm* had been less tense, although she still went a little overboard when it came to taking care of the girls. But now she wasn't any more doting than Chris's mother, who had been by several times to see the twins. Sarah Lynne, who was still struggling with morning sickness, was only able to visit twice, but according to Barbara everything was going well with the pregnancy.

The clicking of the needles abruptly stopped. "I believe I owe you an apology, *dochder*."

Ellie turned her head toward her mother. "For what?"

"For not helping you the way you needed me to."

"*Mamm*, everything has been fine."

"I'm talking about before. I should have trusted you with the twins."

Surprised, Ellie said, "*Danki, Mamm*. I appreciate that."

"I see how *gut* you are with the babies. How organized everything is here." Mamm sighed. "Christopher was right to ask me to leave. I was in the way."

"Is that what he said to you?"

"Not in so many words. But he did the right thing." She started knitting again. "You know I didn't think much of him when we first met."

"You did make that pretty clear."

"Now, Ellie, you couldn't blame me, could you? He had left the Amish. How was I supposed to trust him?"

"By trusting me."

Her mother paused. "You're right. I promise I'll do a better job of that from now on."

The sound of a car turning into the driveway drove Ellie out of the swing. "Is he here?"

"Looks like it," *Mamm* said. She didn't move or stop knitting.

Ellie carefully but quickly went down the steps. She heard the sound of a car door slam. She stopped in the middle of the yard. "Chris?"

"I'm here." He drew her close.

She hugged him tightly, whispering in his ear, "I'm so glad you're home."

"*Mei* too." He pulled away from her. "Hi, Edna," he called.

"Christopher."

He chuckled and said in a low voice, "Same old Edna."

Ellie lifted her head. "*Nee*. She's not the same. She's better."

"What do you mean?"

"I'll tell you all about it. But there are two little girls waiting for you. You won't believe how big they've grown."

"I can't wait to see them. Let me get my duffel bag." When he took her hand, she leaned against him and whispered, "Later I'll give you a proper welcome home."

He laughed, and she smiled. They walked up the front porch steps together, and she stayed back as Chris picked up his daughters, telling them how beautiful they were and how much their *daed* had missed them.

Mamm came up beside her. "It's time for me to *geh* home."

Ellie turned to her. "You can stay, *Mamm*. Chris won't mind."

"*Nee*, Ellie. You all need time together. As a *familye*."

"I'll miss you."

"I'm only down the street, *dochder*. Don't worry. You'll see me soon enough."

Before her mother could walk away, Ellie hugged her, her own heart filling with love as her mother hugged her back. They had both changed since the babies were born. A month ago she wasn't sure if she and her mother would ever get along again. Now she knew they would always be close . . . and she thanked the Lord for that.

READING GROUP GUIDE

1. Do you think Edna's worry over Ellie taking care of the twins was justified? Why or why not?
2. Edna thought she had good intentions when it came to taking care of her grandbabies, but she was really acting out of fear and worry. Have there been times when fear or worry dictated your actions? How did God help you during those times?
3. Do you think Edna would have been as worried about the babies if Ellie wasn't blind?
4. Ellie and Edna both had to learn how to let God be in control of their lives. Have you ever faced this challenge? What helped you "let go and let God"?
5. What advice would you give Ellie about how to deal with her mother?

Acknowledgments

Kelly Long—your encouragement and input as I was writing this novella were invaluable. Thank you!

My editors, Becky Monds and Jean Bloom—thank you for your advice, experience, and support.

A special thank you, as always, to my wonderful family.

Author Bio

Photo by Sarah Debevec

Kathleen Fuller is the author of several bestselling novels, including *A Man of His Word* and *Treasuring Emma*, as well as a middle-grade Amish series, The Mysteries of Middlefield. Visit her website at www.kathleenfuller.com Twitter: @TheKatJam Facebook: Author Kathleen Fuller

An Unexpected Blessing

VANNETTA CHAPMAN

For Becky Philpott,
My friend and editor

GLOSSARY OF
SHIPSHEWANA AMISH WORDS

boppli—baby

bruder—brother

dat—dad, father

danki—thank you

Englischer—Amish person

gem gschehne—you're welcome

Gotte's wille—God's will

grandkinner—grandchildren

gut—good

kaffi—coffee

kapp—prayer covering

kinner—children

mamm/mammi—mom, grandmother

narrisch—crazy

nein—no

onkel—uncle

rumspringa—running around; time before an Amish young person officially joins the church; provides a bridge between childhood and adulthood.

schweschder—sister

was iss letz—what's wrong

wunderbaar—wonderful

ya—yes

"The Lord has done great things for us,
and we are filled with joy."
—Psalm 126:3

Chapter One

Etta Bontrager paid little attention to the north wind that howled and rocked their buggy.

Her husband, Mose, peered out the front window, his weathered hands firmly gripping the reins to their horse. Mose was nearly six feet tall and still had the muscled form of the young man she had married twenty-four years earlier. In her mind, he still was that man in every way. As they passed near a streetlight, Mose raised his hat and reset it on his head, giving her a glimpse of his dark, curly hair and receding hairline. They had both aged, to be sure; nevertheless, in their hearts she felt certain they were the same young man and woman setting out on a life together.

Etta looked past Mose to the scene outside the window. Snow swirled around them, accumulating on the side of the road in three-foot drifts. Beyond the snow was darkness. Little of the northern Indiana countryside was visible. It was as if the rest of the world had virtually disappeared under the weight of the winter storm.

She had kept an eye on the weather all afternoon as an ominous feeling of heaviness in her belly and lower back warned her that her time was near. She'd watched as the snow covered the top of the barn, the maple trees, and the hillside. The east side of the house, where they planted their family garden, had disappeared under the white blanket. The trampoline, which her children had become too old to play on, disappeared under a small white mountain. Their front porch looked like something out of an *Englisch* postcard.

As they rode toward Shipshewana, the temperature held steady at a numbing twenty-four degrees.

Etta was quite aware of the conditions outside their buggy this cold February evening, but she was more concerned about what was happening inside her body. Pushing the blanket down and off her lap, she swiped at the sweat running down her face in rivulets.

She tried to focus on her breathing.

She resisted the fear that insisted on clawing its way up her throat.

She pushed away the memory of that other night nine years ago.

Closing her eyes, she imagined the child in her womb, the babe she would soon hold, the babe she had thought was a mistake. Now she knew it was no mistake. *Gotte* had intended this child for their lives—for her and Mose. He had sent them an unexpected blessing in their later years. She did not believe this child was meant to replace Sarah. One child could never take the place of another. But God had seen fit to bless them one more time, and He would see them through.

No storm was too big.

No night too dark.

The pain washed over her, and she again began to count, panting and praying it would pass quickly. Longer contractions meant the time for their babe's birth was closer, and they weren't yet ready.

Not here.

Not in the middle of the country road.

Mose reached over and clutched her hand.

When she opened her eyes, she saw the worry etched on his face. "The storm is bad, *ya*?"

"We'll get through," he said.

"I'm glad you woke the girls and reminded them to keep feeding wood into the big stove in the living room."

"They're *gut* girls. They'll take turns and handle it just fine—not that any of them would go back to sleep. They were too excited about the arrival of their new *schweschder*."

"Maybe I should have stayed home."

"*Nein*. Doc said you needed to be at the birthing center."

Etta peered out the front window. They had no lights on the front of their buggy, and the streetlights revealed little—snow falling, snow swirling, snow covering everything in its path. The road itself was completely obscured. Etta had no idea how Mose managed to keep them moving in the right direction.

Rather than fret over the weather, which she couldn't control, she prayed for the babe about to be born. She whispered a silent prayer for Sarah, who was now in heaven, and another for David, her lost child. That was how she thought of him now—not gone or vanished but lost. Finally, she prayed for their farm, that Mose might find a way to make the bank payments. She petitioned God for help so they wouldn't need to sell the home where they had raised all of their children.

Each prayer brought heartache.

The ache in her heart over Sarah was steady, constant, familiar. The sorrow over David was fresh, even after two years. Was he safe, sheltered, and warm? When would she see him again? As for their farm, it didn't seem possible that they might lose it. Her thoughts could hardly wrap around that fear.

The questions swirled and collided in her mind, and then her attention was jerked back to the present as the buggy tilted precariously and came to an abrupt stop. Their ten-year-old gelding, Morgan, struggled with the weight of the buggy against the heavy, wet snow, but the drift he'd stepped into was too deep.

The buggy was stuck.

A light from down the street shone into their window, and for a split second, she saw fear bleach the color from her husband's face. Then Mose turned to her and patted her hand. "I have a shovel and lantern in the back. I'll dig him out."

Etta nodded, unable to respond. The next contraction was coming. They were closer together now, barely allowing time to rest in between. It was all she could do to focus on her breathing and continue to pray that this child would wait before entering the world.

Those thoughts all fell away as once again her body was flooded with pain.

She placed both of her hands on her belly, took another breath, forced back the panic, and whispered another prayer.

The contraction subsided, and she glanced to her left.

Mose was gone. He must have stepped out into the storm. The buggy wasn't moving.

Why?

Then she remembered—the snowdrift and the sudden stop.

His promise to dig out the horse.

If there was a way through this storm, Mose would find it.

If not, they'd have the baby here, in the buggy. It wasn't the welcome she'd envisioned for her change-of-life baby, but then often their lives did not follow the path she envisioned.

Like most people, their married life had taken twists and turns she would never have imagined when she was a young woman about to wed.

Another contraction came, consuming her attention with her energy. When it passed, she willed her body to relax, huddled beneath the blanket, and trusted that Mose would be safe as he continued to dig a path around the gelding. Etta could see him now, occasionally, as he passed in front of the light from the lantern. He was a shadow, moving back and forth, side to side, through the blizzard.

She fought to keep her eyes open for a minute, then two, and finally, she relented.

As she rested, her mind traveled back and landed on the day she'd first shared their news . . .

CHAPTER TWO

MID-OCTOBER

FOUR MONTHS EARLIER

Etta adjusted her apron, which was pulling tightly in every place it shouldn't. She would need to do something about that, but she hadn't felt up to tackling any extra sewing projects. Until the last few weeks, she'd struggled to rise from bed in time to feed Mose and the children.

This week had been better. Finally, she felt like her old self, or her younger self. It had been so many years that she'd forgotten the surge of energy she often experienced at the midpoint of a pregnancy. It wouldn't last, but she was determined to take full advantage of it.

She'd risen from bed before Mose and had been in the kitchen warming *kaffi* when he came down. He greeted her with a smile and soft kiss before trudging out to the barn to attend to the morning chores. He'd returned in time to eat breakfast with the children.

Only their girls remained at home. Their two oldest boys had farms of their own—Ben in Middlebury and Christopher, a little closer to Shipshewana proper. Two years earlier their youngest son, David, left the community.

With only the girls, the meal had passed in relative peace. Martha had described the new fabric she would be placing on the store shelves at Lolly's. Beth had told them that business at the pretzel booth was slow, so she planned to stop by the library before her shift and pick up another book. Only Charity had complained, declaring that school was boring and she would be glad to be free of it. All three of her girls were healthy, beautiful, good Amish girls. If one of them was in her *rumspringa*, Etta couldn't tell it. Not that every parent realized when their child entered that time of rebellion. For some teens, it consisted of small, quiet decisions—like choosing to own a phone or going to see *Englisch* movies.

Etta felt the absence of David most keenly in the morning, as he'd always been her bright-eyed and bushy-tailed child, eager to launch himself into the coming day. His seat remained empty at the table. Some families put place settings at each meal to remember the one who had left, but Etta didn't need a plate and silverware to remind her of David's absence. It weighed on her heart each day, and each day she prayed that he would return home. She held tightly to the promise that God would watch over each of her children and that one day David would return.

Once her family had scattered to their various tasks, the house had filled with a silence she'd grown used to. She'd spent the morning cleaning, paused for lunch with Mose, and was now beginning her dinner preparations. For a moment she stood at the kitchen window looking toward the field, hoping to catch a glimpse of Mose. Though many Amish men now worked in factories or businesses, Etta liked having Mose near the house all day. She spotted him at the far side of the field, attending to their large work horses—Abby, Babe, and Chex. All three were black. Abby and Babe were Belgians and Chex was their sole Percheron. Abby and Babe had a single white spot between their ears, stretching down to their eyes. Chex had smaller white patches from the tips of his ears to his nose.

Mose handled the three horses as if they were no more trouble than the neighbor's dogs. In truth, the horses stood over seventeen hands high and weighed nearly two thousand pounds each. They had already harvested the larger soybean crop. Christopher and Ben had come to help with that two weeks ago. Today Mose was beginning to harvest the corn. He would work the field alone as long as the weather remained clear, which it seemed it would.

He'd grimly told her that morning that the harvest was not going to bring in the income they needed. Etta didn't need Mose to point that out to her. She'd been watching the fields for months and realized that the growth had been stunted by a longer than usual winter and rains at the worst of times. They'd make ends meet somehow. They always did. God always provided, though sometimes not as much as they might wish for.

If Etta looked closely, she could make out Pal, their chocolate lab, sitting at the edge of the field, eyes trained on Mose. The dog was exceedingly loyal and wouldn't even consider coming back to the house until Mose did. The afternoon sun splashed through the window, and she stood there for a moment, enjoying the warmth of the October rays against her skin.

When she heard footsteps on the front porch, she knew it would be Rachel, her neighbor, come to share some tidbit of news.

"Come in," she hollered out as she set about mixing together the ingredients for the beef and barley soup they would have for dinner.

She had already chopped the carrots and onion, measured the barley, thyme, and oregano. The spinach leaves lay in a colander in the sink. With a twist of the wrist, she opened the jar of stewed tomatoes—one of the last ones from the previous year's harvest. The girls had recently helped her pull this year's vegetables from the garden. Last week had been spent canning and moving the previous year's bounty to the front of the shelves. Her containers of garlic powder, black pepper, and salt sat beside the stove. The ground beef sizzled in the pan.

Less than two weeks ago, she'd been unable to abide the odor of cooking meat of any kind. Afternoons often found her fleeing to the bathroom. Fortunately her oldest daughter, Martha, had stepped in and helped without asking any questions.

"I have a new letter from Silas and Samuel—" Rachel stopped in the doorway to the kitchen, her fingers on her lips, the letter clutched in her left hand.

Rachel was the same height as Etta, but that was the only physical trait they shared.

Though Etta had gained a solid thirty pounds over the last twenty years, Rachel had somehow managed to keep her girlish figure, even after bearing five children, all of whom were now grown and moved onto farms of their own.

Etta's hair was as brown as Pal's coat. Rachel's remained blond even as gray cropped up here and there. Eight years separated them, with Rachel being the older. She'd turned fifty the previous summer.

No one would mistake them for sisters, but after twenty-four years of living side by side, they had become the best of friends.

"Oh my."

"What's wrong?" Etta asked, her eyebrows arching as she continued to stir the meat. Rachel was staring openly at Etta's stomach. Etta turned the burner off and pushed the pan toward the back of the stove. Then she moved to the sink and washed her hands, taking extra care so she would have a few moments to think of how she wanted to handle this. If she chose to ignore the subject, Rachel would let it drop. But truthfully, she was ready to talk with someone.

She turned and smiled at Rachel. "Perhaps we should have some *kaffi*." She placed a lid over the pan of hamburger meat.

"*Kaffi* and a sticky bun?"

"I haven't been able to abide the sweetness of it, but *ya*—there are several left over and you're welcome to one."

Etta enjoyed the simple task of filling the mugs with the coffee she'd kept hot on the stove and pulling out the milk and sugar while Rachel found the sticky bun and placed it on a saucer. The everyday jobs had brought a sense of joy to her in the last few weeks. It seemed as if everything was new and special—even the chipped mugs for their drinks and the old pitcher that held their fresh milk.

When they settled at the table, Rachel dug into the sticky bun and followed it with a gulp of *kaffi*.

Etta smiled. "I suppose you want to talk about our newest blessing."

"You're with child." It was a statement rather than a question. Rachel wrinkled her nose, accentuating the age lines around her eyes, and took another bite of the sweet roll. Finally, she pushed the plate away. "How did I miss it? You must be—"

"I'm not sure how far along I am. My monthly cycle has been so irregular the last few years."

"Have you felt the *boppli* move?"

"*Ya*. Kicking already. That started a few weeks ago."

"So you're probably five months, maybe six."

"Six, I believe." Etta turned the coffee mug in her hands. She enjoyed the feel of the hot mug against her skin. She'd been limiting her caffeine consumption of late, but that didn't stop her from pouring the occasional cup. Usually she ended up tossing her mugful out onto the roses in the garden.

Rachel shook her head. "In July, when we thought you had a stomach bug—"

"Morning sickness."

"Then in August I was certain you'd somehow caught an early case of the flu."

"I wasn't sure myself at the time. I kept thinking that it couldn't be. I am forty-two."

"Not too old—"

"Apparently not."

"But old enough." Rachel sank back against her chair. "I'm happy for you, Etta. You and Mose are blessed. This is a gift from *Gotte*."

"So Mose said the other night, and I believe him."

"But?"

"But that doesn't stop all the questions I have."

"You know about birthing, Etta. After six children you could probably have this one by yourself, not that I'm suggesting a home birth."

Etta allowed her gaze to travel across the kitchen to the sitting room and out the front windows. The maple tree was dropping red, yellow, and brown leaves around the old wooden swing hanging from its lowest branch. "Mose hung that swing over twenty years ago. Now Noah runs to it as soon as his feet hit the ground."

"He's a sweet grandson."

"*Ya.* That's my point. I'm going to have a child younger than my first grandson?"

"*Gotte's wille . . .*"

"I suppose."

Rachel sipped her *kaffi* and studied her friend. "It's not the age of the children that is bothering you."

"No. It's my age. Will I be able to keep up? I remember clearly enough the long nights when a *boppli* has the colic, trying to ease the misery of teething—"

"You would often come over and help me when the twins went through such spells."

"Two of mine didn't sleep through the night until they were six months old."

"Christopher and David. I remember."

Etta smiled. It seemed as if the two families were one, as if their lives had been entwined as they shared births, deaths, good crops and bad, winter storms and summer droughts. Rachel's twins now lived in Montana. "Any word from David?"

It was one of the things Etta appreciated most about her friend and neighbor. They could talk of the things that mattered the most, the things that often remained beneath the surface of everyday life.

"Not since the message he left at the phone shack—"

"Last spring when he was in Pennsylvania. I'm sure he's fine, or he would have called."

Etta didn't argue the point, but she wondered about its truthfulness. If David were hurt, how would he call? If he were homeless, he could receive help from any Amish community, but would he? After all, he'd left to sample life in the *Englisch* world. She didn't think it likely that he would turn to Amish folk should he encounter trouble. If there was one thing she was sure of, it was David's stubbornness.

"Are you worried about the harvest? Ours was less this year, though the hay crop did well."

"Not really." Etta glanced out the window. "We still have a little savings, though Mose is concerned it won't be enough. Every year is difficult on a farm. Somehow it always works out."

Rachel nodded and waited for Etta to continue. When she didn't, Rachel pursed her lips and finally asked, "Are you worried about carrying this baby to term? Forgive me if I'm prying but—"

Etta shrugged.

"Because many of us have miscarried once or even twice . . ."

"But I didn't miscarry Sarah." Tears clouded Etta's eyes, but she pushed the words, the fears, out. "She was perfect in every way, only so small."

Now the tears fell and splashed onto her hand. She would be embarrassed, but this was her closest friend. This was the person who had patiently sat with her afterward and visited every day that Etta's heart refused to heal.

"I remember. *Gotte* had a special plan for little Sarah, and it didn't include this world."

Etta nodded. *Gotte's wille* was something they were taught to believe in, to accept, even to trust from a very young age. And she did. Honestly, she did trust her savior and Lord, but that didn't erase the ache or the fear.

"If my guess is correct, you're nearly as far along now as you were when Sarah was born."

"*Ya*. I think so." Etta swiped at her tears and attempted a smile. "Another month and perhaps that worry will fade."

"It can fade now." Rachel reached across and grasped her hand. "I will keep you and your *boppli* in my prayers. There's no reason for you to be afraid."

They sat that way for a moment until the cat scratched at the back door. "The girls taught him to do that." Etta stood, found the leftover milk from Martha's breakfast, and set it outside. They'd kept a chipped bowl for the small tabby and regularly left little pieces of their meal for it.

"Tell me about the twins now. If I'm not mistaken, you were clutching a letter when you walked in."

Rachel's twins had joined a different community in Montana. They were both married, had children of their own, and visited each winter. They wrote to their mother at least once a month, a rambling letter that usually included notes from each member of both families.

How had the years swept by so quickly? Etta could clearly remember Silas and Samuel cutting across their fields, heading home in the twilight after they'd been out fishing or swimming. The water had plastered their hair to their heads. In her memory, the boys' laughter rang out as Etta's girls had called out to them.

But it was clear Rachel wasn't ready to talk about her twins. She was still focused on the subject of the new baby.

"We will help you, Etta. You won't be going through this alone. Perhaps I could let some of your dresses out for you. I imagine you don't have much energy left for sewing in the evenings."

"Let them out? That worked when we were in our twenties, but I'm afraid I'm going to need entirely new dresses before this child arrives."

"Then we best go to town and purchase some fabric."

Instead of answering, Etta stood and resumed putting together the beef and barley soup. Rachel read the letter she'd received from the twins—full of information about their harvest, children, and a recent trip fishing for trout in the Bighorn River.

After they'd fully discussed every aspect of the letter, Rachel stood and rinsed out her *kaffi* cup. "I should head back home. Let me know when you want to go to town for that fabric. We'll go together and then follow it up with a sew-in."

"*Danki.*" Etta linked her arm through Rachel's and they walked to the front porch.

"When will you go to see Doc Bennett?"

"I'm not sure."

"Don't put it off." Rachel enfolded her in a hug.

"I wanted to be sure . . ."

"And now you are, so you should go. You know with women our age, they watch for things."

"I've heard . . ." Etta crossed her arms tightly, as if she were suddenly cold, though the day was a fine fall one and the breeze was from the south. "I've heard . . . you know . . . that they will want to do special testing, because of . . . that is, due to my age."

"Not Doc Bennett. He might suggest it, but he won't insist. He understands our ways."

Etta shrugged. She wasn't so sure. She was surprised Doc still delivered babies. He had to be in his sixties. Most *Englischers* retired by that age—most Amish did too, passing the bulk of work on the farm over to a son.

"They'll watch your blood pressure and sugar levels more closely. That's what I was referring to."

"I suppose."

"We'll go together, then stop by Lolly's to purchase some fabric."

Etta realized there was no use arguing with Rachel. Her friend would keep after her until she agreed, and honestly, she knew that it was time to see the doctor. It wasn't that she didn't believe in prenatal care. It was more that she'd been waiting, to be sure about her pregnancy.

Rachel hadn't moved and wasn't about to give up, so Etta pulled in a deep breath and smiled. "I'll send one of the children to the phone shack this afternoon. They can call Doc's office and make me an appointment."

"Then send them over to let me know the day and time."

Etta nodded. Leave it to Rachel to turn a doctor's visit into an excursion into town. But despite her reservations, Etta found herself humming as she added the ingredients to the soup pot— mixing in the stewed tomatoes, fresh carrots, onion, barley, and bouillon granules. The day before she'd pulled thyme and oregano from the garden. She tossed it in the pot as well, along with a pinch of garlic powder, pepper, and salt.

It had helped to speak to someone of their little miracle. To think . . . another child after all these years.

She remembered the Scripture about Abraham and Sarah. Their bishop had spoken on it a few weeks ago, and Etta understood completely why they'd chosen to call the child Isaac, which meant laughter. Best to laugh with life when unexpected blessings came along.

The swollen ankles, indigestion, and birthing would be no laughing matter. But *Gotte's* timing? Well, it was perfect, that she knew. Even when it was something that she could not understand.

CHAPTER THREE

Mose worked in the snow, long past when his fingers and toes had gone numb. The wind had settled, and that was a blessing for sure and for certain. The snow? It continued to fall, covering the landscape around them, even covering the top of the buggy until it looked like something in an *Englisch* snow globe.

He shoveled with the energy of a man much younger than forty-five. It was an energy born of desperation. In truth, the years had taken their toll. His body resisted the labor, muscles and joints screaming against the assault of the cold and the weight of the snow.

It seemed to him like only yesterday that he'd been able to lift the feed sacks for the cattle without breaking a sweat. He had tossed them from the buggy into the barn. He was a different person then.

Now his back ached as he shoveled the snow. The arthritis in his hands begged him to stop, but he thought of Etta—Etta in the buggy about to birth their next child. He thought of her and some of the aches and pain fell away, or perhaps he was becoming too frozen to notice such things.

It wasn't his discomfort that worried him, though. It wasn't the cold that caused him to stop and peer into the darkness. No, it was his concern for Etta. He would prefer she be in Doc's birthing center, not a buggy, when she birthed their child.

And what about tomorrow or next week or next month? Would he have a home for his family to live in? He'd spoken to Etta of their financial situation. She'd patted his hand and said, "*Gotte* will provide a way, Mose."

Maybe.

Or perhaps God's way was for them to move on to a new place. Perhaps He was refining them, allowing them to be tried and tested.

The horse tossed his head, eyes rolling.

"Easy, boy. Easy, now."

How long had he been shoveling? Ten minutes? Twenty? Morgan had walked into the drift, and he could walk out, but not with the weight of the buggy behind him. The buggy would have to be unhitched and pushed backward. He wasn't making enough headway against the snow that piled up on one side even as he shoveled it away from the other.

The snow was falling heavy and fast.

He was making little progress.

He was making no progress.

Reassuring the horse one last time, he turned and trudged back to the buggy. He attempted to slide his door open, but the ice had formed a seal around it. Placing a foot against the side of the buggy, he pulled, and when that didn't work, he faced the opposite direction and pushed. The door didn't budge. His hands were too cold, even wearing the gloves.

So he knocked against the side of the buggy, hoping Etta would hear, but there was no answer. Perhaps she was resting between the pains. Standing next to the buggy as snow continued to fall soundlessly, relentlessly, he waved his arms, slapping them against his body, hoping to restore some feeling to his hands. Turning back to the buggy, he raised the shovel and tapped it against the edge of the door, breaking the ice. This time when he pushed the door, he managed to break the seal.

He jumped inside and pulled the door shut. The inside of the buggy was nearly as cold as outside, but at least no snow was falling on him. They had a propane heater, but he was hesitant to use it. If they were stranded here, they would need what warmth the heater could provide to survive the evening. Fortunately, they did have plenty of blankets. Also, he'd left the battery-operated lantern on, placing it on top of the buggy near the front, its light casting a dim glow around his horse. There was always the chance that someone would see their light and notice they were no longer moving.

Etta had been sleeping, and she didn't stir from his banging on the door or jumping in the buggy. He pulled the blankets more tightly around her, and as he did, he thought of their children—fine men and women, all six of them. Even David, who had felt the need to leave, made him proud. David was a good boy, and he would find his way. It wasn't a matter of *if*, in Mose's mind, but *when*. He supposed that for David, life seemed much like the snowstorm outside the buggy, obscuring his path and confusing his mind.

Mose held firmly to the promise that God would watch over his children, all of his children. His heart ached over the empty seat at his table, but he wouldn't give up on the boy. One day he would return. Mose looked forward to that day as much as he looked forward to this one, which surely would see the birth of their babe.

Each of his children, even this one yet to be born, was a precious gift from the Lord.

He'd sat there for several moments before Etta startled awake. He understood too well why she sat up suddenly, her eyes darting left and right until they finally landed on him and her hands grasping her belly.

"It's okay. Breathe through the pain." He tossed off his gloves and enfolded her hands in his.

Etta nodded, sweat dampening her brow, and clutched his hand. They counted together in German, *"Eins, zwei, drei, vier . . ."* The old language settled around them, calming them, reassuring them. Babies had been born in storms before. Theirs wouldn't be the first or the last.

He knew when the contraction stopped because she smiled at him weakly.

"A bad one?"

"Nein. Not so bad."

He didn't press her, though he knew the truth was somewhat different. She was trying to reassure him, and that was a good sign. The memories of Sarah's birth were never far away. That time Etta had delivered at home, as she had with all the other children. Doc Bennett had assured them that even a hospital birth would not have saved the tiny baby.

Mose would never forget how Sarah had fit into the palm of his hand, how precious and perfect she was. Though they'd had so little time with her, his life had been touched by that trial. He'd learned to appreciate each moment, every sunrise and sunset, and each of his children—even when they were difficult and hard to understand.

"How's Morgan?"

"Unhappy and wishing to be in his barn."

"The storm?"

"Is worsening. I tried digging us out, but the snow falls faster than I can shovel."

Etta closed her eyes, gathering her energy for the next contraction. "This child will be our eighth *boppli*, Mose, and not one of them has been born in a buggy."

"I pray this one will not be either, but if it is *Gotte's wille* . . ."

Etta didn't answer. Instead, she began panting again and counting. How long had it been since the last contraction? Seven minutes or eight? He couldn't be sure, but he did know the pains were closer together than when they'd left the house. And they were more intense. No doubt about it. This child would be born soon.

He waited until she once again relaxed against him. Pulling the blanket up to her neck, he whispered, "Perhaps I should walk."

"In the storm?"

"*Ya.* I believe we're between the Gingerichs' and the Yoders' places."

"Not so far from the birthing center."

"Another couple of miles."

"Which might as well be a hundred in this weather." Etta leaned forward, peering out into the light of the lantern. "We're going to lose Morgan if we don't get him out of this storm. He's been a *gut* horse."

"Don't be worrying about the gelding, Etta. The temperature hasn't dipped below twenty, and although the snow is falling fast, there's little wind with it." He wrapped his arms around her, hoping to transfer the heat from his body to hers. "Morgan is a strong horse and a hearty breed. It will take more than a February blizzard to best him. Focus your prayers on the child."

"I don't want you to leave me."

"Then I'll stay."

But twenty minutes later he knew that he couldn't stay. The snow fell as heavily as when they'd first stopped, and Etta's pains were holding steady—perhaps growing even closer together.

He waited until her contraction eased, then he turned on the propane heater. If he had to leave his wife, he would not leave her with only blankets to ward off the cold.

"You're going," she whispered.

"*Ya*. Rest as much as you can. Don't spend your energy worrying." He gently kissed her forehead. "Persuade our *dochder* to wait for her *dat*."

"Still convinced it's a girl?"

"I am."

"I'd be more likely to believe we're about to have a boy, given how much trouble he's giving us already."

It was good that she could tease. He held on to that and told himself it meant she would be fine. "I'll be back soon."

He grabbed the horse blanket from the backseat. Before he could change his mind, he threw his shoulder against the door, pushing it open once more. He adjusted the wool scarf around his face, then walked to the front of the buggy.

Morgan was now standing silently, head down, conserving his energy to endure the storm. Mose spent another minute—another precious minute—reassuring the horse, speaking quietly and calmly as he brushed the snow off the horse's back and covered him with the blanket. He wished he had hay to give the Percheron, but he hadn't brought any, knowing they had a barn and feed at the birthing center.

He also would have preferred to guide the horse to the trees where he would have some protection against the storm, but that was impossible as well. A blanket and reassuring word was the best he could do. With the promise of extra feed once they reached the center, he squared his shoulders and turned south. If he was correct about their location, the Gingerich farm was closest.

Chapter Four

Etta did not fall asleep between contractions.

Instead, she forced herself to remain vigilant.

There was little she could do to help Mose or the horse, but she could pray. She could be ready for whatever happened next. She could use this time to count their many blessings and anticipate what God had in store. She refused to entertain, even for a moment, that this would be the night she would be called to her heavenly home.

As for losing the child, she'd experienced that once before, but she did not believe it would happen again. Sarah had barely begun kicking when she'd been born. This child had been kicking, turning, and even hiccupping for months. This child was strong and ready to greet the world.

Together, they would endure the night.

As she stared out at the storm, she concentrated on those things. She prayed for her husband's safety and for the well-being of their horse. She prayed for the child soon to be born, and the nurses at the birthing center. She prayed for Doc Bennett. Finally, she prayed that she would have the strength necessary to wait and then to see her babe safely into this world.

Her mind wanted to slide back over the last several months. To when she'd first told Mose, to the children's responses, even to her parents' letters. She wanted to sink into those memories and enjoy the warmth of them, but she was afraid to allow herself that luxury. Better to sit up, to press her forehead against the cold of the buggy wall, to force her eyes open wide.

It was impossible to prepare herself physically while confined to the buggy. At home, she might have paced to quicken the labor. In the buggy, she could barely straighten out enough to ease the pain in her back, so instead she spoke to her child.

She whispered words of assurance.

She described Mose to the babe in her womb—told her of this good, strong man who was battling the storm for the two of them.

She explained what would happen when he returned and they reached the birthing center.

Etta didn't feel at all silly speaking to her stomach, to her child, petitioning her to "wait, a little longer, wait." Something about the fact that they were alone assured her that the child could hear and understand.

As she spoke, her blood pressure lowered, she was certain of it. The contractions remained strong, but no closer together.

Which prompted her to count her blessings. She praised God that her child was waiting, that the contractions remained strong but a good five minutes apart. She thanked God for her husband, who had cared for her these many years. She praised God for her time with Sarah. She remembered that she had six children—nearly all grown—the two oldest boys snug in their own homes and the girls safe and warm back in their house. She prayed that David was also sheltered. Perhaps he was down in Pinecraft, Florida, where many Amish fled during cold spells for a brief vacation. He'd mentioned he planned to catch a ride south in his last phone message. That had been nearly a year ago. He hadn't said why he was going or how long he intended to stay.

Instead of worrying, she forced her mind to focus on their blessings. David had mentioned attending an area church. He still checked in with them occasionally. He sounded as if he was doing well.

Most Amish stayed within the community once they became adults, but when the occasional boy or girl left, the parents didn't always receive communication. Sometimes years could go by with no word. While her hands rested on top of her stomach, comforting the child, she thanked God that they had heard from David, even if it was sporadically.

She also spoke to God of their neighbors, who had always helped, who were bringing Mose back to her even now. She was sure of that.

And so she began to anticipate. She wanted to step outside and reassure Morgan but knew it would be dangerous to leave the shelter of the buggy. Instead, she envisioned what would happen next—Mose arriving, the buggy being pulled free, the lights of the birthing center. Had it been only a few months ago that she had dreaded going there? That she had argued for a home birth? But Doc had explained to her the dangers because of her age, because of her blood pressure.

Instead of focusing on those risks, she once again thanked God for Doc Bennett—for his knowledge and wisdom.

And then she heard the sound of a motor.

Mose didn't have to knock the buggy door free from ice this time. Etta was stretched across the seat, pushing it open even as he hurried through the snow toward her.

"I'll unhitch the horse," Jonas Gingerich called out.

Tom Ramsey backed up to the rear of the buggy and began attaching the towing chain.

Both men were approximately the same age as Mose, though one was Amish and the other *Englisch*. Tonight it would take all three of them to set the buggy free.

"Are you all right?" Mose jumped into the buggy and slid the door shut, hoping to keep out the cold.

"*Ya*. Tom brought his Jeep?"

"He did. We'll pull the buggy out first, then Jonas will back Morgan out."

Etta closed her eyes in relief. Mose squeezed her hand, then hopped out and walked to the front near the hitch.

"Ready here," Jonas said. "I'll calm the horse. Tom can pull anytime."

Morgan was used to the sound of *Englisch* vehicles. He'd been a buggy horse for many years, pulling through the streets of Shipshewana and the surrounding countryside. If the sound of the Jeep's motor agitated him, he didn't show it.

Mose trudged to the back of the buggy and gave Tom the thumbs-up sign.

The buggy wasn't designed to be pulled backward, but it was the best way out of the snowdrift. On the first try, the wheels of the Jeep spun in the snow, and the buggy remained entrenched.

Mose feared he would need to move Etta to the Jeep. Jonas

would have to stay with the horse, and he'd have to ride with Tom. He couldn't imagine carrying Etta over the snow or subjecting her to the bitterness outside the buggy.

He needn't have worried. The Jeep was designed to find traction in the most unlikely of places. Tom changed gears, and the buggy slowly began to move back the way it had come. Though the hitch bounced, then dug into the snow, the jeep had no problem towing it toward the center of the road.

Jonas clucked to the horse, backing it up.

In five minutes, they had the horse once again hitched to the buggy.

"*Danki*," Mose said. He stood with one hand on the door, eager to go and at the same time a little hesitant that they might again become stuck. His friends had been a tremendous help, but he didn't want to ask them to stay in the snow in the middle of the night any longer than necessary, so he said, "We should be fine from here."

"We're already out. Might as well lead you over to the center." Tom blew into his hands. He was a big man, broad shouldered and larger than most Amish at over six feet. He'd worked the land next to Jonas for twenty years, and although he used the *Englisch* tractors, he also had a respect for the land that was akin to the Amish way.

"I agree with Tom," Jonas said. Shorter and rounder, he'd been an elder in their community for as long as Mose could remember. "Naomi won't be happy if I come back home and say I left you on the side of the road. She'd rather have a baby report."

So it was settled.

Tom and Jonas rode in the jeep, its headlights cutting a path through the snow that continued to fall.

The birthing center was located three miles south of town off State Road 5, and within twenty minutes, they could see the lights of the parking area. The single-story building was one of the most welcome sites Mose had seen in a long time. Had they left home mere hours ago? It seemed days to Mose.

The center had been open only a few years. Until that time, most of the local Amish birthed their children at home. He'd recently read in the *Budget* that only ten percent did so now, which seemed like a tragedy to him. He well remembered the cries of their newborns coming from the bedroom, and the tender moment when his sons and daughters were allowed to greet their new sibling.

But it was difficult on Doc and on the midwives. The birthing center had been a good compromise, and a better solution for them than driving to the hospitals in LaGrange or Goshen like a fair amount of Amish did. He realized Doc's center was known to the locals as the "stop and drop" because the Amish tended to wait until the last minute to check in for a delivery. No doubt, they would provide another story for Doc Bennett to shake his head about, but the man was a good doctor. Mose would happily endure the teasing since it meant his wife and child would be in capable hands.

When they pulled into the parking lot, he and Etta both peered out the front window of the buggy. The air practically vibrated with the *whop, whop, whop* of a helicopter landing on the far side of the parking area. The birth must be a real emergency for the father to have called in a helicopter, though the complication couldn't have been too severe or they would have flown them straight to the hospital in LaGrange.

"I'm not surprised another child is insisting on greeting the world this evening." Etta folded the blanket that had covered her the last few hours.

Mose pulled the buggy under the awning. "Three of ours have been born during snowstorms."

"*Mamm* would say it is nature's way, that when the storms come—whatever the season—the babes understand it as *Gotte's* way of sending them into the world."

"A heavenly celebration, though I'd prefer a clear, starry night myself."

As they watched, Doc Bennett helped unload the mother from the helicopter. Another nurse had grabbed a wheelchair and was pushing it toward their buggy.

"Can you tell us who it is?" Etta asked the nurse when she had opened the door and carefully stepped down.

"It's Mary Weaver. She needed an emergency rescue because her water broke three weeks early." The nurse smiled at Etta and patted her hand as she helped her into a wheelchair. "No worries. Doc can handle more than two babies at a time. I've seen him juggle up to four deliveries all occurring within the same hour. He said it was like catching baseballs, and if it kept up, he was going to order a catcher's mitt."

Mose had always been a baseball fan. He enjoyed watching the games some of the members would play after Sunday services when he was full from the meal and the children were dashing around, brimming with energy. He'd once enjoyed playing, though those days were behind him. Yes, he liked baseball, but he certainly hoped it wouldn't come to using a baseball mitt to catch his child.

Thinking back on that younger self, he seemed like a different person, though he knew he was the same. He still had the scar on his left hand from the fishing hook, the pain in his hip on cold nights from jumping out of the hayloft when he was ten, and he still sometimes grew impatient when he knew, he was absolutely certain, that it was best to wait on the Lord.

For some reason, an old saying came to mind that his mother was fond of. "In youth we learn, in age we understand." He almost laughed out loud. He had certainly learned much, but he was doubtful that he understood. He'd simply learned he might not understand, and not to let that hinder his path.

He didn't spend too much time struggling over questions like why the horses fell ill when he needed them most, or why a child chose a different path, or why a babe insisted on being born during a blizzard. He simply worked hard and prayed their way through such times.

As the nurse hurried them into the building, he saw Tom and Jonas parking the Jeep. It was now well past midnight, and the snow that had begun in the early afternoon continued to fall, covering the cars, the sidewalk, and the landscaping. It seemed this child—most certainly his last child—would greet the world on a snowy, wintery night.

CHAPTER FIVE

The nurse's chatter put Etta at ease. That and the fact that she had met the woman when she'd done her prenatal visit. Her name was Linda or Laura. She peeked backward and saw the letters *Lau* . . . Laura then.

As soon as Etta had mentioned to Doc Bennett that she'd rather have a home delivery, he'd insisted she visit the center. "You'll like it, Etta. It's very Amish-friendly." His eyes had twinkled as he'd picked up his phone and dialed the center, telling them that Etta would be over in a few minutes and to give her the grand tour.

Now, as they entered the birthing center, Etta was glad she had visited earlier. At least the rooms and people looked familiar. The blast of warm air was like a welcome caress. She had nearly forgotten that the next day was Valentine's Day. Area school children had made strings of red-and-pink paper hearts, which now decorated the nurses' station.

"Let's get you into a room," Laura said. "Our only patients are you and Mary, so you can choose whether you'd rather have electric lights or gas."

"Makes no difference," Mose muttered. He ran his fingers through his beard as he glanced around.

Priscilla, the area midwife, stopped to check on her as they were moving down the hall. "You made it through the storm!"

"*Ya*, we were stuck for awhile, but Mose walked for help."

"Then you both must be frozen. I'll have one of the aides bring you some coffee."

"I need to tend to the horse, but I don't want to miss . . . anything." Mose had taken off his hat and was twirling it in his hands.

"How far apart are your pains, Etta?"

"Five minutes, I think."

"Holding steady or growing closer?"

"Steady."

"You should be fine to go, Mose. If things change suddenly, I'll send an aide to fetch you." Priscilla had delivered all of their children at their home, and they were both very comfortable with the Mennonite woman. She'd become a fixture in their town, rather like the Blue Gate and Lolly's and Yoder's. She'd become a bridge between the Amish and *Englisch* world.

"Laura will help Etta change into a clean gown, and then we'll check her. By the time you're finished with the horse, she'll be ready for you to come in."

"*Gut.* I'll hurry." Mose turned and fled through the front door, nearly colliding with Tom and Jonas. The three men disappeared into the wintry wonderland.

Priscilla patted her hand and hurried down the hall.

Laura pushed the chair into room three. Decorated in a clean and plain fashion, with off-white paint and a blind on the window, the room reminded Etta of home. No fancy pictures on the wall. No curtains on the window. No television blaring in the corner of the room. There was even a handmade quilt on the bed, done in a simple log-cabin pattern. Etta had asked about the quilts when she was visiting. The aide who had shown her around assured her that the quilts were removed during the actual birth, then put back on the bed for the rest of the mother's visit.

"I feel silly in this chair. I'm perfectly capable of walking."

"Yes, but we wouldn't want you to have slipped on the snow outside." Laura set the brakes on the wheelchair and pointed out the freshly laundered gown hanging on a hook on the wall. "You have your own bathroom, and there's a microwave and small refrigerator to heat and store any food you might have brought."

"I brought soup for myself—for after the babe is born. For Mose I brought some leftover chicken casserole. He's bound to be hungry after trying to dig the horse and buggy out of the snow."

"They were stuck good, huh?" Laura took the bag of goodies and placed the containers in the refrigerator.

"I thought I was going to have this *boppli* in a buggy."

"Well, we're glad that you're here." Laura turned and smiled at her. "If you'll change into the gown on the hook, I'll come back in and help you settle into the bed. Then we can tell Doc you're ready to be checked."

Etta nodded.

But when Laura left the room, she remained still—sitting in the wheelchair and surveying the room. It was different from when she'd visited. Now she was actually staying here. Her child would be born here.

As she stood and reached for the gown, her mind flowed back

to the day a few months ago when she had gone to see Doc Bennett, after Rachel had insisted that it was time.

⋎

Etta sat in the examining room. She'd donned the cotton gown as instructed. Though she was uncomfortable doing so, she reminded herself to be grateful she was seeing Doc Bennett. He understood their ways, having worked in their community since the beginning of his career—for well over twenty years now. He accepted that his Amish patients were very private people, and though they would see a doctor, they preferred to retain as much of their modesty as possible.

She smoothed out the sheet over her lap and tried not to tense up when there was a knock at the door and Doc entered. She'd seen him around town the last few years—in the Blue Gate restaurant, at Yoder's department store, even driving down the road. However, she hadn't been in his office since she'd come in two years ago to ask about the changes in her body, the changes that were due to her going through menopause.

Of course, she knew what to expect. She'd written her mother who lived back in Pennsylvania, and she'd spoken to Rachel as well. No, her concern hadn't blossomed until she'd found the small lump in her left breast. After talking it over with Mose, she'd immediately made an appointment with Doc Bennett. They'd done a test—a mammogram, which showed the lump was not a problem, merely a calcium deposit. At the time, they'd also discussed her menopausal symptoms—everything from hot flashes to fatigue to her recently acquired short temper. Doc had helped her see that these things were normal and would pass with time.

Now she was back in his office, but for a far different reason.

Doc's hair had more gray in it than she remembered. He was tall and still gangly. They all agreed he needed to eat more, or maybe work less. They'd been telling him as much for years, but Doc always nodded as if he agreed, then went on about his former habits. He reminded her of Amish men in that way.

Since his wife had passed, if anything, Doc was working more hours. Or so she had heard.

Today he wore wire-frame glasses, and behind the frames Etta noticed more wrinkles fanning out from his eyes. The thing that had always surprised her about Doc were his hands—big hands, farmer's hands. He'd told her once that God gave him big hands not to till the earth but to catch the babies.

"*Gut* morning, Etta!" Doc feigned an Amish accent for the amusement of his patients. "This is a *wunderbaar* day, yes?"

Etta didn't respond. So many thoughts were flying through her head at the same time that she found voicing any of them too difficult.

Doc washed his hands, thoroughly, slowly, and then he sat down on his stool, studying her file. When he glanced up a smile covered his face.

"According to our test, you're expecting another *boppli*, Etta. Congratulations."

Embarrassed by the tears that suddenly blurred her vision, Etta closed her eyes. She waited for several heartbeats, allowing Doc's words to seep into her heart, answering so many of her questions. Yes, she had known. The baby was already kicking! But to hear Doc confirm the fact, well, it sent a river of joy through her heart. When she opened her eyes, he was studying her and patiently waiting.

"I was afraid I might be going a little *narrisch*."

"Is that so?"

"I recognized all the . . . signs, but I thought it couldn't be."

"Because?"

"Because of my age! Have you forgotten? I turned forty-two recently."

Doc cleared his throat as if to argue with her, but then he motioned for her to continue. So she described her symptoms, and he assured her they were all normal. Some of them hadn't felt normal. She'd never napped when she was pregnant before, and she was embarrassed that she'd done so fairly often with this baby.

"Seems lazy," she admitted to him.

"It isn't."

"I still can hardly believe we're to have another child."

"Now, Etta. Certainly you know that women can have babies at your age. We even spoke about it when you came in for your last checkup."

"*Ya*, I remember, and I know it's possible—for other women."

"Any reason that it shouldn't include you?"

"*Nein*. Only that it's been so long."

"How old is Charity now?" He moved the stool toward her when the nurse walked in and indicated that she should lie back.

"Twelve."

"Seems like yesterday . . ." Doc commented about each of her children as he examined her. Though Priscilla had delivered them all, he had checked on her twice during each pregnancy. It was interesting how Doc and Priscilla worked hand in hand. Still, she was surprised that he would remember their names—even details about their births.

"All done," he said, and the nurse patted Etta's hand as if she needed the extra emotional support, helping her sit up in the process.

"I was thirty years old when Charity was born, a young woman then." Etta checked her prayer *kapp* to make sure it was still on straight, then smoothed the sheet out over her lap again. "Now I'm old."

"You're not as old as I am, but then I only help birth the babies." Doc cocked his head, studying her.

She liked that about him, that he took so much time during his visits with patients.

"Then there's the stillbirth, which happened three years after Charity. After that, I thought I wouldn't be . . . wouldn't be able to conceive."

"That's not how it works. We don't know why some pregnancies carry to term and others don't."

"*Gotte's wille*," Etta whispered. That's what she'd told herself and she could even believe it now, but at the time it had felt as if a piece of her heart had been ripped out and trampled by the big horses Mose used to plow the fields.

"Everything looks good, Etta. This pregnancy is progressing just fine, and I expect that soon you will be holding a healthy baby. I don't suppose you could tell me when your last menstrual cycle was—"

"*Nein*. They've been so irregular."

"I thought so. I would like to do an ultrasound so I can determine exactly how far along you are."

Etta shook her head. She understood that some of the younger women did have ultrasounds, and she knew it wasn't painful. Still, it felt so different from the old ways. "This child will be born when it's ready. I don't need a test to tell me what day that will be."

Doc wrote a note on her file, peering at her over his glasses. "There's something else we need to discuss, Etta. Since you are over forty, the chances that your child could have Down's syndrome go up to one out of forty, according to some studies. A simple test—"

"*Nein*."

Again Doc waited.

Etta knew she didn't have to explain. Doc was well acquainted with their ways, but she found herself doing so nonetheless. "I know the risks, and we have special children here in our community. They are not a burden but a blessing."

"I understand and admire the Amish attitude toward this subject, Etta. However, it would help us prepare."

"*Nein.*"

"All right." Doc didn't look perturbed. No doubt he had expected her response. "However, I insist that we watch your blood pressure and insulin levels. This means you must come in once a month and let us follow up with you."

"*Ya.* All right. Though once a month seems a bit much."

"You'd think she didn't like us," Doc said to his nurse.

"I'll make her another appointment." The nurse bustled out of the room.

"Call the birthing center while you're at it. She'll want to go by and see . . ."

"I was hoping that maybe—"

"No, Etta. Your *boppli* will be born in February or March, depending on how far along you are, and I'd guess the end of February. We won't risk a snowbound, in-home birth. Trust me on this one."

"And Priscilla?"

"Works at the center. She's there most nights. Either she or I or both of us will be there for your babe's birth."

Etta nodded, but her stomach flipped. She'd heard that Doc rarely agreed to home births anymore, but she was hoping that she might be the exception.

"I think you'll like the birthing center." Doc stood and pushed the stool back under the countertop. "It's plain and simple."

Etta rolled her eyes at the pun. Plain and simple—that was the Amish way—or so all the tour guides and fiction books claimed. It was true they were often called the Plain folk, along with the Quakers, Hutterites, and Mennonites. It was true they strove to lead a simple life. But in many ways their lives were anything but plain and simple.

Most folks who said that had never attempted to do their laundry with a gas washing machine or struggled to hang wet garments on the line in the middle of winter.

People who called their life plain and simple didn't realize that they worried about bank payments and crops and new babies in the same way every other farmer did.

Plain and simple indeed . . .

Etta paused beside the bed until her contraction passed. They were as strong as before, but no closer together. She ran a hand over the quilt on the bed, glancing again around the room. Several issues of the *Budget* sat on a small table next to a comfortable recliner. Mose would be happy to learn that it made into a bed, as they might have a long night.

Electric lamps glowed warmly, throwing shadows onto the ivory-painted walls. The blind on the large window was partially open, and Etta could see snow still falling, accumulating steadily across the parking lot, street, and field in the distance—though she couldn't see that far into the darkness.

She'd folded her clothes and set them in the small closet, using the time between contractions to stand and walk around the room. It felt good to be up, to be moving, and to be out of the buggy!

She placed her palm against the coolness of the sink and counter. Beneath it was the small refrigerator and microwave. Her husband would no doubt be hungry when he returned. She removed the chicken casserole from the refrigerator and set it in the microwave, though she'd wait to heat it. No use wasting the electricity and having to do it again.

Beside the bed was a handmade cradle. She walked over and rocked it gently. It looked to her to be made of pine, though she was no expert where types of wood were concerned. A tiny, hand-stitched, nine-patch quilt had been placed inside the cradle. The colors were a soft pink, yellow, blue, and green. Soon her child would lie in the bed and be covered by the quilt.

However, as the next contraction seized her, something deep inside told her she had several difficult hours ahead of her and that this time the birthing would be different.

The pain worsened and the heaviness in her lower abdomen increased. She gripped the back of the chair, afraid to move, afraid to sit or lie down.

Where was the nurse?

Where was Mose?

She suddenly remembered all of the warnings about older women and pregnancy. Now wasn't the time to focus on what could go wrong. She needed to remain positive and use all of her energy to bring her last child into the world.

Chapter Six

Mose stopped at the door with the number three on it. He wasn't normally shy, but none of his family had been in a hospital room before. Certainly none of his children had been born in one. He'd visited a few folks from their community over at the LaGrange Hospital. That had been several years ago, and he remembered clearly disliking the antiseptic smell and impersonal feel of the place. The nurses and doctors seemed efficient enough, but always busy, which seemed to translate into rushing from one room to another.

So he hesitated in the hall, unsure what was proper inside a hospital.

Of course, this wasn't a hospital—not exactly.

Hadn't he just walked by and seen one of the nurses dressing Mary Weaver's new infant in a blue gown?

"A little one you have there," he'd commented.

"*Ya*, he's early, but healthy." The nurse had kept her eyes on the baby, swaddling him in a blanket before cradling him in her arms. Her name tag reminded him that she was Laura, the same nurse who had helped Etta to her room when they'd first arrived. "Soon you will be holding your infant. I believe Etta's time is getting close."

The sight of the small infant had stirred a deep place in Mose's heart. His child, possibly his last child, was about to be born. It could be happening at any moment. He had nodded to Laura and hurried on to room number three, where he now stood hesitating like a donkey unsure it wanted to enter a stall. Then he heard Etta cry out, and he opened the door and stepped into the room.

The moment he entered, he knew something was wrong.

He'd been present at all of his children's births. He'd also been at Etta's side when Sarah had been born. He'd held his wife's hand as the tears slipped down her face, tears that had chipped away a piece of his heart as much as the stillborn child—less than a pound and so incredibly small. That had been a difficult time for their entire family. He'd worried about his wife, and prayed constantly that she would heal, that she would learn to smile and even laugh again.

Images from that terrible day filled his heart and mind as he rushed to Etta's side. He searched her face and saw an expression of such panic that it sent a jolt of fear through his heart.

Laura had been replaced by the midwife, Priscilla. She glanced up at Mose and didn't even attempt a smile.

"Was iss letz?"

"Etta's pain is worse because her time is near, but there's a problem with the baby's heartbeat. Wash up quickly. Lose that coat too. Then come back to Etta's side, Mose. She needs you right now."

He hurriedly did as Priscilla had directed, feeling clumsy with the soap and paper towels, afraid to look at his reflection in the mirror, afraid of the dread he might see there. His heart was beating so quickly he wondered that no one could hear it. Tossing the towels into the trash bin, he hurried back across the room to where Etta lay on the bed. Her forehead was shiny with sweat and her face was deathly pale. Her eyes had a wild look in them—focusing on nothing, seeing nothing. He realized in that instant the depth and relentlessness and intensity of her pain.

Mose clutched her hand as fear seized his heart. "Etta, I'm here."

She squeezed her eyes shut as another spasm of pain consumed her.

"Is it time?" He didn't understand any of this, but he knew when Doc Bennett walked in that things were not proceeding as they should. The man's face was set in a grim line, and he offered none of his friendly chatter. Instead, he went immediately to the sink and scrubbed his hands, then donned a fresh pair of surgical gloves.

Priscilla had been at the foot of the bed. As soon as Doc walked over, she moved to the side. "Your baby's heartbeat has dropped dramatically. I believe we have a looped cord."

Mose knew what that meant.

A lump lodged in his throat, and he prayed that God would deliver his child. He prayed they would not be made to endure the stillbirth of another babe. He began petitioning God in that moment, for Etta's strength, for the health of their child, and for Doc Bennett. "The Lord is my strength and shield. I trust Him with all my heart."

He didn't realize that he'd uttered the words aloud until Priscilla voiced her approval. "The Psalms are a fitting prayer for a child, Mose. Soon you will be holding your *boppli*, and you can whisper those words directly to her."

Though his heart still beat wildly, his emotions settled.

A looped cord.

He'd birthed many calves and even the occasional foal. More than once he'd had to save an animal when the umbilical cord became wrapped around the newborn's neck. It had required him to be quick and decisive at the moment of birth. He understood what lay ahead of them.

Doc spoke from his place at the end of the bed. "All right. Etta, are you ready?"

"Something's wrong . . ." The words were a moan from deep in her soul. Her eyes were fixed on the display of the heart monitor, which was now flashing red, flashing a number that even Mose realized was dangerously low.

"My baby's heart—"

"Don't worry, Etta. Look at Mose and focus. I want you to push with the next contraction. Are you ready?" One of doc's hands was on top of Etta's stomach, feeling the muscles begin to tighten even before she did. "Now, Etta. Push and keep pushing. You can do this."

Etta clutched Mose's hand, her face white with fear.

"It will be fine, Etta." He prayed the words were true, even as doubt seized his heart.

Doc and Priscilla shared a glance when the monitor began to beep.

"What is wrong?" Etta cried.

"It's the baby's heart, Etta." Doc's voice was now gruff, focused. "Push one more time."

There was a mirror in the corner of the room. It reflected what was happening at the end of the bed, and Mose glanced up in time to see his baby girl slide into Doc's hands. The child was unnaturally pale, unlike his other children—they had been screaming and red, a healthy color. The cord was indeed wrapped around her neck, but Doc slipped it off as if he were tossing away a shawl.

Mose couldn't tear his eyes away from the mirror. He willed her to pink up, prayed with everything in his heart that God would bless them with this child.

The baby's arms began to wave, slowly at first and then with more vigor. As her tiny fists pumped in the air, her color turned first to a light pink and then to a darker rose.

Doc handed the baby to Priscilla, who said, "You have a beautiful girl, Etta. She is doing fine and looks happy to have arrived."

As she spoke, she'd been clearing the mucus out of the baby's mouth. Mose watched as their daughter took her first and then second breath. Suddenly her robust cry filled the room. The glorious sound filled Mose's heart until he thought it might burst.

"She looks and sounds like a healthy baby girl," Doc noted as he continued working on Etta.

"May I hold her?"

"Of course you may. Let's set her on top of your belly while Mose cuts the cord." Priscilla placed a clamp on the cord, close to the baby.

As he'd done with his three sons and three daughters, Mose accepted the scissors, reached forward, and cut the cord between mother and infant.

Etta watched Mose fit his large fingers into the scissor handles. He smiled at her once—his eyes filled with tears of so much love and joy that she thought they might overflow. Then he reached forward and cut the cord that connected her to her daughter. The baby looked perfect in every way—her skin was pink and wrinkled, her hair a chestnut brown, and her cry continued to fill their room.

A moment earlier Etta had been filled with such fear. Her vision had clouded as she imagined all that could go wrong, all that had gone wrong before.

Then Mose had slipped his hand over hers and he'd quoted the Psalms, a verse she had clung to many times. His kind eyes had looked into hers, and she'd known—she'd positively known at that moment—such bottomless love from him that her fear had melted away like snow on a sunny day. Her worries for the new babe, for David, even for their home had fled.

Now it felt as if a hundred butterflies had taken up residence where her child had been. She was consumed with happiness as tears continued to slip down her cheeks. Her hands shook as she reached to hold the child Priscilla placed in the crook of her arm.

"She's perfect," Priscilla assured her.

"*Ya*, that she is." Etta touched her daughter's cheek, rested the palm of her hand on top of her babe's stomach. She was a warm bundle of blessing, and Etta could not imagine being happier than she was in that moment. "Her eyes are shaped like Martha's."

"And she cries like Beth."

Mose ran a finger down the baby's face. "But her nose—it is the same as Sarah's."

Laura walked into the room, all smiles and bustle. "It sounds as if there's a recent arrival for me to clean and dress. Do we have a name for the newest Bontrager?"

Mose ran his fingers through his beard. "We'd thought about Peaches."

"That was for the horse, Mose!"

"*Ya, ya.* That's right."

"Hannah." Etta breathed the word like a prayer. "We decided upon Hannah."

"Merciful and blessed by *Gotte*." Mose ran his thumbs under his suspenders.

"A *gut* strong name for a *gut* strong girl." Laura smiled as she picked up the infant. "I will have her back to you in a few minutes."

Etta might have protested, but she was suddenly aware of Doc speaking to her at the end of the bed. There was still work to do.

"We'll be finished here by the time she's back." Priscilla seemed to read her thoughts.

The next few moments passed quickly. Free of the fear for the health of her child, Etta found the work of delivering the placenta uneventful. Doc finished and was once again scrubbing his hands. Priscilla had changed the bedding and Etta was sitting up crunching on ice chips when Laura returned.

Hannah was clothed in a long light-pink gown that had been hand sewn by one of the women in their community. She was sucking on her fist, and her wide eyes seemed to take in everything around her.

"She's beautiful."

"Like her mother," Mose agreed. "For sure and certain, she does look like you, Etta, and would you look at all that brown hair."

Though four of their babies had been born with no hair at all, Hannah's hair curled around her head, like a soft cap.

Her skin, soft and wrinkled, reminded Etta of the raisins she put into the children's lunches—only they were children no longer and had been making their own lunches for several years. She had spent much of her pregnancy worrying about whether she could physically handle the work of a new child, but now she delighted in the thought of all those days ahead of her, when Hannah would crawl and then walk.

Her first words.

Her first day to school, carrying a lunch that Etta would pack.

The day she would join their church.

Those events stretched out in front of them, like a road that led into the future. Etta could hardly wait, but at the same time she'd learned the importance of enjoying the moment. Even when that moment was a screaming *boppli*.

"Sounds as if she wants her *mamm*." Mose had accepted the child from Laura, but now he placed her next to Etta.

Etta repositioned herself so that Hannah could try her first attempt at nursing.

"I believe I'll go out and tell Jonas and Tom we have a fine, new baby girl."

Laura plumped Etta's pillows, refilled the cup with ice chips, and moved the cradle closer to the bed. Hannah finished nursing, which took only a minute or so—the darling wore out quickly. Then Laura placed the baby girl in the cradle, tucking the small handmade, nine-patch quilt tightly around her.

"You both had a long night. It was hard work, too, and now you should rest."

Etta nodded, but she couldn't quite take her eyes off the tiny miracle sleeping beside her. She turned on her side and stared at Hannah, praying that God would bless and protect her. She longed to allow herself to relax for the first time since her labor had begun, but a nagging worry kept her eyes open. Now that her baby was born, her mind turned to their financial problems. It was a silly thing to dwell on mere moments after her child was born, but the urge to protect this small one was strong.

Would they need to sell the farm?

And if they did, where would they go?

Would Hannah be raised in a new community, one full of strangers?

Her heart ached to think of what might lie ahead, even as she vowed to be strong for Mose and all of their children. Deep within her soul, though, she cried out to God and prayed again for His mercy and grace.

CHAPTER SEVEN

It seemed to Etta that she didn't sleep deeply, as if she was remembering as much as she was dreaming. She was aware of Laura quietly moving around the room, of the gentle suckling noises as Hannah again claimed her fist, of morning sunlight peeking through the blinds.

But her eyes slid shut, almost against her will, and she felt herself drifting back.

Her dreams were filled with memories from the past Christmas morning. It had been a time of quiet reflection, fasting, and shared Bible study. Since the holiday did not fall on a Sunday, there was no church service. Instead, Etta spent the time with Mose and the girls, gathered in their sitting room, the Bible turned to the recounting of Christ's birth. Martha, Beth, and Charity asked their dad questions about the Scripture, especially how it was foretold in Isaiah. Mose did his best to answer them, and Etta realized what a good father he had been to their children—what a good father he would be again.

By early afternoon, their oldest, Ben, had arrived from Middlebury.

Soon after that, another buggy *clip-clopped* down the lane, carrying Christopher, his wife, Jana, and their two-year-old child, Noah.

The only one missing was David. Etta whispered a prayer for his safety, then pushed the worry away. God would care for the son who was gone in the same way He cared for the rest of her children now noisily filling their home.

Her family gathered around the table, and together they prayed. Before they bowed their heads for that silent time, Mose reminded them to be thankful for the birth of God's son, for the meal before them, for the closeness of family, and for David—wherever he might be. Mose didn't specifically mention the child they were expecting, but asked each of them to petition God's blessing on any who might join their family in the coming year. There were several chuckles and after the prayer, a few whispers.

Etta studied Jana. Could her daughter-in-law be pregnant again? Yes, she supposed it was possible. In fact, it was time. Noah was two. If Jana was three months pregnant now, Noah would turn three before another baby was born. Amish children often arrived two to three years apart.

Which made her family something of a rarity because there was a gap of five years between her three boys and three girls. As they passed the plates of chicken, candied yams, potato casserole, corn, and fresh bread, Etta thought of those five years. It had been a difficult time.

She'd had three children in a row—when she was twenty, twenty-one, and twenty-two. Yes, she'd been exhausted. Yes, her body had been depleted. Maybe that was why the next five years were so difficult. Did Mose realize she was struggling? Is that why he'd held himself apart from her?

Likely it was. She could see that now, as she glanced up and met her husband's gaze. He was perceptive in that way, kind and caring. He wouldn't have spoken of it, wouldn't have wanted to offend her in any way. Instead, he spent many a night working in the barn—after the boys were asleep and while she was struggling to stay awake with some bit of darning or needlework.

She had felt so unwanted and unloved.

She had convinced herself that Mose regretted ever marrying her.

It was a challenging time in their marriage, but eventually the boys began sleeping all night. Her body began to grow strong again, and her old energy and positive outlook returned. But soon after, when all three boys were still not in school, they had been bombarded with financial woes. Amish life might be simple, but they had to pay taxes on the land like everyone else. The boys constantly needed new shoes. The house always had one thing or another in need of repair or replacement.

By the time she was twenty-seven, the financial hardships had abated somewhat. The boys were five, six, and seven, and she delivered their first baby girl, followed soon by another and then a third. Again, there was a three year gap, but not for lack of trying. No, she simply failed to conceive during that time—until she became pregnant with Sarah.

After the stillbirth, she had assumed something was wrong with her, that she was unable to have any more children. She'd found happiness and contentment, eventually—once her period of mourning over Sarah had passed. Though a part of her heart would continue to grieve—to ache for the tiny girl—she had learned to trust.

The baby in her womb kicked, as if to agree.

"Aren't you hungry?" Charity asked. Their youngest was the worrier of the family.

"*Ya*, I am." Etta glanced down at her plate and then back up. "I was remembering each of your births."

"All here in this very house." Mose grinned as he filled his plate.

"And the new *boppli*?" Ben reached for another fresh roll, broke it open, and slathered butter on both sides.

"The new *boppli* will be born at Doc's birthing center." Etta popped a forkful of chicken into her mouth—the meat was moist and well-seasoned. She was certainly a better cook now, better than when she'd been a first-time mother. It was a wonder Mose had survived.

The meal proceeded with plenty of conversation, a few secrets shared, and everyone proclaiming it was the best Christmas ever.

Then they moved into the sitting room to exchange gifts. Etta worked all year to put back a little money for Christmas presents. She kept a jar to store her savings, and any money she earned from her crocheted and knitted items was put there. Virtually all of the gifts they gave to the children were handmade—buggy blankets and winter scarves for the boys and a set of gloves for each of the girls. Usually the children pitched in and purchased one thing for their mom and dad—a gift for the house. One year it had been a new coffee maker, another year a new flashlight for each of the bedrooms. Etta always looked forward to this time of gift giving because it showed how much they understood each other, how much they knew of each other's needs.

When Christopher and Ben stood and walked out of the room, she nudged Mose. "Something's up."

"*Ya?* Christmas time . . . usually brings a few surprises." But his eyes were twinkling, which caused Etta to realize he knew what was going on.

Then the boys walked in carrying the cradle and placed it in front of her. It was the cradle Mose had built so many years ago, when Etta was a first-time mother. The wood shone, and when she reached out to touch it, to run her fingers over the tiny rails, a thousand memories poured from her heart.

"You made her get all emotional," Charity whispered.

"*Nein.* I didn't!" Christopher protested. "It's only the way women are when they're expecting."

"Are you saying that we're overly emotional?" Jana asked.

"Careful how you answer that one, *bruder.*" Ben's voice bordered on laughter as he slapped his brother on the back.

The cradle was filled to overflowing with all manner of items—several packages of disposable diapers, new cloth diapers, baby teething rings, tiny handmade blankets, and two crib quilts.

Etta's eyes filled with tears as she pulled her attention from the cradle and gazed around the room. Though they hadn't spoken much about the new baby with their children, she realized in that moment that they understood what a shock it had been. They knew she no longer had the things a woman would keep for the next baby. She'd given them all away long ago, including the cradle, which had gone to Christopher before Noah was born.

Noah ran over to the cradle and began pushing it so that it would rock. Glancing up at Etta, he proclaimed, "*Boppli!*" Then he picked up his wooden horse from the floor and placed it in the cradle.

"*Danki,*" she said, swiping at her eyes.

"You did make *Mamm* cry." Beth pushed her brother playfully.

"*Nein.* You're the one who had the idea. It's your fault if she cries."

"It's no one's fault. Your *mamm* is happy, and we both appreciate what you've done. It was very thoughtful." Mose beamed at his children and caught up young Noah into his arms.

Soon there was laughter and oohing and aahing over gifts. It was an hour later before Etta had a chance to speak with Christopher.

"You shouldn't have returned the cradle. No doubt you'll be needing it again soon."

"*Ya*, maybe." Her son had outgrown her by a good four inches. He slid into a chair as he studied her. "But we don't need it now, and you do. You can return it when the *boppli* is too big to sleep in it."

"Thank you, Christopher." Etta cut him a piece of the chocolate cake and pushed it in front of him. Then she poured him another cup of coffee. Her middle son had been a coffee fan since he was fourteen and helping his dad in the fields. "I noticed that you cleaned up the cradle before returning it. The grain of the wood, it looks brand new."

"I sanded it a bit, then worked in some of the furniture oil Ben keeps in his woodshop."

"That takes several coats to be done properly, and I can tell you did a fine job. *Danki*."

"*Gem gschehne*." Christopher stared down at his cake, not bothering to pick up a fork.

"Go ahead and say whatever's on your mind. You never were able to eat when you were tossing something around in there." She reached out and messed his hair as she had when he was young.

"It's just . . ." He sipped the coffee and then met her gaze. "I was twelve when Sarah was born. I remember how hard that was on you."

"*Gotte's wille*." The words were softer than a whisper of wind in the trees.

"*Ya*. Surely it was, but still, you suffered. I remember asking Ben what we had done wrong."

"You didn't—"

"I know that now. I bring it up because I want you to know how much we care about you. I've heard pregnancy is harder on . . . older women."

Etta placed her hands on top of her stomach, closed her eyes, and envisioned the child growing there. When she opened her eyes, Christopher was still studying her. "I'm nine years older now than I was then."

"Exactly."

"But Doc says age has nothing to do with whether a *boppli* survives the birthing. He says that some babies are just not . . . meant for this world."

"And I would agree with him. But now that I'm a parent, I understand better what that must have been like. If there's anything at all we can do, promise me you'll tell us."

"Of course I will."

Christopher paused, then pushed on. "What about the bank payments? *Dat* mentioned things were tight—"

"Tight, yes. But we're doing all right, Christopher."

"And you would let me know if you couldn't make the payments?"

"We would, but, son, we do not expect you to help with our financial obligations. We've had bad crops in years past. *Gotte* always provides, and your *dat*—he's a hard worker."

Satisfied, Christopher sunk the fork into the moist, rich cake and plopped it into his mouth, a smile spreading across his face. "*Wunderbaar.*"

"Is it now?"

"It is." He reached out and covered her hand with his. "Know that we are praying for you and the *boppli*. Know that we are all eager to meet this new child that *Gotte* is sending into our family."

Etta nodded, then stood and took several moments to refill her own cup. She needed the time to rein in her emotions. Her children had grown into fine men and women, and she was proud of them. She didn't want to spoil their Christmas by tearing up—again. She didn't want to share with the children that Mose had asked the bishop for help. He'd loaned them the money to make the current month's farm payment. Mose was trying to find work at the stores in town. Something would turn up, and even if it didn't, Christmas morning was not the time to dwell on such things.

The kitchen was soon crowded and the mood jovial.

"Oh, you get the first piece?" Martha asked.

"*Ya*, because I'm special."

"I think the special one would have the first piece of apple pie."

"There's pie?" Ben shouldered Martha away from the counter, Martha pretended to be offended, and Christopher insisted he could eat cake and pie.

Etta turned and watched her children, watched her family.

It seemed God had blessed her beyond what that twenty-year-old girl could have imagined, and it seemed that He wasn't finished yet. She was suddenly ashamed of her doubt. God would provide for their financial needs, if only she knew how.

CHAPTER EIGHT

"You look eager to leave. Did the chair sleep so badly?"

"Nein." Mose folded the blanket he'd used for cover and placed it on the seat of the recliner, then paced to the window and stared out at the sunrise spilling over the winter landscape. "I'm ready to be off is all. I'm ready to take you and Hannah home."

Etta nodded, and Mose realized it wasn't a meaningless gesture. She understood him, sympathized with his need to be in his own home. The birthing center had been good. He was glad they'd been there, especially with the looped cord situation. But now he was ready to be with the rest of his children, to be home.

"Did you talk to the girls?"

"Christopher came by when you were sleeping earlier. He said he'd go out and deliver the news."

"Did he hire an *Englisch* driver or did he drive his buggy?"

"The buggy. Seems the city has done a *gut* job clearing the roads. The trip home should be no problem."

"No snow banks for Morgan to step into?"

"I think one was quite enough."

When the nurse walked into the room with Hannah, Mose could feel the beat of his heart clattering against his chest. When he looked at his new daughter, he was overwhelmed by the depth of his love and gratitude. He was immensely grateful that she had been born healthy, pink and crying, and ready to bring some chaos to their household. He loved her more than he would have thought possible. Already it seemed this little one had always been a part of their family.

"She's beautiful." He accepted the baby from the nurse and cradled her in the crook of his arm. He had worried that he might have forgotten how, but it seemed some things—once learned—became second nature.

"You're going to spoil her, *Dat.*" The nurse smiled as she walked to Etta's side and had her sign the release papers. Her name was Marilyn, and she'd arrived before the sun was up. Apparently they'd called her in because they needed extra help. She was short, plump, and quite motherly.

"*Nein*, but I am going to appreciate every moment. They grow up too fast. Don't they, Etta?"

His wife nodded as she swung her legs over the side of the bed. "Indeed, though I might have to remind you of that when she cries in the middle of the night."

Mose didn't think so. He didn't think interrupted sleep could temper his enthusiasm for this child. Hannah stared up at him with her large eyes—eyes that seemed to be memorizing his face, watching for what? Such curiosity in one so young. He was sure the child smiled. Not even twenty-four hours old and already she was smiling! The nurse would say it was gas, but he knew better. Dads could tell.

"So I can go?" Etta asked the nurse.

"You sure can. Doc said everything was fine after he checked you on his predawn rounds."

"Does he ever go home?" Mose asked.

"Some nights he does, but last night we received a new delivery every few hours." Marilyn turned toward Etta. "He did want me to remind you about your appointment in a week."

Etta met Mose's eyes, and they both nodded.

Mose would have scoffed at such things with their earlier children, but they would be following Doc's advice this time. Things were different with Hannah, not only because of her birth and the looped cord, or because of Etta's age. Things were different because times had changed.

He pondered that as he went to fetch the horse and buggy from the large barn behind the birthing center. As Plain people, they valued consistency and didn't embrace change. In fact, they fought against it rather valiantly. But Mose had accepted one thing long ago—certain changes couldn't be resisted. Certain changes were actually for the better. Many Amish would argue with him about that, but only a few of those had suffered through the experience of a stillborn child.

Though Doc had assured them it wouldn't have been any different had they been in a hospital, Mose was grateful that the birthing center had been built. Doc was always there, as were the midwife and the nurses. In many instances, this would make the difference for a child. The medical community had found a way to bridge the gap between technology and the Amish lifestyle. He thought it was a good compromise.

It was one of many things he liked about their community. They knew and trusted the doctors, the merchants in town, and even the bank. The thought of having to move caused his stomach to twist and turn.

Pulling the buggy even with the front door, he set the brake and jumped out to help Etta.

Once she was settled beside him, the floor heater providing a little warmth and the blanket wrapped firmly around her and the babe, he picked up the reins and directed Morgan toward home. The gelding tossed his head once, then set off at a merry trot.

Etta was relieved to be home, in her rocker, with baby Hannah in the cradle that was set between her and Mose. It had been a long day, and yes, she had taken a short afternoon nap. That was something out of the ordinary, but the night before had been long and they'd risen early. She'd made it through lunch and fed Hannah when her arms grew incredibly heavy and her eyelids felt as if they'd been basted shut.

Martha, Beth, and Charity noticed instantly and suggested the nap. They'd spent the morning oohing and awing over Hannah. Her stomach full from soup and sandwiches the girls had fixed, Etta suddenly wasn't sure she could walk up the stairs to her bed.

Martha had taken Hannah into her arms and insisted. "We'll wake you if she needs feeding."

"*Ya*, and I already have dinner started—chicken and dumplings." Charity worried the strings to her prayer *kapp*. "Hopefully I didn't add too much onion this time."

"And I've made dessert." Beth smiled confidently. "Apple crisp. *Dat* loves it, and I thought he could use something special."

"Plus, you're going to ask him about letting you spend Friday evening with your *Englisch* friend."

Beth didn't deny it. "We're working on our recipe book. It's another reason I made the apple crisp. I'm trying a new ingredient."

Etta would have loved to hear more, but instead she surrendered and trudged up the stairs. Her baby was beautiful, and she no longer questioned why God had sent her such a blessing in her later years. As her eyes closed, she realized it would only be harder physically. Emotionally and spiritually she felt more prepared than ever.

The nap had revived her and now she sat in the rocker, the baby in her cradle, and Mose pretending to read the *Budget*. The paper hadn't rustled in quite some time, so she suspected he was close to drifting off.

Glancing down at her lap, she picked up the letter from her *mamm*.

"What does *Mammi* say in her letter?" Beth was paging through a library book looking for more recipes.

"She says she misses each of you."

"Two-page letter." Martha glanced up from her sewing. "She must say more than that."

Hannah began to cry, a piercing, healthy cry that caused them all to laugh.

"You read it to your *schweschdern*, Martha. I'll take care of little Hannah."

Martha glanced down at the letter, then set aside her sewing and began to read.

Dear Etta and family,

    We are happy to hear that you all are well. We still have plenty of snow here in Pennsylvania. Yesterday your dat showed

Reuben's boys how to use the snow shoes. Do you remember the time you were determined to walk to town in them? You made it to the end of the lane before turning around.

"Seriously, *Mamm*?" Beth looked at her curiously.

Etta shrugged and motioned for Martha to continue reading.

The next portion contained details about various family members in Pennsylvania. Etta hadn't been home in two years, and it was good to hear how everyone was doing. Perhaps when Charity was done with school, they would take the bus for a visit, just her and the girls. Hannah would be big enough to travel then, and she wanted her parents to meet their newest *grandkind*. She wanted Hannah to meet them. Family was precious, and she didn't want to put off something that she might wish she had done. Her parents were in their seventies, and though her mother's health was good, her father had been hospitalized twice with heart trouble. Etta understood there would only be so many chances to enjoy family reunions.

Then she remembered about their financial situation. The bus tickets were something they definitely couldn't afford. It would have to wait at least a year, until the summer crops were harvested and sold, and that still might not give them much extra.

Etta suddenly realized that Martha had stopped reading and was staring at the paper, a look of surprise on her face.

"*Mammi* wrote a special note for Hannah."

"*Ya?*"

"But Hannah wasn't born yet when she wrote this letter."

"True."

"She wrote it to *our new baby girl* . . ."

"Melinda had a fifty-fifty chance of getting that right," Mose muttered.

"Huh." Martha flipped the page over and then back again before she resumed reading.

Tell our new baby girl that we pray for her each morning and each night. Tell her that she is blessed to have three wunderbaar older schweschdern to help care for her. And tell her not to let the boys turn her into a tomboy.

Etta smiled briefly as she rocked Hannah. A lump lodged in her throat at the thought of her missing child, but she pushed it away. Hannah's first night home wasn't a time for sadness.

Remember to share our love with Martha, Beth, Charity, and Mose. Tell Christopher, Jana, and Noah that we think of them often. Hug Ben for us, and know that we keep David continually in our prayers.

Above all, know that our heavenly Father cares for you and your family. He will see you through the sleepless nights ahead, as He has done before. He will be your rock and your redeemer.

Much love,
Mammi

Martha passed the letter to Beth, who studied it for a moment and then passed it on to Charity. The next evening they would write a letter back with each person adding their own paragraph of tidbits and news. Etta hadn't told her parents about the problems with the bank note. She hadn't wanted to worry them, but now she realized she was underestimating her parents. They would pray with them and encourage them. They couldn't do that unless Etta was completely honest with them, which meant she had to stop holding back.

Etta realized that her family might not be all under one roof anymore, and the roof they were under might change, but her mother was correct. God cared for each one of them, and He could be trusted.

CHAPTER NINE

The first two months of Hannah's life passed in a blur of late-night feedings and too little sleep. It was a precious time that Etta vowed to enjoy and remember. When April arrived with blossoming trees and warmer temperatures, she felt as if she were seeing the rebirth of everything around her for the first time. She felt as if God's blessings filled her life to overflowing.

The only dark cloud was the *For Sale* sign Mose had placed next to the fence where their property bordered the main road.

"The crops are barely in the ground. The harvest won't come in time. I'm sorry, Etta, I know you would like to stay here."

"What I'd like is for my family to be together," she'd assured him, though she fought the tears threatening to fall.

"That we will, dear."

She'd sold several of the quilts her mother and grandmother had made. While they were precious to her, they were only quilts— material things. She didn't need quilts to remember the two most influential women in her life. The money had purchased groceries, the few disposable diapers they used, and paid off part of Doc's bills.

Etta glanced out the window at the April sunshine as she placed Hannah in the cradle near her rocking chair. Soon it would go to Jana and Christopher, for the next *grandkinner* was due in the summer.

To Etta, the cradle was a thing of art. The wood was smooth and worn. The small mattress had been made from old quilt pieces sewn inside a homemade sheet. It had been recovered more than once. The cradle, fashioned by Mose's hands so many years ago, seemed like a constant reminder in their lives—of the love of family, the grace of God, and the importance of faith.

Etta shook her head at the absurdity of her thoughts.

Could an infant's bed, a simple piece of furniture, represent all of that?

Placing her hand on the cradle and rocking it gently, she decided perhaps it could. Mose had made it when they were first married, when they were a young couple and expecting their first child. Now it held their seventh, an unexpected blessing for sure. It had also been used for their single grandchild, and would soon be used for another. They passed the cradle back and forth, and sometimes laughed that the day would come when they'd need two, if the babies kept coming as quickly as it seemed they would.

Etta lowered herself into the rocking chair next to the cradle, determined to finish some darning. Hannah smiled up at her, raising and waving a tiny fist before stuffing it into her mouth. It was hard to believe her daughter was already two months old!

And what a blessing she was.

Though Hannah was just beginning to sleep through the night, Etta had found she didn't mind rising to feed her at two in the morning. Those were precious moments that the two of them shared, when the usual bustle around the house turned to quiet and the rest of the family slept. She used that time to pray for her sweet baby—her blizzard baby. Etta wondered that she had actually questioned whether she could do this. Caring for an infant was the most natural thing in the world, and though many days Etta's eyes stung from lack of sleep and her cooking was more often thrown together casseroles . . . that all faded into the background when she held Hannah in her arms.

She picked up a pair of Mose's work pants and began darning the persistent hole he managed to wear into the right knee—always the right because he went down on his right knee when mending fences or caring for a calf or playing with Hannah on the floor. Etta worked the needle and thread through the tough fabric, sewing a patch to the back of the worn area. Her mind was on the patch and the stitches, so it took her a moment to realize the sound she heard was that of stomping feet on the back porch—someone clearing the mud off their shoes.

Mose back so early?

That wasn't like him, but perhaps he'd decided he did want one of the sweet rolls Rachel had brought over the day before. He'd claimed he needed to watch how many sweets he ate, not because of his weight, but his blood sugar. "I need to take care of myself so I can teach this little girl to throw a baseball."

Etta had laughed at that. The girls in their family had always been better ball players than the boys, a constant source of teasing.

Peering out the window, she saw the April day was heavy with clouds. Perhaps he'd decided an extra cup of coffee and something sweet wasn't such a bad idea. Before Hannah's arrival he rarely came back to the house in the middle of the morning. More and more it was becoming a daily occurrence. They'd talked about it a few evenings ago, and Mose admitted that he understood too well how quickly children grew.

"It's *gut* you don't work away from home, like so many *Englisch*. You would miss too many precious moments with her."

"Amish too," Mose had reminded her. "More and more of our men are going to work in the factories."

Not their sons, and for that she was grateful.

At least not Ben and Christopher.

She even found it in her heart to be thankful that Mose had been turned down for the factory job he'd sought. She wanted him home, even if home was someplace else. He was a good farmer, and he would provide for them in spite of crops and bank payments.

The sound of the back door opening and closing brought a smile to her lips.

She set the darning into her basket and stood, prepared to go to the kitchen and fetch a snack for Mose while he played with Hannah.

And that was when her youngest son stepped into the room.

At the sight of David, Etta felt her heart jump in her chest. A small cry must have escaped from her lips, because Hannah startled and began to fuss.

Etta flew across the room into David's arms.

He laughed and returned her embrace, even lifting her off the ground. When he set her back down, she reached up to touch his jaw—clean-shaven and sturdier. He'd grown since she'd seen him last. He was now taller and broader in the shoulders. While he'd been away, he had become a man.

"Has it really been more than two years?"

"*Ya*, it has."

"It's so *gut* to see you." She cupped his right cheek in her palm, kissed him on the left, and then grabbed his hand. "Come and meet Hannah."

"I thought I heard a *boppli's* cry. So I'm an *onkel* again."

Etta picked up the babe and placed her in David's arms. "Say hello to you *schweschder.*"

David's eyes widened. *"Schweschder?"*

"*Ya.* We were as surprised as you are, but then, we've had longer to get used to the idea."

At that moment, Mose came in the back door. "I saw someone walking up the lane. Looked like it might be—"

Etta thought the next moment would remain crystal clear in her mind should she live to be one hundred. David turned toward Mose. Hannah was nestled against his shoulder and chose that moment to reach over and touch his face. Mose froze where he stood, and her husband's face changed in an instant, changed as hers must have. It seemed to her that he went through disbelief, shock, and then joy. In that moment, the years fell away as the worry he had carried over his son all this time evaporated in a moment of grace.

He moved toward David, not having said a word.

David stood completely still, as if he had been sure of his mother's reception but wary of his father's. Had words passed between the two? Possibly. She suddenly couldn't remember the precise details of the day he had left. Did it even matter? Since that day many prayers had been lifted in hope and trust and yes, a degree of anxiousness, perhaps on both sides.

The moment held, frozen in Etta's mind, and then it was broken.

Mose wrapped his arms around David.

David smiled over his dad's shoulder, smiled at Etta.

Hannah let out a squeal as she was embraced between father and son.

As they gathered around the kitchen table, David described his trip from Pennsylvania and the effects of the recent heavy rains there. The Amish and Mennonite communities were pulling together to assist those with flooded homes and crops that would need to be replanted.

"So you're helping with disaster relief." Mose leaned back in his chair. He'd limited himself to half a sweet roll, which wasn't a big concession since each was as big as Etta's plates.

"*Ya*. I've been working with MDS the last two years."

"Mennonite Disaster Service does fine work." Mose stood and refilled his coffee cup, waving the pot toward them, but Etta and David declined.

"It's *gut* to know you've been using your time away to help others." Etta reached across the table and squeezed her son's hand. How many of her prayers had been answered in the last hour? She was ashamed that she had ever doubted God's will in their lives, in her son's life.

"Why is the place for sale, *Dat*?"

Etta thought Mose might avoid the question. Instead, he looked at David and said, "Because we don't have the money to pay the note. Last year's harvest was bad—"

"What about your savings?"

"Gone. Used for the doctor bill, birthing center, and to help make ends meet all winter."

When David shook his head, Mose added, "We'd been behind all of last year. Two of the work horses took sick and died. I tried to work without replacing them, but I had to reduce the size of the crop."

"And then the crop didn't make it," Etta said.

"Why didn't you ask for help?" David asked.

"From you?" Mose folded his arms. "How would we have found you?"

David cleared his throat. "I'm sorry. I didn't know—"

"There's no need to be sorry. *Gotte* has provided, and He will again. Just not here. We'll start over somewhere else—maybe Ohio or Kentucky. The farm should fetch a good price. I've put in a crop, so whoever purchases the house and fields will be able to walk in and start immediately rather than waiting a year."

David stared at Hannah, then asked, "Do you want to move?"

"Makes no difference what we want." Mose's tone reflected his growing impatience.

"But if you did have a choice—"

"There's no use talking *ifs*." Mose stood, kissed Hannah on the head, and touched Etta's shoulder. It hurt her to see conflict between them, but she also understood that these were things that needed to be aired.

"Now I have work to do."

He moved toward the mudroom but stopped when David stood and said, "They've offered me a job."

"Who?"

"MDS."

"There's plenty of work here. We could use your hand with the farming and with the move." Mose offered this in a neutral tone. He wasn't reprimanding his son. He was stating a fact.

"I'm sure there is, but my *bruders*—"

"Each has places of their own. We always hoped you would return, David. We always prayed and expected that you would. It's past time for you to act like a man, not a boy."

"You have no idea what I do, and how is accepting a job acting like a boy?"

"You have responsibilities to your family. I think it's time you lived up to those."

David walked to the sink. He rinsed his cup and plate and set them aside. When he turned back to his parents, Etta realized that his mind was made. A small part of her heart broke then, because she understood that it meant this was a temporary visit.

"I'm joining the Mennonite church. It's where I belong."

Neither Etta nor Mose spoke.

"The job, it's disaster response coordinator for the East, an area that stretches from Pennsylvania to Florida." He returned to the table. Instead of looking apologetic, his expression was one of excitement. "I've worked in many of these areas the last two years. I enjoy the labor, and I've overseen jobsites determining the most effective place to direct folks who show up to volunteer and also coordinating with the local community. It's a job I'm *gut* at, and one that brings me satisfaction."

"You feel called—" Etta placed Hannah across her knees. The *boppli* had fallen asleep as soon as they'd sat at the table.

"I do."

Mose ran a hand through his beard. "You needn't join the Mennonite church to work for MDS. There are many Amish who—"

"There are."

"Why do you always have to rebel? Why can't you do the normal thing for once?"

"Because it's not what I'm supposed to do." David closed his eyes and pulled in a deep breath. "Don't you see? My experiences—the way you raised me—they're part of the reason I'm perfect for this job. I've grown up in the heart of one of the largest Amish communities in the country. I understand, better than our friends within the Mennonite community, how to work with different groups of Plain folk."

"And their beliefs?" Mose again crossed the room. "Their beliefs are different from ours. They do not remain separate. They embrace much that we have rejected. There are reasons for this!"

"Their ways are not so different from ours—"

"Different enough." Mose frowned at the table, ran his hand over the pine wood.

"It's true that we—Mennonites—accept more of the technology."

"Cars . . ." Mose shook his head.

"Yes, cars, which are quite helpful if you're moving up and down the East Coast coordinating jobs—a distance of more than fifteen hundred miles." He held up his hand to stop his father's protests. "I realize I could use the buses. Were it only the inconvenience of traveling by bus, I would still do so. However, it's also impractical. Often when we need to be on a jobsite, the situation is dire and it's important that I arrive as quickly as possible. On more than one occasion, the people we were serving were without homes."

Mose grunted but didn't respond.

"The Mennonite rules for living are different, but our faith is the same. You know this, *Dat.* I am sure that working with the MDS is where *Gotte* would have me."

"And you've prayed about it?" Etta asked.

"Of course. That's the reason I'm here. I want your blessing, and I'd like the blessing of the bishop as well."

Mose stared out the window. Etta realized that he was releasing his dream in that moment. He was accepting that his son wouldn't work beside him in the fields.

When he turned around, a hint of a smile returned to his

expression. "There will be no shunning, if that's what you're worried about."

"*Nein*. I didn't think there would be, since I didn't join the church before I left."

"As far as the bishop, Simon will be pleased. He works closely with MDS. I have no doubt he will give you his blessing."

"And what of you?" David's voice cracked slightly. "Will you give me your blessing? It means a lot to me."

Etta feared then that Mose would ask David to stay, that he would attempt to talk him out of this thing that obviously meant so much to him.

He didn't, though. Instead, he walked around the table. David met him halfway, and Mose enfolded him in an embrace. "You have it."

Etta joined them, placing Hannah in Mose's arms and turning to David. She put one hand on each of his shoulders, marveling again that he had grown so much since he'd left.

God had been faithful to answer their prayers, though He'd done so in a way they couldn't have anticipated.

"You're following *Gotte's wille*, David. That's all we ever wanted. Now, tell me you're staying longer than for one meal. Your *bruders* and *schweschder* will want to see you."

"I have the entire week off."

Seven days. That was what she would have with her son who had been lost, but was no longer. It wasn't what she'd dreamed of, but she vowed to be grateful nonetheless. She would make sure that she stored up enough memories to last until he could visit them again.

David smiled, then turned to follow his father out into the fields. He might only be staying a few days, but Etta had the feeling he would spend that time working. She could tell by the look of him that he wasn't accustomed to sitting still.

As she carried her infant back to the sitting room and placed her in the cradle, Etta's heart was full with prayers of gratitude and hope.

She returned to her darning, and as she sewed, she prayed. Gotte, *bless David in all he does. I've known since he was a* boppli, *as small as Hannah, that he would find a place in Your plan. Cover him with grace, and fill his heart with Your mercy.*

She continued sewing, pulling the thread and needle through the rough, blue fabric. *And please provide us a place to live. Send a buyer for our home—a* gut *family who will raise healthy, faithful children here. Prepare us for whatever lies ahead.*

CHAPTER TEN

Mose watched his family as they settled into their Saturday-evening activities. The boys, men actually, had trudged out to the barn to see to the animals. The girls cleared the dishes from the table and helped their *mamm* return the kitchen area to its orderly condition.

The meal had been a special one—with all seven of their children present. Ben had traveled over from Middlebury and was planning to stay through the weekend, attending the worship service with them the next day. Christopher was also present, with Jana and Noah, which brought the total of their *kinner* and *grand-kinner* to nine. A good number, in Mose's opinion. A full family, and each one of them a blessing to him and Etta.

Mose brought in more firewood for the stove and paused now and again to check on Hannah. She was sleeping peacefully in her cradle, there in the sitting room. Mose found it a marvel each time he stared into her sweet little face—to think he and Etta had produced such a miracle even in their middle ages. To think that God had blessed them yet again.

Within the hour, everyone was gathered in the sitting room.

"What kind of disasters do you see?" Charity asked David. At twelve, she was full of questions, which was perhaps why she read so much. He rarely saw the girl when she didn't have her nose in a book, even when she was feeding the chickens.

"All sorts." David was sitting on the floor, rolling a wooden horse back and forth with Noah. "Floods, fires, blizzards—you name it and it seems to eventually happen."

"Will you be going on for more education?" Beth was now out of school and worked at the pretzel stand in town, but she'd recently confessed that she dreamed of one day opening her own bakery. "I don't need schooling to be a *gut* cook, but it seems that what you do might call for it."

"*Nein.* I don't think so. Most of what I need to know I can learn from those more experienced than I am. If I decide to go back to school, though, it would be for my high school equivalency and then, I suppose, to pursue a construction science degree."

"With all that studying, your head would grow so big your hat wouldn't fit anymore." Ben had always enjoyed teasing his younger brother.

Instead of rising to the bait, David smiled and nodded.

Mose nearly laughed to see his children scattered around the room. Saturday evenings had been this way when they were young, and little had changed in that regard. Ben and Christopher set up a game of checkers. Charity plopped into a chair and opened a book, though her gaze kept darting from its pages to her brothers and sisters. The older girls were huddled over their yarn and needles, having discovered a new pattern for baby blankets, which they sold at Davis Mercantile. Christopher spoke of the weather and the prediction for more rain.

Finally, Etta entered the room, appearing at the same moment Hannah began to fuss. She scooped the baby out of her cradle and settled in the rocker.

"What of the land, *Dat*?" Ben asked as he made his first move in the checker game.

"What of it?"

"Have you had any offers?" Christopher asked.

"Yes, one, but it wasn't what I hoped for. It would barely be enough to pay off the note. We'll wait and see if someone else offers more."

"Maybe you don't have to sell."

Everyone turned to stare at David.

"We've been through this, son."

"I spoke with my boss this afternoon." The room fell silent. Mose had no idea what David was getting at, but he was sure that it wasn't going to solve their problems. How could it? Mennonite Disaster Services helped families who had suffered disasters—his finances were bad but he couldn't blame them on a flood, blizzard, or fire.

"There's a program with the university over in South Bend." David stood and began pacing the room. "They have an agricultural program that visits Amish farms, because acre for acre, Amish farms produce more than *Englisch*."

Mose ducked his head and muttered, "He's telling this to a man about to lose his farm from crop failure."

"That's just it, *Dat*. What happened to you was due to a wet year and late planting, but walk out into your fields now. You've recovered."

"Not in time."

"You don't understand. They'll pay to send students out. They want to learn our ways of farming, ways that combine the best of the old *Englisch* ways and what we've learned since about rotating crops, leaving stalks in the field, things that to you and me are common sense."

"And they would pay *gut* money to come and watch me work?"

"They'll pay to learn from you."

All of their children started talking at once.

Mose stopped them by raising his hand, palm out. "I wouldn't be comfortable having *Englischers* traipsing around my fields."

"The program lasts for eight weeks each semester. They'd be here three days a week. Students are carefully screened to be sure they are a good fit—that they understand our ways and respect them."

When Mose didn't stop him, David continued, "I was talking to my boss about the details, and he thinks this place would be perfect. I also took the liberty of speaking with our bishop—"

"You did what?"

"You told me to take responsibility, to act like a man. Well, a man doesn't sit around and watch his family lose their home." Then David named the amount the university was willing to pay. "Not only will they watch, but they'll also help. They'll be training *Englischers* who have family farms, so it's important they have hands-on experience."

"The money we need and free labor in the fields." Etta looked at him, her eyebrows cocked and a smile tugging at her lips.

"I like David's idea." Ben turned from the game and studied his father. "But if you don't, I'm still willing to sell my place in Middlebury and move back."

"*Nein.* You found prime land there and at a *gut* price."

"I could try to cut back on my time at the farrier's." Christopher exchanged glances with his wife.

Mose realized too well that they needed the extra income Christopher was able to earn working in town. It was difficult to be a full-time farmer these days, particularly when you were first starting out, as Christopher and Jana were.

"You need that money, especially with another *boppli* on the way."

Jana blushed at the mention of her pregnancy, but she didn't contradict him about the need for additional income.

"*Gotte* has provided for us, all of these years, and we can trust that He will provide again. What David has suggested, I will need to think and pray on it. I'm an old man and decisions take longer than they used to." That statement brought a chuckle from several of his children.

The future—it was often uncertain. Most men in the Amish community, when they reached the age of fifty or fifty-five, began handing over their farmland to one of their sons. It was unclear how this would work in their case, but Mose had learned to accept such unknowns as a part of life. Though he had to admit that he had thought about the question often over the last twenty-four hours, actually since the day that David had left. God had provided part of the answer with David's commitment to disaster relief work. The question of the university's help? His heart wanted to agree, but he needed to speak to his bishop first. At least now they had an option that would allow them to stay.

When Mose reached for Hannah, his hands lightly brushed against Etta's. The contact sent a river of warmth through her arms, and the smile Mose gave her—it seemed to reach deep into her heart.

Etta realized she was more emotional since Hannah's birth. She cried more easily—like last week when she had burned the cornbread—but she also smiled more. It seemed as though she felt things keenly, as though before she had kept her emotions at a distance so that there were few highs and lows. Now she felt things sharply—sorrow, joy, happiness, love, and even loss. The people and happenings around her touched her heart more than ever before.

She understood this was a result of her hormones, as Doc Bennett had warned her. "You'll be dealing with postpartum hormonal changes at the same time you're coping with hormonal fluctuations due to menopause. Give yourself time and rest when you need it—and come to see me if your mood swings feel severe."

She hadn't needed to see Doc Bennett.

She had found herself next door at Rachel's several times a week. More than once she had sat and wept over some inconsequential thing as Rachel had made them both a cup of hot tea. But just as often she'd hurried next door because she needed to share a joy.

Some new thing Hannah had done.

A kind moment that had passed between her and Mose.

The way the landscape around them was coming to life in the trees, the gardens, and the fields. Those times Rachel had smiled and walked with her out into their yard where they'd sat and enjoyed the day for a brief moment before returning to their work.

Etta realized more than ever the value of a good friend, one who was near and kind and wise.

She also realized the blessing of her family—whole again, if only for the weekend.

And David's suggestion for saving their farm? She thought

Mose would agree. It allowed them to stay within the community, and it provided the income they needed. The fact that David had already spoken with their bishop about it confirmed in her heart that it was the right thing to do.

Picking up a baby blanket she was quilting, she spoke to David. "Perhaps when you are in Florida, you can check out Pinecraft. I've heard it's a *wunderbaar* place to visit in the winter. Who knows, your *dat* and I might even make it down there one day."

"You and *Dat*? Taking a vacation?" David smiled as Noah climbed onto his lap, then plopped down. His expression quickly turned to one of puzzlement, then unpleasant surprise. "I believe this one has a full diaper, Jana."

Everyone laughed at the way David picked up Noah, holding the child out and away from him.

"*Ya*, a vacation is a *gut* idea." Mose cradled Hannah in his arms. She immediately began reaching for him, eventually coming into contact with his beard and smiling broadly when she did so.

Hannah . . . Hannah, their unexpected blessing. They would enjoy her more than the rest, perhaps because they did understand how quickly time passed. And a vacation to Pinecraft? Suddenly it didn't seem like such a wild idea. Not that they would be vacationing soon, but in a year or two? Anything was possible.

Though there might not be many grandparents with a young *boppli*, she had a feeling there would be a few.

"Florida sounds like a *wunderbaar* place to spend a week during the winter," she admitted. "Much better than being stuck in a buggy in a blizzard."

"We'll try not to repeat that experience," Mose agreed.

Their eyes met. Mose winked, and Etta didn't even try to stop the smile spreading across her face.

"*Mamm* and *Dat*, they're growing a little *narrisch* in their old age," Charity explained to David. "Must be the lack of sleep from baby Hannah."

"*Ya*, no doubt that's hard for someone in their golden years."

The teasing continued until Noah came running back into the room proclaiming he had on clean, dry pants. Soon the boys returned to discussing the weather, and the girls once again took up their needlework.

Hannah began insisting on her nighttime feeding, so Etta took her into the bedroom, changed her into her evening gown and a fresh diaper, and nursed her.

When she returned to the sitting area, Mose was waiting to say good night to his youngest. He held Hannah high in the crook of his arm and softly whispered to her in German. Etta was suddenly aware that all of their other children were watching. Perhaps they were remembering similar moments, if it was possible to remember something that had happened to one so young.

"You are a blessing, little Hannah." He kissed her on the cheek and then placed her into the cradle, covering her with the small quilt Jana had brought over as a gift.

Etta sat in the rocker and resumed her needlework, but Mose kept his hand on the cradle, rocking it gently until their little blessing was peacefully dreaming.

READING GROUP GUIDE

1. At the beginning of this story, we see the friendship between Etta and Rachel. In what ways does this friendship help Etta through a trying time?

2. Change is something that is difficult for all of us. Etta is dealing with several changes in this story—from where she will birth her baby to having a newborn at age forty-two. What Bible verse helps you most during times of change?

3. How would you describe the relationship between Etta and Mose? They've had trouble in the past, but they seem to have weathered it. What do you think helped them retain their love and respect for one another?

4. David is described as Etta's "lost child." However, the family has never actually given up on him. What can we do when someone we love has chosen a different path?

5. This is a story of unexpected blessings. Discuss a blessing in your life that seemed like more of a trial at the beginning. How did God show you that it was something to be grateful for?

ACKNOWLEDGMENTS

This book is dedicated to my editor, Becky Philpott. Becky has seen me through several manuscripts. She never fails to provide timely advice, good suggestions, and the occasional cat picture to brighten my day. For this story, she also provided me with my main characters—a lovely couple she met in Indiana. I adore you, Becky. Big hugs and thank you for all you do to bring my fiction to readers.

Thanks also to my pre-readers: Donna, Dorsey, and Kristy. You girls are faithful and true and always come through for me. I'd also like to once again thank Mary Sue Seymour, who has been my agent since the beginning of this journey. A special thank-you to Connie Voight, who provided and made the soup recipe for me, and to Marie Daugherty for the cornbread recipe. Also, I owe a debt of gratitude to Kris Stutzman from Lolly's Fabrics in Shipshewana. She always faithfully answers my questions. I enjoyed this return visit to northern Indiana. If you're in the area I encourage you to visit the Amish communities in Elkhart, Goshen, Middlebury, Nappanee, and Shipshewana.

And finally . . . "always giving thanks to God the Father for everything, in the name of our Lord Jesus Christ" (Ephesians 5:20).

Blessings,
Vannetta

AUTHOR BIO

Photograph by Jason Irwin

Vannetta Chapman is the author of the bestselling novel *A Simple Amish Christmas*. She has published over one hundred articles in Christian family magazines, receiving over two dozen awards from Romance Writers of America chapter groups. In 2012 she was awarded a Carol Award for *Falling to Pieces*. She discovered her love for the Amish while researching her grandfather's birthplace of Albion, Pennsylvania. Visit Vannetta's website at www.vannettachapman.com Twitter: @VannettaChapman Facebook: VannettaChapmanBooks

RECIPES FROM BETH WISEMAN'S
In His Father's Arms

RUTH ANNE'S CHICKEN NOODLE SOUP

1 broiler/fryer chicken (3 to 4 lbs.) cut up
10 cups water
1 large carrot, sliced
1 large onion, sliced
1 celery rib, sliced
1 garlic clove, minced
1 bay leaf
1 teaspoon dried thyme
1 teaspoon salt
¼ teaspoon pepper
2 large carrots, sliced
2 celery ribs, sliced

1 medium onion, chopped

2 cups egg noodles, uncooked

1 cup frozen peas

½ cups cut green beans, frozen

In a large soup kettle or Dutch oven, combine the first ten ingredients. Bring to a boil. Reduce heat; cover and simmer for 1 ½ to 2 hours or until the meat is tender.

Remove chicken and cool. Remove and discard skin and bones. Chop chicken and set aside. Strain broth, discarding vegetables and bay leaf. Return broth to the pan; add carrots, celery, and onion. Bring to a boil. Reduce heat; cover and simmer for 10 minutes or until the vegetables are tender.

Add noodles and chicken. Bring to a boil. Reduce heat; cover and simmer for 6 minutes. Stir in peas and beans. Cook for 2 to 4 minutes or until beans and noodles are tender. Yield: 6 to 8 servings.

Susanna's Cinnamon Raisin Bread

2 cups warm water

2 packages (1/4 ounce each) active dry yeast

1 cup sugar, divided

¼ cup canola oil

2 teaspoons salt

2 eggs

6 to 6 ½ cups all-purpose flour

1 cup raisins

Extra canola oil

3 teaspoons ground cinnamon

Using a large bowl, dissolve yeast in warm water. Add ½ cup sugar, oil, salt, eggs, and 4 cups flour. Beat until smooth. Stir in enough remaining flour until it forms a soft dough.

On a floured surface; knead until smooth and elastic, about 6 to 8 minutes. Place in a greased bowl, turning once to grease top. Cover and let rise in a warm place or until doubled, about 1 hour.

Punch dough down. Turn onto a lightly floured surface; divide in half. Knead ½ cup raisins into each; roll each portion into a 15x9-in. rectangle. Brush with additional oil. Combine cinnamon and remaining sugar; sprinkle to within ½ in. of edges.

Tightly roll up, jelly-roll styled, starting with a short side; pinch seam to seal. Place, seam side down, in two greased 9x4-in. loaf pans. Cover and let rise until doubled, about 30 minutes.

Preheat oven to 375. Brush with oil. Bake 45-50 minutes or until golden brown. Remove from pans and cool on wire racks. Yield—2 loaves (16 slices each).

Recipes from Amy Clipston's
A Son for Always

Carrot Bread

3 large eggs

1½ cups vegetable oil

2 cups sugar

3 teaspoons vanilla extract

3 cups all-purpose flour

1 teaspoon baking soda

1 teaspoon salt

3 teaspoons ground cinnamon

2 cups grated carrots

1 cup crushed pineapple with juice

¾ cup chopped nuts

Place eggs, oil, sugar, vanilla, flour, baking soda, salt, and cinnamon in a large bowl and beat together. Add carrots, pineapple with juice, and nuts, and mix until combined. Pour into two large, greased loaf pans and bake at 325 degrees for one hour.

Makes 2 loaves.

RECIPES FROM KATHLEEN FULLER'S
A Heart Full of Love

STEW

1 qt. canned steak or chunk meat, chopped
3 cups water
Bring these ingredients to a boil then add:
½ pk. noodles (4 oz.)
Cook 10 minutes, then add:
3 medium potatoes, diced
4 medium carrots, diced
1 small onion, diced (optional)
Cook another 3 to 4 minutes. Add:
2 cups cooked corn
2 cups cooked beans

Simmer 10 minutes. Add salt to taste (about 1 tsp.)

MARINATED CARROTS OR COPPER PENNIES

SAUCE

1 can tomato soup
½ tsp. salt
½ tsp. pepper
1 Tbsp. mustard
½ cup sugar
½ cup cooking oil
¼ cup vinegar
chopped onions (optional)
chopped peppers (optional)

Slice and cook 1 lb. carrots. When done, add sauce, 1 sliced mango, and 1 onion. Marinate overnight.

MOCK PECAN PIE

½ cup sugar
¼ melted butter
1 tsp. vanilla
¼ tsp. salt
3 whole eggs
1 cup Karo syrup
1 cup oatmeal

Mix in order given. Pour into unbaked pie shell and bake at 350 for 35 to 40 minutes, or until center is almost set.

All recipes from A Taste of Home From the Schlabach Family

Recipes from Vannetta Chapman's
An Unexpected Blessing

Ground Beef, Spinach, and Barley Soup

12 ounces ground beef
4 cups water
14 ounces stewed tomatoes
1½ cups sliced carrots
1 cup chopped onion
½ cup quick-cooking barley
1½ teaspoons beef bouillon
1½ teaspoons dried thyme
1 teaspoon dried oregano
½ teaspoon garlic powder
¼ teaspoon black pepper
⅛ teaspoon salt
3 cups spinach leaves

Brown beef in large saucepan over medium heat until no longer pink. Drain grease. Add all water, stewed tomatoes, carrots, onion, barley, bouillon granules, thyme, oregano, garlic powder, pepper, and salt.

Bring to a boil, then reduce heat to medium-low. Cover and simmer 12 to 15 minutes or until barley and vegetables are tender, stirring occasionally. Stir in spinach. Cook until spinach starts to wilt, usually within 1 or 2 minutes.

Makes 4 servings.

*Adapted from *Amish Country Cookbook*, Publications International, Ltd.

CORNBREAD

2 cups self-rising cornmeal
1 cup self-rising flour
½ cup buttermilk
3 tablespoons oil
water

Grease a 10-inch cast-iron skillet with vegetable oil. Put skillet in 400-degree oven to warm while mixing up your cornbread ingredients.

In large bowl, mix cornmeal, flour, and buttermilk. Mix in enough water to make mixture look like cake batter. Remove skillet from oven and pour batter into hot skillet. Return skillet to the oven, and bake until golden brown on top, approximately 20 minutes.

*Recipe provided by Marie Daugherty.

The garden plays a pivotal role in every Amish household. Explore the different ways the garden provides for four different women in this new collection of Amish novellas from Beth Wiseman, Kathleen Fuller, Tricia Goyer, and Vannetta Chapman.

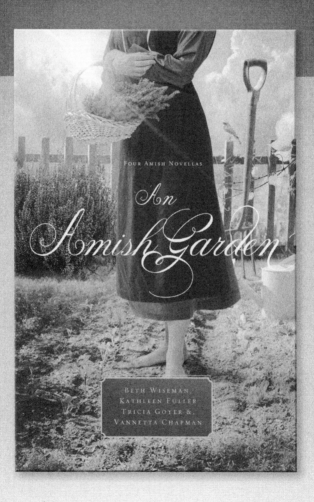

FOUR AMISH NOVELLAS

An

Amish Garden

BETH WISEMAN
KATHLEEN FULLER
TRICIA GOYER &
VANNETTA CHAPMAN

AVAILABLE IN PRINT AND E-BOOK

ENJOY THESE AMISH NOVELLAS
FOR EVERY SEASON